TOP 60 CUSTOM SOLUTIONS

BUILT ON MICROSOFT SHAREPOINT SERVER 2010

YAROSLAV PENTSARSKYY

ISBN: 145287736X

ISBN-13: 9781452877365

Library of Congress Control Number: 2010907231

INTRODUCTION

Many of you are already familiar with functionality and features available in past versions of SharePoint. However, the new version of SharePoint has many great improvements and new features to offer. As with every technology, many features are backwards compatible, and you can continue building solutions as you do now, as most of those are still going to be understood in the new version. The best approach, however, is to get complete coverage of what's available for you in the new release, especially components that you had to build from the grounds up before. Every time a new technology such as SharePoint is released I see new books and materials available in the market. Most of the time, books are released few weeks before the technology reaches the release to manufacturing stage, which is understood, because many of us have access to the pre-release version of various tools. The pre-release version of tools usually is almost complete and usually resembles the release to manufacturing version ... right? I mean what major features could change in next three months? Well, if you're like me, you probably know that there are many things that usually change before the product reaches release to manufacturing stage. In fact, the time span from beta to release to manufacturing is when the product team hopes to fix all of the issues reported by the early adopters. This book has been in its initial stage since the latest beta of SharePoint to early adopters. After new version of SharePoint was released, all of the examples you will see in chapters here were reviewed for changes to their original scenarios. I do hope you will find this book resourceful and complete with examples that closely resemble your scenarios and actually work from the first time.

WHOM THIS BOOK IS FOR

This book is intended for two types of audiences:

A .NET developer with little experience in SharePoint looking to start developing using the latest release of SharePoint.

A SharePoint developer gearing up for the new release of the product.

Whoever from the two above you might be, here are some of the assumptions I made about why you would buy this book. If I'm going to buy a book that will tell me everything that I can read by pressing F1 in Visual Studio, or everything I can ready by going to the "What's new" section of the product page, I probably wouldn't buy it. Also, I don't want to buy a book to learn abstract scenarios that I will never work with. I assume you're thinking the same.

Here are the three objectives that this book is trying to achieve:

Get you familiar with technical and business scenarios rather than features of the product.

When you're in the middle of reading vague requirements on what you actually need to implement, it's hard to see how all of those great new features you're reading about will fit together to solve your problem on time. This book navigates through business and technical scenarios and, hopefully, it will get you to the correct solution right from the table of contents.

Give you a real code with all of the steps you need to do to run it.

We've all been there. You have a technical problem, you find the solution someone has posted online, you put it together ... - it doesn't work. The last thing you want to see is a sample that's broken, and then few hours later find that post author forgot to include one step that you never thought you would be required to do. This book comes with references to downloadable solution files that have been compiled and tested.

Get you thinking about what else you can do with features described and scenarios used.

Association is a powerful thing. You can read about a feature or a sample that is not related to your case in any way, yet sometimes you will get enough information to get started on your own solution. Through-out each sample you will find pointers that will get you thinking how else you could use the feature discussed.

With this set of objectives, I really do hope you will find this book everything you ever wanted a developer book to be and nothing less, nothing more. I understand you may not be as excited reading it, as I was writing it; after all, it's just a manual organized a bit differently to help you get things done easily.

With that, I hope you have fun reading this book and if you want to give me your feedback – visit my blog and drop me a note: www.sharemuch.com.

ABOUT THE AUTHOR

Yaroslav Pentsarskyy has been architecting and implementing SharePoint solutions since its 2003 release. Yaroslav has extensive .Net and SharePoint development experience working with medium-sized businesses, non-profits, and government organizations.

As a recipient of the Microsoft Most Valuable Professional (MVP) 2009 Award, Yaroslav is also a developer audience leader for VanSPUG (Vancouver SharePoint Usergroup) and actively contributes to local and not-so-local technical communities by presenting at local events and sharing his findings in his almost-daily blog: www.sharemuch.com.

Outside of work, Yaroslav enjoys travelling and maintains a growing "places-to-visit" list.

ACKNOWLEDGEMENTS

Throughout my career in software development I have been involved with variety of organizations. I want to give a special thanks to my dynamic team at Habanero Consulting who actively supports and contributes to local and worldwide communities, and especially local SharePoint community here in Vancouver. A lot of my knowledge comes from interacting and exchanging ideas with my team.

My thanks also extend to local and worldwide usergroup leaders with whom I have been involved with over the last few years. Your involvement in the community helps people tremendously, please keep doing what you're doing.

I also would like to mention and thank to all of the bloggers out there who share their ideas online. It takes a lot of effort and dedication to post all of those tips and innovations on your blogs almost every day. Without those posts we wouldn't have such a great community and so many innovative ideas and solutions.

BOOK SOURCE CODE

This book comes with a source code for each chapter. As you go through the book – you will see many examples and source code. The source code in the book is for you to follow the flow of the logic that is referenced, not to type it out into your Visual Studio. If you would like to see actual example in action, download the corresponding chapter source code that is ready for you to compile and use. The source code samples assume you're running the system with:

- Microsoft SharePoint Server 2010 installed.
- Visual Studio 2010 Professional or higher installed.
- PowerShell enabled.
- Sufficient account permissions to access SharePoint 2010 Central Administration and Service Applications.

All source code can be downloaded from the 'Downloads' section at www.sharemuch.com. Below is the source code index for each sample:

CHAPTER 1

Solution Packaging
Custom Solution Deployment Script
Referenced Assemblies in Your SharePoint Solution

CHAPTER 2

List Item Validation
List Item Security
Excluding List Items from Search Crawl
Creating Custom Permissions Levels
Enforce SharePoint List Relationship Behavior
Working with SharePoint List Event Receivers
Aggregating Contents of Lists, Queries, and Rollups

CHAPTER 3

Creating Custom List Item Detail Forms
Field Level Security in Your SharePoint List Forms
Manage Behavior of SharePoint 2010 Composite Fields
Defining List View Look and Feel in Your Custom List Schema
Adding Web Parts to Item Detail View Form

CHAPTER 4

Creating External Content Types with Visual Studio
Exporting and Importing Your BDC Model
Importing BDC Models into Visual Studio
Provisioning SharePoint External List Schema Programmatically
Executing Queries on External Lists

CHAPTER 5

Process Automation and Scheduling Long Running Operations

CHAPTER 6

Creating Your Own User Profile Properties
Creating SharePoint User Profiles Programmatically
Add New Terms to SharePoint User Profile Properties
Retrieving Taxonomy Types Properties from SharePoint User Profile
User Profile Integration with Out-of-the-box Features: Update
MySite Status Message Programmatically
Programmatically Enable Rating on SharePoint Lists and Libraries
Adding Item Rating Control to Your Custom List Forms
Tagging Content Programmatically with Managed Metadata
Service

CHAPTER 7

Creating Basic SharePoint Ribbon Controls
Creating a Fly out Anchor on Your Ribbon
What if your Ribbon Java Script is Too Large for One File
Working with Ribbon Groups and Tabs
Creating Site Level Ribbon Tabs
Determining the State of Ribbon Tabs and Hiding Ribbon
Opening Modal Windows upon Ribbon Control Clicked

CHAPTER 9

Defining Site Templates and Driving Site Content
Provisioning Page Content to Your Pages Programmatically
Provisioning Other Web Parts and Views on to the Page
Provisioning Several Pages with One Module
Privisioning Web Parts directly to page layouts
Rendering Additional Page Specific Metadata during Page Edit
Programmatically Hide SharePoint Web from default Navigation
Limiting Allowed SharePoint Page Layouts on a Desired Web
Setting Automatic Page Title for SharePoint Default Pages

CHAPTER 10

Limiting the List of Available Page Layouts with an Application
Page
Displaying SharePoint "Processing" Page during Your Long Running
Operations

CHAPTER 11

Extending Visual Studio Server Explorer Window with New Nodes
Creating Visual Studio Project and Item Templates

TABLE OF CONTENTS

Introduction v

Whom this book is for vii

About the Author. xi

Acknowledgements xiii

Book source code. xv

Chapter 1 Setting Up for Success: Visual Studio 2010 Solution Structure 1
and Deployment Scripts
    Solution Packaging 7
    Custom Solution Deployment Script 10
    Referenced Assemblies in Your SharePoint Solution 19
    Debugging Your SharePoint Applications. 24

Chapter 2 Lists and Libraries: List Rollups, Security, ...31
and Integration with the Rest of SharePoint 2010 Components
    List Item Validation. 37
    List Item Security. 41
    Excluding List Items from Search Crawl. 43
    Creating Custom Permissions Levels 44
    Enforce SharePoint List Relationship Behavior 47
    Working with SharePoint List Event Receivers. 50
    Aggregating Contents of Lists, Queries, and Rollups. 52

Chapter 3 Lists and List Items: Changing the Look of Forms 61
and Incorporating Custom Logic into Item Forms
    Creating Custom List Item Detail Forms 61
    Field Level Security in Your SharePoint List Forms 66
    Manage Behavior of SharePoint 2010 Composite Fields 71
    Dynamically Changing SharePoint 2010 List Form Rendering Templates . .74
    Making Changes to List View and List Item Detail View Using XSL. 76
    Defining List View Look and Feel in Your Custom List Schema 79
    Adding Web Parts to Item Detail View Form 83

Chapter 4 Using External Data with SharePoint 2010 Out-of-the-Box 91
Components and Custom Features
    Connecting to SQL Server Data Source 91
    Creating External Content Types with Visual Studio 98
    Exporting and Importing Your BDC Model 105
    Importing BDC Models into Visual Studio 108
    Provisioning SharePoint External List Schema Programmatically 111
    Executing Queries on External Lists 114
    SharePoint External List Item Throttling and Limits 117

Chapter 5 Process Automation and Scheduling Long Running Operations . .121

Chapter 6 Metadata, Tags, Rating: Working with and 129
Extending Social Features of SharePoint 2010
    Creating Your Own User Profile Properties 131
    Creating SharePoint User Profiles Programmatically 135
    Add New Terms to SharePoint User Profile Properties 138
    Retrieving Taxonomy Types Properties from SharePoint User Profile 141
    User Profile Integration with Out-of-the-Box Features: 144
    Update MySite Status Message Programmatically
    Getting Started with SharePoint Social Rating Feature. 149
    Changing Update Frequency of SharePoint Rating 150
    and Social Data Synchronization
    Programmatically Enable Rating on SharePoint Lists and Libraries 152
    Adding Item Rating Control to Your Custom List Forms. 156
    Working with Managed Metadata Service and Tagging Features 161
    Tagging Content Programmatically with Managed Metadata Service .163

Chapter 7 Creating SharePoint 2010 Ribbon Components 171
and Managing Existing Ribbon Elements

   Creating Basic SharePoint Ribbon Controls 171

   Creating a Fly Out Anchor on Your Ribbon 175

   What If Your Ribbon Java Script Is Too Large for One File. 178

   Working with Ribbon Groups and Tabs 181

   Creating Site Level Ribbon Tabs. 185

   Determining the State of Ribbon Tabs and Hiding Ribbon. 188

   Where is SharePoint Out-of-the-box Ribbon Defined? 190

   Opening Modal Windows upon Ribbon Control Clicked. 191

Chapter 8 Search: Extending Search Components 199
and Incorporating Search Features in Your Portal

   Add Your Own Search Refinement Categories 200

   Adding New Metadata to Your Search Results View 208

   Adding Graphic Representation of Item Rating to Your Search Results. .215

Chapter 9 Working with SharePoint 2010 Publishing and Custom Pages 221

   Getting Started with Creating Custom SharePoint Pages 222

   Defining Site Templates and Driving Site Content 227

   Provisioning Page Content to Your Pages Programmatically 238

   Provisioning Other Web Parts and Views onto the Page 242

   Provisioning Several Pages with One Module 245

   Provisioning Web Parts Directly to Page Layouts .248

   Rendering Additional Page Specific Metadata during Page Edit 251

   Using SharePoint Publishing Site Navigation Properties. 256

   Programmatically Hide SharePoint Web from Default Navigation 258

   Hide Unused SharePoint Site Templates 260

   Limiting Allowed SharePoint Page Layouts on a Desired Web. 263

   Setting Automatic Page Title for SharePoint Default Pages. 268

Chapter 10 Adding Custom Logic to Your Site Using Application Pages 273

   Limiting the List of Available Page Layouts with an Application Page . . .274

   Displaying SharePoint "Processing" Page during. 279
   Your Long Running Operations

Chapter 11 Extending Visual Studio 2010 to Speed Up 283
and Standardize Your SharePoint 2010 Projects

Extending Visual Studio Server Explorer Window with New Nodes 284

Creating Visual Studio Project and Item Templates 293

CHAPTER 1

Setting Up for Success: Visual Studio 2010 Solution Structure and Deployment Scripts

Getting Visual Studio 2010 solution structure right for your SharePoint 2010 projects is a crucial element for successful solution deployment, future maintenance, and enhancements a few months from now. With Visual Studio 2010, you have much better support in terms of creating solution elements such as modules, event receivers, and features. With that support, you can create solution elements almost anywhere and really confuse your sustainment team (even if it includes you) three months down the road, or confuse other developers trying to pick up where you left off.

Each SharePoint solution will have few logically separated Visual Studio projects serving various functions.

For example, if part of your SharePoint solution will deliver content to a site, the other part will provision Web Parts and lists, and yet another part will provision workflow— it will be fairly confusing and irrational to place them all together as the same Visual Studio project.

Instead, it's best to create a:

- Platform project –to handle provisioning of core components; all the Web Parts and list definitions will go here.

- Content project – to provision default content to pages when the site is deployed –after all you don't want to have a site with nothing on it when customer receives it.
- Services project – to store all of your constant classes as well as any logic that will interact with non-SharePoint systems such as reading and writing to your **web.config** file.
- Branding project – to place all of the components that will take care of your solution branding –items like themes, along with their CSS files, images, and even any footer and header controls.

Here is a typical solution structure for a Platform project:

Platform Project Root

- Features
  - ☐ Master Page provisioning feature
  - ☐ Page layout provisioning feature
  - ☐ Page provisioning feature (s)
  - ☐ General Web Part provisioning feature
- Pages
  - ☐ Page Module
  - ☐ Page specific Web Part module
  - ☐ Page specific list instance
- Page layouts
- Master pages
- ControlTemplates *
  - ☐ Project specific custom user control
- Template *
  - ☐ 1033
  - ☐ Project site template definition
  - ☐ Site Templates
  - ☐ Project site template
- Controls
  - ☐ Custom controls

- **■** Layouts *
  - ☐ Folder (project name)
  - ☐ Layouts ASPX page
- **■** List definitions
  - ☐ List definition
- **■** Lists
  - ☐ List Instance
- **■** Web Parts
  - ☐ General Web Part

aaThe rule of the thumb here is that you should keep all of your solution items hierarchical unless they are generic enough for other elements to reuse. For example, you see that I have "Page specific Web Part module" right under pages; this is mainly due to those custom Web Part modules being used on that page only, and nowhere else. If you anticipate using your Web Part modules throughout your site on multiple pages, the modules for such Web Parts should sit under Web Parts of the root of your SharePoint project (see General Web Part in my tree).

- **■** Content Project Root
- **■** Features
  - ☐ Page provisioning feature (s)
- **■** Pages
  - ☐ Page module

You will notice that this Visual Studio project is much simpler than Platform, here we'll only place content provisioning XML files for your pages.

Services Project Root

- **■** Constants
- **■** List constants
  - ☐ Site constants
  - ☐ Web Part constants

- ■ List Helpers
    - □ Service query helper

The above structure is for a Visual Studio project that is a type of a **Class Library** and not SharePoint project at all. The above project will produce a DLL with all of the classes you might create as you create artifacts for your solution, but in its essence, this is just a container for everything that helps your SharePoint solution but doesn't necessarily belong to it. There is one more benefit to keeping those artifacts separate; when it comes to bug fixes or functionality upgrades, it's easier to replace one DLL that keeps all of the supporting functionality than replacing core **Platform** DLL.

Branding Project Root

- ■ Features
    - □ Theme installer
    - □ Theme setter
- ■ Controls
    - □ Optional header control
    - □ Optional footer control
- ■ Template *
    - □ Layouts
    - □ 1033
    - □ Styles
    - □ Themable
    - □ Project folder (containing images and style artifacts)

The above project will hold your entire theme related artifacts and elements. This way if you need to upgrade a few images or maybe a CSS markup, you can always do it separately without disturbing the rest of the **Platform** solution items.

The above four Visual Studio projects are not mandatory, of course, and if you have really small projects that require no branding or content provisioning, you would not include those respective Visual Studio projects.

Now that we know what goes where, let's go through a few small technicalities on how to create all of those projects in Visual Studio 2010.

We will start by firing up an instance of Visual Studio 2010 and creating a new SharePoint 2010 project as shown below.

Figure 1-1 Creating SharePoint 2010 project in Visual Studio 2010

Remember, despite all of the .NET 4.0 goodness available in Visual Studio, we will use .NET 3.5 since this is the framework that SharePoint 2010 uses.

Next, you will be asked to choose whether your solution is a **Sandox Solution** or **Farm Solution**. In this book, we will be deploying all of our applications as **Farm Solutions**. You will also be asked about the name of the site you wish to use for debugging. It is handy to specify the site that most closely resembles the site template you are creating solutions for— for example: **Team Site**, or **Publishing Site**.

After you picked the site and the type of solution, click **Finish** and your SharePoint project will be created. Your Visual Studio Solution Explorer will contain a single solution with a project in it.

NOTE:

One of the few advantages of creating **Sandoxed Solution** is when the administrator of the farm deploys your solution; they have a choice to decide what level of access to give to your application as well as define a threshold when to disable your solution if it reaches the limits defined in SharePoint 2010 configuration. Some types of project components—for example, Web Parts—require being deployed on a farm, and therefore, cannot be used in a Sandbox Solution.

The project you created will be your Platform project, not because it has to be in that sequence.

Next, navigate to your **Platform** project properties and give a meaningful name to your assembly and namespace. You can see the convention that I recommend, below.

- Assembly Name: **SolutionName.Platform** – for **Platform** project.

- Default Namespace: **SolutionName.Platform** – assuming it's a **Platform** Visual Studio project.

If you remember our **Platform** project structure, it had number of folders and modules. There is a difference between a regular Visual Studio folder and a special mapped folder. A mapped folder is a folder that is mapped to a specific SharePoint 2010 directory under the SharePoint Root (aka: *[Drive]:\Program Files\Common Files\ Microsoft Shared\Web Server Extensions\14*).

To create a mapped folder:

1. Right click on the Platform project.

2. Select Add.

3. Select SharePoint mapped folder.

4. Pick the folder you would like to map (TEMPLATE for example).

5. Click OK.

Now you will see a new folder in your solution structure. In the **Platform** project structure, all of the mapped folders are identified with an asterisk (*).

After I populate my solution structure with the hierarchy we discussed earlier, my Solution Explorer will look similar to what is shown below.

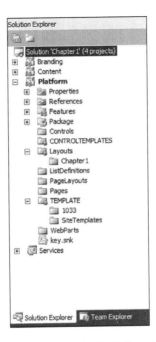

Figure 1-2 Platform project solution structure

Now the remaining pieces left are, at least, **Services** and **Branding** project structure, which follow the same principle.

Solution Packaging

You have created your Visual Studio solution structure and are eager to add components. You can perform manual solution deployment to your SharePoint 2010 farm using tools in SharePoint 2010 Central Administration. As an alternative, you can choose to automate your deployment steps so that every time you do a test deployment—we all know how often that happens—you don't have to go through a series of pages and clicks.

In Visual Studio 2010, you have a great new feature allowing you to build, package, and deploy your solution with a right click of all of the three options in Solution Explorer. In most cases, when you're dealing with a simple set of tasks, the separation between build and package and deploy is OK; In more complex scenarios, you may want to build and package all at once or maybe even copy your resulting solution files (aka WSP) to a destination folder where your automated scripts pick it up and deploy. If the latter is the scenario that sounds like you, we're onto our first custom mini-solution: setting Visual Studio to package on build.

Each SharePoint project you create will come with a project definition file that will outline solution variables such as solution name and whether you're in configuration or release mode. You can modify the project configuration file on each of your SharePoint projects (**Platform, Branding**, etc) to perform your own build tasks when the solution is built in our case package task.

Build tasks are a set of commands you want to execute during build, and most of them are pretty standard. In fact, Visual Studio 2010 comes with a great set of SharePoint tasks, which in past many development teams created manually. You can find a set of tasks here, by opening the file in Notepad: *[Drive]:\Program Files (x86)\MSBuild\ Microsoft\ VisualStudio\ v10.0\SharePointTools\ Microsoft. VisualStudio.SharePoint.targets.*

NOTE:

On a topic of simple code editors I prefer Notepad ++ which is a free for download editor that also numbers your lines and colors your code keywords in all sorts of programming languages making it very easy to navigate through XML files and other code.

In this case, we're after a **CreatePackage** command that creates solution packages (aka WSP files). As you see, the **CreatePackage** is already defined in *Microsoft.VisualStudio.SharePoint.targets.* Here is how we add it as a build task.

To change the standard Visual Studio build order execution, we'll follow the steps below.

1. In your Visual Studio Solution Explorer, right click on the Platform project, and in the menu select Unload Project.

2. Right click on the project again and select Edit Platform.csproj. This will load the solution definition file in an XML compatible editor.

3. Scroll down to the very bottom until you see the following SharePoint targets are loaded.

LISTING 1-1

```
<Import Project="$(MSBuildExtensionsPath32)\ Microsoft\
VisualStudio\v10.0\ SharePointTools\Microsoft.VisualStudio.
SharePoint.targets" />
```

4. Right below is where you define your own build commands. To package, you add the contents below.

LISTING 1-2

```
<PropertyGroup>

<BuildDependsOn>$(BuildDependsOn);CreatePackage</
BuildDependsOn>

</PropertyGroup>
```

This means that whatever build targets are already defined, add **CreatePackage** to the list. If you're thinking about automating the development processes in your team, this is a great place to start. You can add as many of your own or existing targets here to complement a standard build sequence. Here, for example, is how you can copy the output WSP file from the BIN folder, where it usually gets generated to the main solution directory, and where your custom deployment scripts can pick it up.

LISTING 1-3

```
<TargetName="CopyPackage">

    <ExecWorkingDirectory="$(PackagePath)"

        Command="copy$(TargetDir)$(TargetName).wsp

        $(SolutionDir)$(TargetName).
        wsp"ContinueOnError="false"/>

</Target>

<PropertyGroup>

<BuildDependsOn>$(BuildDependsOn);CreatePackage;CopyPackage</
BuildDependsOn>

</PropertyGroup>
```

NOTE:

Ensure the package names for each Visual Studio SharePoint project (**Platform, Branding, Content**) follow below convention: **[solution name].[project name]**;

Example: '**Chapter1.Platform**'. This will make sure the solution files (WSP) are copied successfully to the root folder of your Visual Studio solution.

Once done, you can save your Visual Studio project definition file and reload the project again by right clicking on the **Platform** and choosing **Reload Project**.

Custom Solution Deployment Script

You've created your project structure and you followed all the rules, what else there is to the successful SharePoint custom solution deployment? The deployment comes next. I'm sure you have heard a lot about how easy it is to deploy Visual Studio projects with built-in deployment tools.

Depending on how you have set up your SharePoint and Visual Studio, you may run into an issue with deploying your solution right from Visual Studio. One of the most common issues you may get is the error message when trying to deploy your newly created Visual Studio solution using the **Deploy** command from within Visual Studio.

Error occurred in deployment step 'Recycle IIS Application Pool': The local SharePoint server is not available. Check that the server is running and connected to the SharePoint farm

Or this:

Error occurred in deployment step 'Recycle IIS Application Pool': Cannot connect to the SharePoint site: http://localhost/. Make sure that this is a valid URL and the SharePoint site is running on the local computer. If you moved this project to a new computer or if the URL of the SharePoint site has changed since you created the project, update the Site URL property of the project

Visual Studio uses the following process to deploy your solution: **vssphost4.exe**.

Open your task manager and find the process in the list; take a note of the **User Name** under which this process is running—let's say it's **myadmin_account**.

Next, we'll ensure the SQL server your SharePoint install is using has proper permissions set up for the account Visual Studio is using, here are the steps:

1. Open your SQL Server Management Studio with the user account that is able to manage SharePoint databases.

2. Expand Object Explorer and drill down to **Security -> Logins**.

3. Locate the **myadmin_account**.

4. Right click on the username and select **Properties**.

5. Open **User Mappings** tab.

6. Ensure all three databases below have **myadmin_account** added as a **DBOWNER**:

■ SharePoint_Config

■ SharePoint_AdminContent_[guid]

■ SharePoint Site Content DB

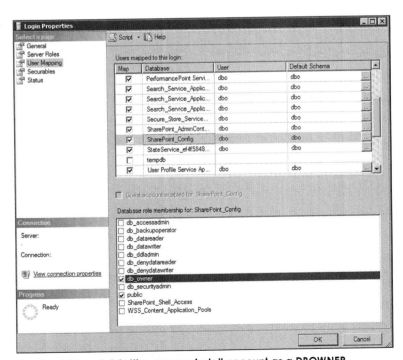

Figure 1-3 Setting up your install account as a DBOWNER

After the changes to the SQL login have been applied, close and launch your Visual Studio. This will ensure the deployment service is recycled, and consequently fix the deployment problem. If you're still seeing the same issue after restarting your Visual Studio, open your task manager and end the **vssphost4.exe** process manually; restart Visual Studio.

Although manual, the deployment method from within Visual Studio is quick and easy—there are more deployment scenarios requiring better approaches. Chances are that your client, and even your QA environment, will not have Visual Studio installed on the server. In order to have a solid deployment strategy and not a hundred pages of deployment documents, it really pays to create install and deployment script. With PowerShell available (which I assume you have by default or will install shortly while finishing reading this sentence) and SharePoint 2010 support of PowerShell commands, the deployment experience is more flexible and robust. After performing several SharePoint 2010 deployments, below is my generic script that will read your configuration and deployment preferences from an XML file to drive the deployment.

If you already have solution files (WSP) in your script directory, you can execute deployment commands with that assumption. The deployment script will consist of three files, plus any WSP files from your solution:

1. SetupSite.bat.

2. SolutionStructure.xml.

3. SetupSite.ps1.

We'll start with **SetupSite.bat**, as this is file's sole purpose is to call PowerShell script (PS1), which actually performs operations. Here is what the file looks like.

LISTING 1-4

```
@echo off

powershell -Command "& {Set-ExecutionPolicy bypass}" -NoExit

powershell -Command ".\SetupSite.ps1" -NoExit

pause
```

SolutionStructure.xml is the file that defines variables that will be used in PS1 script, such as Web Application names, features to be activated, and so on. Let's take a look at the contents.

LISTING 1-5

```
<SetupWebAppUrl="http://localhost">

<Solutions>

    <SolutionWebApplication="True">MyProject.Platform.wsp</
    Solution>

    <SolutionWebApplication="False">MyProject.Branding.
    wsp</Solution>

</Solutions>

<SiteCollectionName="MyNewSite"

Url="/sites/MyNewSite"OwnerAlias="administrator"

Template="STS#0">

    <Features>

        <Feature>MyCustomFeature</Feature>

    </Features>

    <SiteName="MySite" Url="MySite" Template="STS#0">

        <Feature>FeatureName</Feature>

    </Site>

    <SiteName="MySite1" Url="MySite1" Template="STS#0">

    </Site>

</SiteCollection>

</Setup>
```

Here are the variables we are using in the script.

1. **WebAppUrl** –is the Web Application URL. If you're deploying to a different Web Application than a root site, this is where you specify that exact URL.

2. **Solution** –is one of the solutions that will be deployed into the solution gallery in SharePoint Central Administration. You can list as many as you require. Solutions that require deployment on a

Web Application level specified in #1 will have **WebApplication** parameters set to **true**; otherwise, your solution will be deployed to all Web Applications.

3. **SiteCollection** –is a pretty descriptive element denoting a new site collection. Here, we define a site collection administrator user name as **OwnerAlias** and **Template** used for site collection root. If you have a custom template provisioned as a part of your solution, this is where you'd specify its respective ID. For example, **STS#0** is a template ID of a team site.

4. **Feature** –is one or more features that you'd like to see activated at the site collection. Those, for example, are features that will provision your content types.

5. **Site** –is one or more sites that will be created under the site collection. Unless your site is a test site that has nothing but site collection with many pages underneath it, you will have at least few sub-sites.

6. **Site -> Feature** –is the feature that will be activated under the sub-site. When you provision a generic site template—in this case we use team site (STS)—you are likely to provision additional pages under that site. Since your pages will be contained in **Modules**, you will need a feature that will provision them to the proper destination sub-site and not to all of the sites. For that same purpose, you will dedicate a page provisioning feature and activate it under the site where pages should be delivered.

Now that we've looked at the XML file that holds configuration settings, let's take a look at the script that reads all of those settings and makes proper provisions.

LISTING 1-6

```
Write-Host

#define variables for script

[xml]$SiteStructure=get-content SolutionStructure.xml

$WebAppUrl=$SiteStructure.Setup.Attributes.Item(0).Value

$SiteCollectionUrl=$SiteStructure.Setup.SiteCollection.
Attributes.Item(1).Value
```

```
$SiteUrl=$WebAppUrl+$SiteCollectionUrl

#check to ensure Microsoft.SharePoint.PowerShell is loaded

$snapin=Get-PSSnapin | Where-Object{$_.Name-eq 'Microsoft.
SharePoint.Powershell'}

if($snapin —eq $null){

Write-Host "Loading SharePoint PowerShell Snapin"

Add-PSSnapin "Microsoft.SharePoint.Powershell"

}

#delete any existing site found at target URL

$targetUrl=Get-SPSite | Where-Object{$_.Url —eq $SiteUrl}

if($targetUrl.Url.Length —gt 0){

Write-Host "Deleting existing site at " $SiteUrl

Remove-SPSite-Identity $SiteUrl -Confirm:$false

}

#add the solution package

$solutions=$SiteStructure.Setup.Solutions

foreach($solutionInstance in $solutions.ChildNodes)

{

if($solutions.Solution.Count —gt 0)

{

$targetSolution=Get-SPSolution | Where-Object{$_.Name —eq
$solutionInstance.InnerText}

if($targetSolution.Deployed —eq "True")

{

Write-Host "Uninstalling existing solution package: "
$targetSolution.Name

$WebAppInstallTarget=$solutionInstance.Attributes.Item(0).
Value

if($WebAppInstallTarget —eq "True")

{
```

```
Uninstall-SPSolution—Identity $targetSolution.Name —
WebApplication $WebAppUrl-Confirm:$false

}

else{Uninstall-SPSolution —Identity $targetSolution.Name-
Confirm:$false}

do

{

$targetSolution=Get-SPSolution | Where-Object{$_.Name —eq
$solutionInstance.InnerText}

} while($targetSolution.JobExists —eq "True")

Write-Host "Removing existing solution packages"

Remove-SPSolution —Identity $solutionInstance.InnerText
-Confirm:$false

}

Write-Host "Adding solution packages"

Add-SPSolution —LiteralPath $solutionInstance.InnerText

Write-Host "Installing solutions"

$WebAppInstallTarget=$solutionInstance.Attributes.Item(0).
Value

if($WebAppInstallTarget —eq "True")

{

Install-SPSolution —Identity $solutionInstance.InnerText

—WebApplication $WebAppUrl —GACDeployment -force

}

else{Install-SPSolution —Identity $solutionInstance.InnerText
—GACDeployment -force}

do

{

$targetSolution=Get-SPSolution | Where-Object{$_.Name —eq
$solutionInstance.InnerText}

}while($targetSolution.JobExists —eq "True")

}
```

```
}
#creating site structure
$SiteCollectionName=$SiteStructure.Setup.SiteCollection.
Attributes.Item(0).Value;

$SiteCollectionOwner=$SiteStructure.Setup.SiteCollection.
Attributes.Item(2).Value;

$SiteCollectionTemplate=$SiteStructure.Setup.SiteCollection.
Attributes.Item(3).Value;

Write-Host "Creating new site collection at" $SiteUrl

$NewSite=New-SPSite -URL $WebAppUrl $SiteCollectionUrl

-OwnerAlias $SiteCollectionOwner -Template
$SiteCollectionTemplate

-Name $SiteCollectionName

$RootWeb=$NewSite.RootWeb

$features=$SiteStructure.Setup.SiteCollection.Features

if($features.Feature.Length -gt 0)

{

foreach($SiteColFeature in $features.Feature)

{

$ActivatedFeature=Enable-SPFeature $SiteColFeature -url
$RootWeb.Url

Write-Host "Enabled Feature:" $SiteColFeature-
foregroundcolorGreen

}

}

Write-Host "Site collection created successfully"

Write-Host "Title:" $RootWeb.Title -foregroundcolor Green

Write-Host "URL:" $RootWeb.Url -foregroundcolor Green

Write-Host "-------------------------------------"

for($i=1; $i -lt $SiteStructure.Setup.SiteCollection.
ChildNodes.Count; $i++)

{
```

```
$childsite=$SiteStructure.Setup.SiteCollection.ChildNodes.
Item($i);

$WebName=$childsite.Attributes.Item(0).Value

$WebUrl=$childsite.Attributes.Item(1).Value

$WebTemplate=$childsite.Attributes.Item(2).Value

Write-Host "Creating new web at " $SiteUrl/$WebUrl

$NewWeb=New-SPWeb $SiteUrl/$WebUrl —Template $WebTemplate —
Addtotopnav —Useparenttopnav —Name $WebName

Write-Host "Web created successfully"

Write-Host "Title: "$NewWeb.Title —foregroundcolor Green

Write-Host"URL: " $NewWeb.Url —foregroundcolor Green

$features=$SiteStructure.Setup.SiteCollection.ChildNodes.
Item($i)

if($features.Feature.Length —gt 0)

{

foreach($WebFeature in $features.Feature)

{

$ActivatedFeature=Enable-SPFeature $WebFeature —url $NewWeb.
Url

Write-Host"EnabledFeature: " $WebFeature —foregroundcolor
Green

}

}

Write-Host "-------------------------------------------------"

}

start-process —filepath iexplore —argumentlist $SiteUrl
```

The main purpose for dropping this script in front of you is not so you can practice your typing skills. Rather it is to take a look at some of the sections in the script and take note of the syntax and how to access objects and process logic. The next time you need to extend this PowerShell script to include new scenarios, you will have a better idea where to start and what to copy where. This is definitely not the catchall scenarios script, but it will work for most of your small to medium site solution deployments, and definitely reduce your deployment time from one environment to another.

Referenced Assemblies in Your SharePoint Solution

If you're developing a SharePoint 2010 solution that works with third party components or even if it's your own Service project that produces a separate DLL, you will have to instruct SharePoint to deploy those libraries. You may think that just by providing a project reference in your solution, SharePoint project will take care of your extra DLLs and use them in WSP it generates; however, there are few extra steps you need to take to make that happen.

Assuming you are referencing an internal assembly from another project residing in the same Visual Studio solution, here are the steps you need to take:

1. Create a reference in the SharePoint project that uses your **Service** project

   ■ Right click on your SharePoint project and select **Add a Reference**.

   ■ Select **Projects** tab.

   ■ Add a new reference.

2. In the Solution Explorer of your SharePoint project locate **Package** and expand it.

3. Double click on expanded child element of **Package**.

4. Click **Advanced** from the newly opened window and click **Add**.

5. Here pick the option **Add Assembly from Project Output**.

6. Pick the assembly from the drop down and click **OK**.

NOTE:

The assembly you will be referencing from your project must be signed with a strong name key if you're planning to deploy it to Global Assembly Cache.

Now, if you're referencing third party assemblies that you have already copied into your solution structure, you'd perform the steps below to make your DLLs part of the SharePoint project package.

In your Solution Explorer, in SharePoint project, locate **Package** and expand it.

Double click on expanded child element of **Package**.

Click **Advanced** from the newly opened window and click **Add**.

Here pick the option **Add Existing Assembly**.

Locate an assembly from the disk and click **OK**.

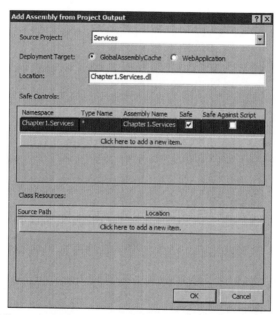

Figure 1-4 Adding a project output assembly to the package of SharePoint project

A nice feature about Visual Studio is that it will provision all of the necessary Safe Control attributes into your IIS site **web.config** file to make sure your assembly is loaded properly. In some cases, you may want to make additional changes to web.config at the time of your solution deployment. You may want to set variables in your **web.config** so that your custom application will consume, connection strings, custom error pages, custom login pages, authentication providers, and so on. You can either write a one – or two—page deployment instruction for your administrators on all of those settings or you can programmatically provision those changes and save yourself and everyone user errors. Here, we'll see how to create a SharePoint Web Application scoped feature allowing to provision variables to **web. config** at the time of deployment.

The reason why our feature will be activated on Web Application scope is so that application changes can take place before other potentially dependent features on site collections and sites are deployed.

We'll start by creating new **Web Application** scoped feature in your Solution Explorer in **Platform** project.

1. Locate **Features** node in your Solution Explorer; right click on it and select **Add Feature**.

2. Specify feature title.

3. Select **Scope** to be a **Web Application** and save the feature.

4. Right click on newly create feature from Solution Explorer and select **Add Event receiver**.

5. Locate **FeatureActivated(SPFeatureReceiverProperties properties)** and uncomment the section.

6. Right above the definition for the **FeatureActivated** you uncommented add the following security identifier on a class:

LISTING 1-7

```
[SharePointPermission(SecurityAction.LinkDemand, ObjectModel
= true)]
```

7. Add the following namespace reference section:

   □ using System.Collections.Generic;

   □ using Microsoft.SharePoint.Administration;

8. Define the class variable that will hold all of your configurations:

```
List<SPWebConfigModification> webConfigModifications =
new List<S
   PWebConfigModification>();
```

9. Add the helper methods (below) right under your **FeatureActivated**; those will serve as helper methods entering various elements and attributes in the **web.config**

LISTING 1-8

```
protected void SaveConfig(SPWebApplication app)

{

foreach (SPWebConfigModification mod in webConfigModifications)

{

app.WebConfigModifications.Add(mod);

}

webConfigModifications.Clear();

}

protected void AddSection(string name, string xpath)

{

SPWebConfigModification mod = new SPWebConfigModification(name,
xpath);

mod.Sequence = 0;

mod.Type = SPWebConfigModification.SPWebConfigModificationType.
EnsureSection;

webConfigModifications.Add(mod);

}

protected void AddNodeValue(string name, string xpath, string
resource)

{

SPWebConfigModification mod = new SPWebConfigModification(name,
xpath);

mod.Sequence = 0;

mod.Type = SPWebConfigModification.SPWebConfigModificationType.
EnsureChildNode;

mod.Value = resource;

webConfigModifications.Add(mod);
```

```
}

protected void AddAttributeValue(string name, string xpath,
string value)

{

SPWebConfigModification mod = new SPWebConfigModification(name,
xpath);

mod.Sequence = 0;

mod.Type = SPWebConfigModification.SPWebConfigModificationType.
EnsureChildNode;

mod.Value = value;

webConfigModifications.Add(mod);

}
```

Lastly, we'll enter our **web.config** changes to illustrate the syntax we use. Place the listing below into the **FeatureActivated** method body

LISTING 1-9

```
SPWebApplication app = properties.Feature.Parent as
SPWebApplication;

string customErrorPath = "configuration/system.web/*[local-
name()='customErrors']";


AddNodeValue("error", customErrorPath, "<error
statusCode='404☐ redirect='~/Pages/404.aspx' />");

AddAttributeValue("mode", "configuration/system.web/
customErrors", "On");


string authenticationPath = " configuration/system.
web/*[local-name()='authentication']";


AddNodeValue("forms", authenticationPath, "<forms
name='MySignIn' loginUrl='SignIn.aspx' path='/Pages/' />");


SaveConfig(app);
```

```
app.Farm.Services.GetValue<SPWebService>().
ApplyWebConfigModifications();

app.Update();
```

As you can see, we're calling the helper functions we created earlier to specify:

- Custom 404 error page
- Turn on custom errors
- Set forms authentication
- Set custom form to handle forms authentication

Now, when this solution is deployed the feature will be activated and all of the defined changes will automatically get provisioned to the relevant configuration file.

Debugging Your SharePoint Applications

So far, you have learned how to create your solutions and deploy them automatically. What else could you possibly need before starting your custom component development? Debugging is next. Knowing how to debug your application in various scenarios can make a difference between painful guessing, traversing through thousands of lines of logs and stepping through the code and identifying the problem in just few minutes.

In SharePoint 2010, there has been significant improvement in terms of debugging information that is emitted when errors happen. By default, SharePoint holds all of its logs in the following location: [Drive]:\Program Files\Common Files\Microsoft Shared\Web Server Extensions\14\LOGS.

If you open this location you will see at least few log files that log the activity happening on your SharePoint install. If you open one of the files, you will be instantly overloaded with the volumes of information those logs contain. One of the useful pieces of information SharePoint provides when errors occur is the **Correlation ID** of the error. **Correlation ID** is the number in a GUID format that links the error with the corresponding record in the log file. If you copy the ID from the error message on the screen and search for it in the log file, you will narrow down troubleshooting from a few thousand lines to ten or so.

One of the other issues you might be having is that SharePoint doesn't collect enough logging information in the log files and, therefore, they become useless. The good news is that you can adjust the verbosity and type of the logs in SharePoint Central Administration; here is how.

1. Navigate to your SharePoint Central Administration with the install account credentials.

2. Click on the **Monitoring** link on the left side navigation.

3. Under the **Reporting** section, click **Configure Diagnostic Logging**.

4. Here, pick the category of SharePoint activity you wish to monitor.

5. Set the **Least critical event to report to the event log** to **Warning** or other appropriate level.

6. In the next dropdown select **Verbose** to get the most detailed log information. Keep in mind that this will cause general system slowdown and produce large volume of logs.

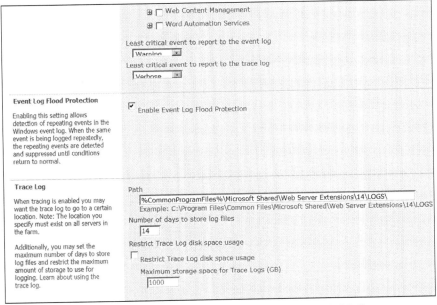

Figure 1-5 Diagnostic logging settings for your SharePoint site

7. In the **Trace Log** section, you can also pick where the log will be stored if different from the current location.

Setting up verbose logging may be helpful at the time you have a problem but as soon as you don't need the option to be available, give your SharePoint server a break and set the logging to be less verbose and you will notice an increase in performance.

Information in logs is only the data that SharePoint was able to catch from its modules. If you're trying to find an issue with your customizations, SharePoint logs may not be the first place you want to look.

We have all seen generic error pages and know how frustrating it can be to determine the cause of the problem.

At first, it's quite clear that you have to disable custom error reporting that IIS site SharePoint is running. However, there is at least site collection you're working with, as well as the Central Administration site, not to mention the entire out-of-the-box virtual directories have their own configuration files. So which **web.config** file do you have to modify to get to the bottom of the error message clarity issue?

If your error occurred while performing out-of-the-box activities in SharePoint or custom Web Parts loaded into the page, you need to make the following changes.

1. Open **IIS Manager** on your SharePoint server with an install account credentials.

2. Expand **Sites** node and locate the site that represents your SharePoint site.

3. Right click on the Site node, select **Manage Web Site -> Advanced Settings**.

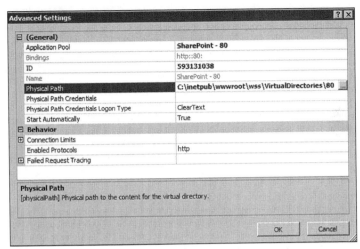

Figure 1-6 Determining the physical path of of your SharePoint site using IIS

4. Locate the physical path and copy the location. You path is likely to be something like this: *[Drive]:\inetpub\wwwroot\wss\ VirtualDirectories\80*.

5. Locate the **web.config** file and open it in **Notepad**.

6. Find the following in the file: **customErrors**.

7. Replace the value of the **mode** attribute to **Off**.

8. Find the following in the file: **debug** and change its value to **true**.

9. Find the following in the file: **CallStack** and change its value to **true**.

10. Save the file and refresh the page on which you received an error originally.

Now, you should get a more detailed description of the error and debug your application.

If you have received an error while executing custom functionality in SharePoint Central Administration, your steps of troubleshooting would be exactly as above except in your IIS Manager, you would located the **Physical Path** of your SharePoint Central Administration site.

Things can be a bit confusing to most folks who have enabled those options in their corresponding **web.config** files and still get a cryptic error when trying to debug their custom page in the **_layouts** folder or a custom web service in the **_vti_bin** folder.

As mentioned before, those are virtual folders in IIS and, therefore, they have their own **web.config** which you guessed right ... has its own values set for debugging and error handling.

As you've see how to extract the path to the appropriate **web.config** location in IIS for web sites, the same approach applies to virtual directories such as **_layouts** and **_vti_bin**. Once you have the physical location of the file, go ahead and make modifications that apply to your scenario.

Now, when you open **web.config** files in your virtual directories, they will look much smaller and with less detail. This doesn't mean you have to specify debugging parameters here. If you specified **debug='true'** in your site **web.config**, this value will be inherited. Only the values that are defined in the virtual directory explicitly need to be overwritten— usually it's **CustomErrors**.

Options above turn on heavy logging on your SharePoint server and produce significant overhead in processing, meaning it's not OK to have those on by default in your production environment.

CHAPTER 2

Lists and Libraries: List Rollups, Security, and Integration with the Rest of SharePoint 2010 Components

Working with lists is one of the most common tasks you will do in SharePoint. After all, lists are nearly everything in SharePoint. Blog articles, discussions, calendars, document libraries are all lists. Understanding some of the enhancements in how lists work will make a difference when creating your custom applications.

We'll start by adding a simple list to the Visual Studio structure we have created before. The concept of list includes list definition and list instance. As the name suggests, the definition will define what fields your list is going to have, views, and queries. The instance will create a new instance of this list and possibly set some initial data into the list. In most cases many lists are already defined, and in fact, SharePoint comes with variety of available list types. If you're happy with any of the list definitions that SharePoint comes with, the only task to do is to create an instance of the list. Let's see what involved in creating a list instance using Visual Studio. Since our list instance is going to be a generic instance not tied to any specific page, we'll create a new Visual Studio folder under the root of our **Platform** project and call it **Lists**. Following the steps below, we create a list instance.

1. Right click on **Lists -> Add -> New item**.

2. Select **List Instance** from the dropdown and give it a name.

3. Click **Add**.

4. On the next window, besides the obvious name and description parameters, examine the list of available list definitions you can instantiate and pick **Custom List**.

5. Click **Finish**.

You will notice that a new module has been created for the list, and also a new feature has been added to the project. If you double click on the feature name, you will see a form where Visual Studio tells you that your list instance has been added to the feature and now will be provisioned wherever the feature is activated. Since the feature that Visual Studio created is set to activate by default, your list instance will be provisioned right away to the root site.

Let's deploy the solution using Visual Studio deployment command:

1. Right click on the Visual Studio solution name.

2. Select **Deploy** and wait for Visual Studio to complete deployment.

When deployment is complete and you open your SharePoint test site - you will notice that the list has been indeed created, but the only field that it has available is the **Title** field.

I don't know about you, but in most cases, I would like my list to be able to hold my custom metadata fields. Metadata of the item is defined with a **Content Type**. A content type will be based on one of the existing content types such as **Page** or Item, and will enhance that content type to include additional fields you need. Let's go ahead and create a custom content type for the new type of item and define any custom columns it might have.

1. In your Solution Explorer, locate **ListDefinitions** folder and right click on it.

2. From the menu select **Add -> New Item**.

3. Pick **Content Type** and set the name.

4. SharePoint will provide a long list of existing content types on which to build your custom one. Let's pick an **Item** from a list of content types.

5. Click **Finish**.

Now, the new content type is created, but it's useless until we add some fields to it. For the reference of existing fields that are provisioned in SharePoint by default, check out the **fields** feature located here: [Drive] :\Program Files\Common Files\Microsoft Shared\Web Server Extensions\14\TEMPLATE\FEATURES\fields.

There you will find a variety of different fields and their types; this is a great reference to build your own field if required, just as I will do now.

1. Double click on the newly created content type to ensure you are editing its **Elements.xml** file.

2. Right after the content type closing tag **</ContentType>**, insert the following field definition:

LISTING 2-1

```
<Field ID="{658D3426-DA8B-488A-80D1-C8A62E0B71EB}"

Name="MyField"

Type="Text"

DisplayName="My Field"

SourceID="http://schemas.microsoft.com/sharepoint/v3" />
```

NOTE:

To create random GUID, I use Visual Studio Create GUID tool from the tools menu.

3. Create a new field reference right between **<FieldRefs>** node like this:

<FieldRef ID="{658D3426-DA8B-488A-80D1-C8A62E0B71EB}" Name="MyField" />

Your field reference is just the field you have created.

The entire code will look something like this, without the same **IDs** of course:

LISTING 2-2

```
<Elementsxmlns="http://schemas.microsoft.com/sharepoint/">
<!--ParentContentType:Item(0x01)-->
<ContentTypeID="0x010038333e0117c245669287b96037d5fe60"
        Name="Platform-ContentType1"
        Group="CustomContentTypes"
        Description="MyContentType"
        Inherits="TRUE"
        Version="0">
<FieldRefs>
        <FieldRefID="{658D3426-DA8B-488A-80D1-C8A62E0B71EB}"
        Name="MyField"/>
</FieldRefs>
</ContentType>
<FieldID="{658D3426-DA8B-488A-80D1-C8A62E0B71EB}"
        Name="MyField"
        Type="Text"
        DisplayName="MyField"
        SourceID="http://schemas.microsoft.com/sharepoint/v3"/>
</Elements>
```

Now that we have our content type, let's create a list definition that
uses it.

1. In your Solution Explorer, right click the **ListDefinitions** folder and
   select **Add -> New Item**.

2. Pick **List Definition from Content Type** and give it a name.

3. Pick any name and find the newly created content type name
   from the list of content types that Visual Studio suggests. Notice
   that you are suggested to create a list instance from this list
   definition; set that checkbox too.

4. Click **Finish**.

You will notice Visual Studio has created a list definition and the list instance folder is right in the folder of a list definition. Let's take a look at how Visual Studio defined our new field in your list definition.

1. Locate the **schema.xml** from the folder that Visual Studio created for your list definition.

2. Open the **schema.xml** file.

3. Take note how the **schema.xml** now has a reference to your **Content Type ID** and the new field.

The generated code for the content type will look something like this:

LISTING 2-3

```xml
<?xml version="1.0" encoding="utf-8"?>
<List xmlns:ows="MicrosoftSharePoint"
        Title="Platform-ListDefinition1"
        FolderCreation="FALSE"
        Direction="$Resources:Direction;"
        Url="Lists/Platform-ListDefinition1"
        BaseType="0" xmlns="http://schemas.microsoft.com/
        sharepoint/">
<MetaData>
<ContentTypes>
        <ContentType ID="0x010038333e0117c245669287b96037d5
        fe60"
            Name="Platform-ContentType1"
            Group="CustomContentTypes"
            Description="MyContentType"
            Inherits="TRUE" Version="0">
        <FieldRefs>
            <FieldRefID="{658D3426-DA8B-488A-80D1-
            C8A62E0B71EB}"
                Name="MyField"/>
        </FieldRefs>
```

```
    </ContentType>
  </ContentTypes>
```

If you open the same feature Visual Studio created for you the first time you create a list instance, you will see that now there is a content type, list definition, and new list instance. Whether all of those components are going to be provisioned with the same feature is entirely up to you. You may decide that all of the content types and definitions must be available on each site of your solution, but only one site should have instances of those lists. In this scenario, you would create a separate feature to provision your lists and keep the initial feature to provision your content types and other artifacts.

Assuming you created a site to deploy your Visual Solution to, right click on your solution and select **Deploy**.

You will be asked whether you would like to upgrade a schema of the first list that you created in your Visual Studio solution, select **Resolve Automatically** to upgrade the schema. Althought in our case we haven't made any changes it`s nitce to see that Visual Studio takes care of resolving schema conflicts for you.

Once the solution has deployed successfully, open the site and let's take a look at the second list instance you have created based on your custom **Content Type**. If you accepted all of the default changes when created content list definition, the name of your list will be **Platform – ListInstance1**.

Click **Add new item** button and you will see a new form with your custom field in it.

That's how easy it really is to create your own custom fields and lists. Now that you're still excited about this task, check out some of the field types available and create your own fields based on the ones you find here: *[Drive] :\Program Files\Common Files\Microsoft Shared\Web Server Extensions\14\TEMPLATE\FEATURES\fields*.

If you switch back to your Visual Studio and the list definition folder, you can change the name of your list instance by editing the **Elements.xml** file in the **ListInstance1** folder.

Take a look at the contents of the file and some of the attributes available for editing.

Also, remember how our initial list instance was created in **Lists** Visual Studio folder? It's good idea to be consistent and move the **ListInstance1** to the **Lists** folder by dragging the list instance folder to a new location in the Visual Studio tree structure.

Both instance and definition will still be able to find each other by the equal attribute in **ListInstance1 -> TemplateType and ListDefinition ->Type**.

Try deploying the solution again using Visual Studio **deploy** command. You will notice that deploy has failed with a message that our custom field id we has been already installed in the solution. Remember in our **Elements.xml** for the content type we added the definition of our custom field? When we create a new list definition based on the content type, Visual Studio defined the field again in the **schema. xml** file. In order to resolve the error we're getting you will have to delete the duplicate field definition Visual Studio added to the **schema.xml** file.

After this manuall correction, your solution will deploy with no problem.

List Item Validation

One of the most common requests when working with lists and libraries is to enable validation of list fields. One of the great improvements in SharePoint has been made particularly to that functionality. SharePoint has entire field validation syntax that you can set in your list definition.

Assuming you still have a list definition from the last list provisioning example we looked at, let's now make the title field validate user input and return custom error if validation fails.

1. In your Solution Explorer, locate the list definition you created in the previous example.

2. Open the **schema.xml** file and scroll all the way to the bottom until you see the **</MetaData>** closing tag.

3. Right before the **</MetaData>** closing tag, enter the following validation syntax:

LISTING 2-4

```
<Validation Message="Something is not quite right with this
value" >

=Title="My Value"

</Validation>
```

4. Save the file and right click on your solution to deploy the project with Visual Studio resolving all of the schema conflicts you're prompted to resolve.

Once deployed, open your list instance on the test site and try adding a new item with the title equal to any other value than **My Value**. You will get the error message you have set earlier.

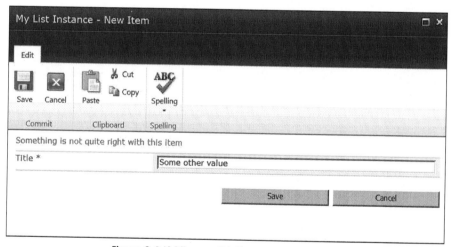

Figure 2-1 List item validation on item entered

Obviously, the example with the text comparison has little business value, so I thought you might like a more comprehensive list of validation logic. Search MSDN with the keyword – **Calculated Field Formulas** to find more options.

Now if you're not a fan of adhering to calculated field rules, you have an option to specify your validation logic with JavaScript. In this example, you will see that validation logic can be specified right in the field definition (when we're creating our content type).

Here is an example of what the validation XML element will look like within the custom field definition added to the content type to verify that the number entered in the field is greater than zero. Switch to the **Elements.xml** file on the content type definition in your solution and add the following code right after the definition of **MyField**:

LISTING 2-5

```
<Field Type="Number"

    DisplayName="TestNumber"

    ID="{e47ae7ad-fb63-4ead-a50c-4143f86e727f}"

    StaticName="TestNumber"

    Name="TestNumber">

    <Validation Message="Test Number must be greater than 0"

    Script="function(x){return SP.Exp.Calc.valid(SP.Exp.
    Node.f('GT',[SP.Exp.Node.a(0),SP.Exp.Node.v(0)]),x)}">

    =TestNumber&gt;0

    </Validation>

</Field>
```

Additionally, in order for the field to appear in the list instance entry form we'll add the reference to the list definition **schema.xml** of our custom list.

Right after:

<FieldRef ID="{658D3426-DA8B-488A-80D1-C8A62E0B71EB}" Name="MyField" />

We add:

<FieldRef ID="{e47ae7ad-fb63-4ead-a50c-4143f86e727f}" Name=" TestNumber" />

To test this method of field validation – deploy the solution with Visual Studio and try adding new item in our test list instance on your SharePoint test site.

When you enter a value below zero into the **TestNumber** field – you will receive a corresponding error message.

If you think that hardcoding validation logic inside schema is not something you want to do because your logic may change and you can't afford recreating the list schema, there is an approach to setting validation rules with the event receiver code.

Event receiver is attached to the SharePoint feature and is executed upon the feature being activated. The code within the event receiver is just like any other code, plus you get access to event receiver context variables that let you access contextual information about the site the that the receiver was called from, and from there you can access other object that might be useful in your logic.

Here is how you create an event receiver in a feature that will assign validation logic to a field in the list.

1. Add a new feature in your Solution Explorer **Features** folder.
2. Give a feature a name (Ex.: ProvisionListValidation)
3. Right click on the feature name and select **Add Event Receiver**.
4. A new CS file will be added to your feature. Double click to open the file.
5. Uncomment the **FeatureActivated** section of the file and replace the code to match below:

LISTING 2-6

```
public override void FeatureActivated(SPFeatureReceiverProper
ties properties)
{
SPWeb web = properties.Feature.Parent as SPWeb;
SPList list = web.Lists["My List"];
if (list != null)
{
        list.ValidationFormula = "=Title=\"My desired value\"";

        list.ValidationMessage = "Something is not quite right
        with this item";
```

```
list.EnforceDataValidation = true;

list.Update();

}

}
```

Ensure that the value of **My List** is actual value of the list instance title you have provisioned earlier.

6. In the Solution Explorer double click on the new feature folder to open its properties. On the bottom of the properties window you will see **Feature Activation Dependencies**. Expand the section.

7. Here we need to ensure that our event receiver will start working on a list only after the list is provisioned with its parent feature. Therefore, in the **Activation Dependencies** section click **Add** button to add feature name that is used to provision lists.

8. Deploy the solution and navigate to your SharePoint test site.

On your site, locate the list you have added custom validation to. When you enter values other than defined in the validation code, your list will have the same validation messages as entered through the **schema.xml**. One benefit of this approach is that you can grab the formula configuration string dynamically and therefore in a future change it without recreating the list schema.

List Item Security

Since lists represent and store all sorts of data in SharePoint, every developer wants to have as much flexibility with the concept of lists as possible. One of those flexibilities is list item security. One of the features that SharePoint has is the ability to restrict whether users can read and edit all items in the list or only their own. This setting is not tied up to a permission definition and doesn't validate whether user belongs to a specific group. The implementation simply compares the author or the item and determines whether the user is allowed to read or edit the item.

Here is how you can set this setting:

1. Navigate to the list instance you created in the previous example or create new list.

2. On the ribbon tab, click **List** and select **List Settings** option.

3. Click **Advanced Settings** and take a look at the available options for **Item-level Permissions**.

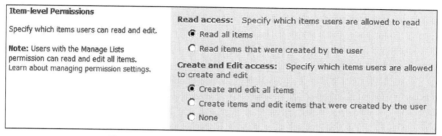

Figure 2-2 Item level permissions for list items

When you provision your solution along with all the other definitions and settings you would set **Item Level Permissions** automatically by using a feature receiver just like we attached it in the previous example.

Here are the steps involved in setting your list security programmatically:

1. Add a new feature and call it **ProvisionListSecurity**.

2. On the feature property page add new **Feature Activation Dependency** on the list provisioning feature just like you did in a last sample.

3. Add an event receiver to our feature and replace its **FeatureActivated** code with the following.

LISTING 2-7

```
public override void FeatureActivated(SPFeatureReceiverProper
ties properties)
{
SPWeb web = properties.Feature.Parent as SPWeb;
SPList list = web.Lists["My List"];
list.ReadSecurity = 1;
list.WriteSecurity= 1;
```

```
list.Update();
```

}

4. Deploy the solution with Visual Studio. Navigate to your
    SharePoint test site and a list you have referenced in your feature
    to verify whether new security settings have been successfully
    applied during the deployment.

The value of **ReadSecurity** we used in our code is a 32-bit integer with
the following range:

> 1 - All users have Read access to all items.
>
> 2 - Users have Read access only to items that they create.

WriteSecurity is a 32-bit integer with the possible values including:

> 1 - All users can modify all items.
>
> 2 - Users can modify only items that they create.
>
> 4 - Users cannot modify any list item.

This is particularly handy if you're creating a list that will be used for
system purposes and that only has to store values of users accepting
terms of service. In this scenario, you can ensure that no one can
modify the item once it's created.

Excluding List Items from Search Crawl

As the last example illustrated, you can set list settings to have certain
limitations on the way users access the items in the list, which can
be used for your custom system settings. One of the most common
concepts that go along with securing your lists is to exclude lists
from search crawl. Search crawl has pretty granular settings and
configuration, and the easiest way to exclude the list from search
crawl is from the same settings page you manage list item permissions.

Same as in my last example I will be using a feature receiver that
will initialize on the web where I host my list. The feature receiver
FeatureActivated code will look like this:

LISTING 2-8

```
public override void FeatureActivated(SPFeatureReceiverProper
ties properties)

{

SPWeb web = properties.Feature.Parent as SPWeb;

SPList list = web.Lists["My List"];

// Specify whether this list should be visible in search
results

list.NoCrawl = true;

// disabling list item attachments

list.EnableAttachments = false;

// Specify whether the "New Folder" command is available

list.EnableFolderCreation = false;

list.Update();

}
```

In the example above you've got a couple of other settings on top of search crawl activation settings. One of them, **EnableAttachments**, specifies whether users can add attachments to their items. Another one, **EnableFolderCreation** –specifies whether users can create new folders or if the list is flat.

Creating Custom Permissions Levels

One thing that happens quick with SharePoint is that because it's so easy and allows so much, everyone gets on it and tries to create their sites, document libraries, and so on. Then after a while, you end up with a situation where you have confidential or sensitive data exposed to unprivileged users. To avoid situation like this, here we'll take a look at how you can create custom permission levels and roles to manage which groups can do what in SharePoint.

Let's access the list we have created as a sample in our last example, or create a new list. Open the list, and on the **List** ribbon tab, click **List Settings**. On the settings that that you will see right after, click **Permissions for this list**.

Among few other items, you will notice this message: **This list inherits
permissions from its parent.** This option means that everyone who
has access to the site can see the list. Click the **Stop Inheriting** ribbon
button and click **OK** to the info message that comes up.

Now if you click the **Grant Permissions** button on the ribbon, you will
be presented with a modal window that allows you to pick users from
your site and set various levels of access for them.

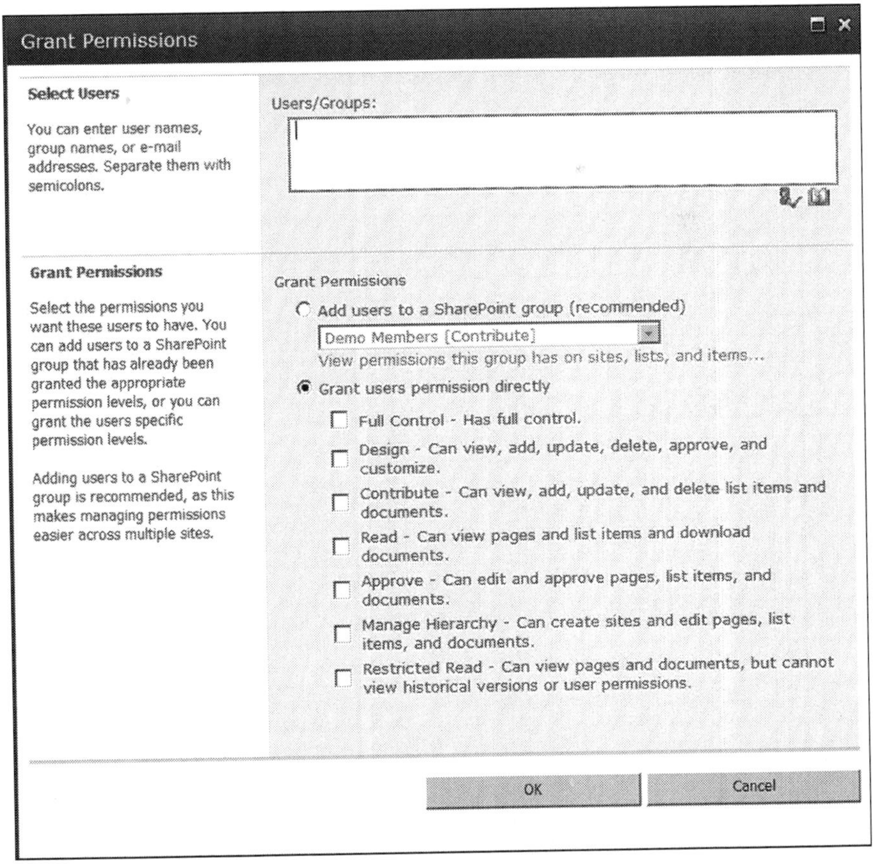

Figure 2-3 Levels of access offered when granting permissions

Notice how the **Contribute** level gives the ability to add, edit, update,
and delete. In some cases, you may not want to let users delete
content—just add and edit or just add. In this case, you will have to

create your custom permission level, which you will see in the list of
levels shown above.

To create a custom permission level, assign a set of permissions to it,
and to bind it to the group, we will use the feature and its receiver logic.
Here is the code I will have in my **FeatureActivated**:

LISTING 2-9

```
public override void FeatureActivated(SPFeatureReceiverProper
ties properties)

{

// Create custom permission level with a set of permissions

SPWeb web = properties.Feature.Parent as SPWeb;

SPRoleDefinition role = new SPRoleDefinition();

role.BasePermissions = SPBasePermissions.OpenItems

 | SPBasePermissions.EditListItems

 | SPBasePermissions.ViewListItems

 | SPBasePermissions.ViewPages

 | SPBasePermissions.Open

 | SPBasePermissions.ViewFormPages;

role.Name = "My Role Name";

role.Description = "My Role Description";

if (web.RoleDefinitions[role.Name]!=null)

{

    web.RoleDefinitions.Delete(role.Name);

}

web.RoleDefinitions.Add(role);

// Then we assign a set of permissions to an

// existing group in this case called MyGroup

SPRoleAssignment roleAssignment =

    new SPRoleAssignment(web.SiteGroups["MyGroup"]);
```

```
roleAssignment.RoleDefinitionBindings.Add(role);

web.RoleAssignments.Add(roleAssignment);

}
```

To test this feature, right click the solution name in the Solution Explorer and select **Deploy**. When the solution deploys and feature activates, you will notice a new permission level that was added to the list of permission levels on the **Grant Permissions** page we looked at initially. If you notice, I added assignment of my custom permission level to a group on the site. This step is optional and you don't have to have a group on the site with the specified permission level. However, it is a good example that you might need to use in a future. After all, all of SharePoint maps out-of-the-box permissions levels to groups such as Members, Owners, and Visitors.

Also, here are some great references on various permissions available, which you can add to your permission levels. Search MSDN site with the following **SPBasePermissions**.

Enforce SharePoint List Relationship Behavior

List relationship is a new concept in SharePoint 2010 that allows you to have one list to have a lookup into another one and, if delete is performed on the dependent items, you can either choose to cascade delete on related child items or restrict deletion.

To set this list relationship up, you will need two lists. One of them will be your child list and another main list. The child list will have a lookup field created in it, which will link to a field in the main list.

Let's set this up with new list in our Visual Studio solution structure.

1. Locate the **Lists** node in our Visual Studio solution you created in the beginning.

2. Create a new **List Instance** called **Main** and use **CustomList** definition for it.

3. Once the list instance is created, open the **Elements.xml** file and take a note of URL node of the list instance. In my case, it's **Url='List/Platform-Main'**.

4. Locate the **List Definitions** folder in your solution and create new **Content Type** in it.

5. For your content type parent choose **Item**.

6. Open the **Elements.xml** file of your newly created content type and add the following field definition right after **</ContentType>** node:

LISTING 2-10

```
<Field Name="MyLookupField"

        Type="Lookup" Required="TRUE" DisplayName="MyField"

        List="Lists/Platform-Main" ShowField="Title"

        ID="{29B8A30E-7CB9-463F-A295-9EEE815C0F71}"

        Indexed="TRUE" Sealed="TRUE"

        RelationshipDeleteBehavior="Cascade"

        SourceID="http://schemas.microsoft.com/sharepoint/v3"

        StaticName="MyLookupField">

</Field>
```

In here, the ID is auto-generated; the name and the title can be whatever you choose. The **List** attribute will point to the list URL you have taken note of Step 3. The **RelationshipDeleteBehavior** attribute is set to cascade, meaning that child items will be deleted when the main items are deleted. There are two more options available: to restrict deletion and take no action. For up to date information on those, search for **RelationshipDeleteBehavior** on MSDN.

7. Add newly create field to the **<FieldRef>** section of your content type:

```
<FieldRef Name="MyLookupField" ID="{29B8A30E-7CB9-463F-A295-9EEE815C0F71}"/>
```

8. Verify that your content type definition looks something like this:

LISTING 2-11

```
<?xml version="1.0" encoding="utf-8"?>

<Elements xmlns="http://schemas.microsoft.com/sharepoint/">
```

```
<!-- Parent ContentType: Item (0x01) -->
<ContentType ID="0x01004b64c1007ac1481994c0bd3b6e3a2b60"
        Name="Platform - ContentType1"
        Group="Custom Content Types"
        Description="My Content Type"
        Inherits="TRUE"
        Version="0">
<FieldRefs>
        <FieldRef Name="MyLookupField"
          ID="{29B8A30E-7CB9-463F-A295-9EEE815C0F71}"/>
</FieldRefs>
</ContentType>
<Field Name="MyField"
        Type="Lookup"
        Required="TRUE"
        DisplayName="MyField"
        List="Lists/Platform-Main"
        ShowField="Title"
        ID="{29B8A30E-7CB9-463F-A295-9EEE815C0F71}"
        Indexed="TRUE"
        RelationshipDeleteBehavior="Cascade"
        Sealed="TRUE" SourceID="http://schemas.microsoft.com/
        sharepoint/v3" StaticName="MyField">
</Field>
</Elements>
```

9. Right click **ListDefinitions** folder to create a new **List Definition from Content Type**.

10. Accept all the defaults and specify the name of the content type you created earlier as your content type.

11. Locate the schema.xml file in your newly create list definition and remove field definition located within **<Fields>** section of your XML. Similar to earlier example Visual Studio created duplicate field definition, which will result in error when solution deployed the second time.

12. Deploy your solution from within Visual Studio.

Both lists will be provisioned to the site. Now let's test the behavior.

1. Open the **Main** list and create an item in it.

2. Open the child list (called **Platform – ListInstance2**, if you accepted defaults) and create a new item in it; you will see the name of the item from the **Main** list will show up as a drop down box selection.

3. Open the **Main** list again and try deleting the one and only item. You should receive a message like this:

    Sending this item to the site Recycle Bin will also send any related items in the following lists to the site Recycle Bin: [Platform – ListInstance1]. Are you sure you want to send the item(s) to the site Recycle Bin?

4. Click **OK** and both items will be deleted from both lists.

If you chose **Restrict** attrbiute value as your referential rule in the **MyLookupField** definition, the delete action would fail.

For more reference on various rules available and their behavior search MSDN for **RelationshipDeleteBehavior**.

Working with SharePoint List Event Receivers

Just above, we looked at how you can enforce the simplest of the business rules by using out-of-the-box features to preserve the parent-child relationship for list items. However, you might have more complex rules in your scenario. This chapter would not be complete without mentioning list event receivers. Event receivers are attached to list items and other SharePoint objects and trigger various actions and code execution based on several predefined events. The simplest way to learn event receiver is to see them in action, let's create one.

1. In your Visual Studio solution structure create a new list instance of **Custom List** instance. Let' call it **EventReceiverSample**.

2. Right click on the newly created list folder, select **Add -> New Item -> Event Receiver**.

3. After giving a name to your receiver, you will be given a choice to determine the type of the receiver. Let's pick **List Item Events**.

4. For the event receiver source, select **Custom List**.

5. For the events to handle pick: **Item was added**.

6. When finished, Visual Studio will create a receiver for you and open a code editor.

7. In the newly create event receiver folder, locate and open the **Elements.xml** file. You will notice the event receiver is set to listen to events of our custom list template. You can tell it by **ListTemplateId** attribute equal to **100**, which is a template of a **Custom List**. If you want your receiver to only listen to events from specified list instance, replace **ListTemplateId** with **ListUrl** attribute. Let's set **ListUrl** attribute to **Lists/EventReceiverSample**. Ensure the URL matches the URL of the list defined in **Elements.xml** file in the list instance folder.

8. Switch to the code behind file of the receiver.

9. Replace the **ItemAdded** event method with the following content:

LISTING 2-12

```
public override void ItemAdded(SPItemEventProperties
properties)

{

if (properties.ListItem.Title.Length <10)

{

        properties.ListItem.Delete();

}

base.ItemAdded(properties);

}
```

The method above will get a hold of the current item that fired an event and verify if one of its properties, **Title**, is less than **10** characters. If so, the event will be cancelled and no changes will be made to the item.

10. Navigate to the **Features** folder in your Visual Studio solution and ensure both your new event receiver and a list instance have been provisioned with the same feature.

11. Deploy the solution and test adding items to the list with the **Title** value less than **10** characters.

This simple example demonstrates some of the capabilities you can achieve with event receivers. One of the great new additions is the ability to redirect users to an alternative page upon logic in the code, which can be achieved by using the value of **properties.AfterUrl**.

Aggregating Contents of Lists, Queries, and Rollups

As previously mentioned, SharePoint lists are used to build many out-of-the-box and custom features in SharePoint. One of the most common questions I often get asked is whether it is possible to show data stored in one list on a dashboard of the main site; or is it possible to aggregate content from multiple lists on the site and display them in a custom view on a home page of the portal. The answer is yes, and in fact, we have already looked at some of the techniques that drive that functionality. One of the advantages of having a custom content type for your list or library items is that you can run site-wide queries against the content type and get results.

For this sample, we will be using SharePoint publishing template. If your SharePoint test site is of a **Team Site** template – delete the site and create a new instance of s site based on **Publishing** template.

Let's create a new **Content Type** under **ListDefinitions** folder in our solution structure.

1. Add new item as content type under **ListDefinitions** folder with any name of your choice.

2. Set your content type to inherit the **Item** base type.

3. Open the newly created content type **Elements.xml** file and take
    a note of the **Name** attribute. In my case, it's **Name="Platform -
    ContentType1"**.

Create a new list definition and instance that uses your content type.

1. Add a new item as **List Definition** based on existing **Content Type**
    under the **ListDefinitions** folder with any name of your choice.

2. Ensure the content type that your list definition uses is the name
    you noted in Step 2 of the last sequence.

3. Right click on **Lists** folder in your solution structure and create a
    new list instance.

4. Ensure the list instance is based on the definition you created in
    Step 2 in this list.

The reason why we created a list template with content type separate
from the list is because we want our content type to be provisioned
on the site level rather than individual Web. The steps above are not
the only ones required to provision the content type and list definition
of a site level, we look at the remaining steps in a moment. When the
content type and list definition is provisioned on the site level, our users
can create instances of our definition on new Webs. This means that
even if we have a hierarchy of sites one day, and some of them or all
of them have the instance of our list, we can query the data from all
of them anywhere on the site.

We'll create a custom Web Part to handle our presentation and logic
for the rollup component.

1. Locate the **Web Parts** folder in your Visual Studio solution
    structure we created earlier.

2. Right click on the folder and select **Add -> New Item -> Visual
    Web Part**.

3. In the newly created Web Part, switch to the code view of the
    ASCX control.

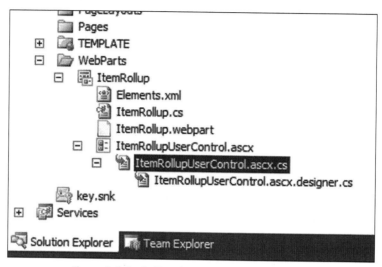

Figure 2-4 Code file of the Web Part user control

4. Add a new **Reference** to your Visual Studio SharePoint project
   (in my case **Platform**): *Microsoft.SharePoint.Publishing*

5. Add new namespace references to your Web Part class:

   using Microsoft.SharePoint.Publishing;

   using System.Data;

   using Microsoft.SharePoint;

6. Add the following helper method to query items from your site:

LISTING 2-13

```
protected virtual DataTable RetrieveData(SPWeb web,
CrossListQueryInfo query)

{

DataTable resultTable = null;

CrossListQueryCache queryCache = new CrossListQueryCache(query);

resultTable = queryCache.GetSiteData(web.Site,

        CrossListQueryCache.ContextUrl());

return resultTable;

}
```

7. Next, replace your **Page_Load** with the following:

LISTING 2-14

```
protected void Page_Load(object sender, EventArgs e)

{

CrossListQueryInfo query = new CrossListQueryInfo();

query.Query = "<Where><Eq><FieldRef Name='ContentType'
/><Value

        Type='Choice'>Platform - ContentType1</Value></Eq></
        Where>";

query.ViewFields = "<FieldRef Name='Title'/>";

DataTable table = RetrieveData(SPContext.Current.Web, query);

MyTable.DataSource = table;

MyTable.DataBind();

}
```

In here, we've got a query that pulls all items from the site with
the **Content Type** value matching the following name **Platform -
ContentType1**; if you have another name in your content type
Elements.xml file, that's the value that is required to match here.

8. Lastly, switch to the **ASCX** part of your user control and place the
   repeater control as follows:

LISTING 2-15

```
<asp:repeater runat="server" ID="MyTable">

<ItemTemplate>

        <asp:Label ID="Title" runat="server" Text='<%#
        Eval("Title") %>' />

</ItemTemplate>

</asp:repeater>
```

Here, the repeater control will have an item template that will get a
hold of one of the items in the result table and render it on the page.
In Step 7, we have the repeater control data source bound to a table
with results of the query.

Remember at the beginning of the Web Part creation walkthrough I mentioned that we needed to perform couple of steps to make the content type and site definition available on a site level? That's the time to do it. You may have noticed, or not, that Visual Studio has created a new feature in its structure under the **Features** folder. The reason why we have a new feature is because Web Parts always have to be provisioned on a site level due to their nature. Since we didn't have a site scoped feature before, the Web Part Creation Wizard created one for us. The only difference between a Web scoped and site scoped feature definition is a **Scope** drop down choice when you open a feature.

Since we want our content type and list definition to be provisioned on a site scope, we will repurpose the feature used to provision a Web Part to provision our content type and list definition too.

Here is how my site scoped feature will look after I add list definition and content type to it:

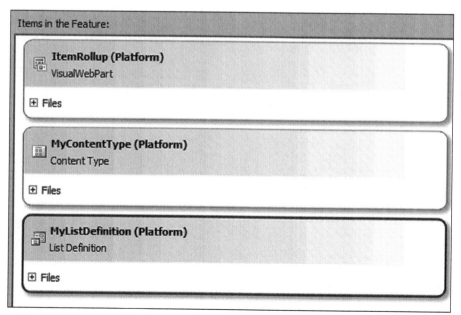

Figure 2-5 Site scoped feature provisioning Web Part, Content type, and List definition

Here is how my Web feature will look after I shuffle items in and out in it:

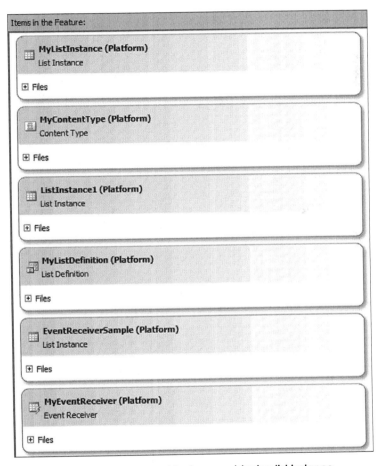

Figure 2-6 Web scoped feature provisioning list instance

This feature will provision the list instance on a root site, all of the other list instances you can create manually when you deploy the solution.

What's left now is to deploy your solution from the Visual Studio and navigate to your portal to add a newly created Web Part:

1. Deploy your solution from Visual Studio.

2. Navigate to your SharePoint test site based of publishing template and ensure your Web Part feature as well as list feature have been provisioned activated with deployment:

- Click **Site Actions -> Site Settings -> Site Collection features** and ensure the name you gave to the Web Part provisioning feature is active.

- Click **Site Action -> Site Settings -> Manage site features** and ensure the names you gave the features provisioning content types, list definition, and list instance are active.

3. Navigate to the main page of your site and click **Site Actions -> Edit Page**.

4. Select any Web Part zone on a page and click **Insert** ribbon tab.

5. From the **Insert** ribbon tab, click **Web Part**.

6. From the **Categories** section select **Custom** and from the **Web Parts** section pick the Web Part you have just created.

7. Click the **Add** button.

The Web Part is now placed on the page, and you can save the page. Now, when you add more items to the list instance you created earlier, their title will all be rendered in your repeater control. Feel free to experiment with the query in the Web Part code and look at various methods of how you can rollup items.

CHAPTER 3

Lists and List Items: Changing the Look of Forms and Incorporating Custom Logic into Item Forms

SharePoint functionality and features are built upon lists and libraries of various types. When you create a calendar event – you're working with a list; when you create a blog post – you're looking at the list item form. All lists and libraries have basic interface for users to create items, edit, and view them. If you compare calendar event entry form and blog post entry form – you will see a significant difference. In this chapter we'll take a look at why there is a difference between different types of list item entry forms. We'll also take a look at how to modify list item forms for out-of-the-box lists and custom lists; we'll see how you can add a new content to your forms and custom controls that change the behavior of the form and other controls on it.

Creating Custom List Item Detail Forms

In the last chapter, we created list instances and content types that drive the way your lists look. When you add a new field to your content type, your field gets rendered in a pre-defined way, depending on the template that has been specified in SharePoint. When you create a new column in your list, you have a set of radio buttons allowing you to choose the kind of field you want to create and some basic settings around it. For example, if you choose a choice field, you can define choices available to users when they create new items. In few cases, users will ask to have their own look and feel to the list item forms. Whether its custom rendering they are after or they require some logic around when to display the field and when not, this can be achieved by creating your own list item details template.

SharePoint understands three types of templates:

1. **New** form – used to create new items. Users can enter values into fields that get saved.

2. **Edit** form – used to edit existing items. Users can edit values in fields and save them.

3. **View** form – used when the item is viewed and all fields are in read only mode.

By default, SharePoint implies that you're going to be using default templates for all of those forms, but you don't have to. Let's see how you can define a content type that will have your own custom templates.

1. In your Visual Studio **ListDefinitions** folder create a new **Content Type** called based of the **Item** content and call it **MyListItem**.

2. Open the **Elements.xml** file of the new content type.

3. Locate the **</FieldRefs>** element in the XML document; right after it, place the following code:

LISTING 3-1

```
<XmlDocuments>

<XmlDocument NamespaceURI="http://schemas.microsoft.com/
sharepoint/v3/contenttype/forms">

<FormTemplates

    xmlns="http://schemas.microsoft.com/sharepoint/v3/
    contenttype/forms">

    <Display>MyTemplate</Display>

    <Edit>MyTemplate</Edit>

    <New>MyTemplate</New>
```

```
</FormTemplates>
```

```
</XmlDocument>
```

```
</XmlDocuments>
```

Notice how there are three types of templates defined, and the corresponding form value for each. We will be using the same template for each of the forms and you will see why in a moment.

4. In your Visual Studio **ListDefinitions** folder create a new item which is going to be a list definition based on the content type from above. Let's call our list definition **MyCustomList**.

5. Open the **schema.xml** file of the newly created list definition and locate the **<ContentTypes>** section.

6. Replace the contents of the section with the reference below:

    <ContentTypeRef ID="ID" />

    Replace the ID value in brackets with the corresponding automatically generated ID in your content type's **Elements. xml** file.

7. You will notice Visual Studio has created a feature that will provision all of your components. Ensure only your list definition and list instance are provisioned in a feature scoped to a Web.

8. Create a new feature and change its scope to **Site**; add a content type definition to that feature.

    By now, you're probably curious where **MyTemplate** is and how you can make it look like you want. SharePoint keeps its default rendering templates in the following file: *[Drive]:\Program Files\Common Files\Microsoft Shared\ Web Server Extensions\14\TEMPLATE\CONTROLTEMPLATES\ DefaultTemplates.ascx.*

    We're not going to make any changes to the **DefaultTemplates.ascx** file. Any changes to that file will take an effect on all of the instances in your farm. We'll use it as a reference to create our own rendering template. Here is how.

1. In your Visual Studio solution structure, locate the following mapped folder: **CONTROLTEMPLATES**. It's capitalized by default in SharePoint.

2. Right click on the folder to create new item, a **User Control** template.

3. Give the newly created template a nice name, like **MyRenderingTemplate.ascx**.

4. Ensure your **ASCX** file has the new name within its control definition just like mine here:

LISTING 3-2

```
<%@ Control Language="C#"

AutoEventWireup="true"

CodeBehind="MyTemplate.ascx.cs"

Inherits="MySolution.Platform.CONTROLTEMPLATES.MyTemplate" %>
```

5. Open the default templates file ([Drive]:\Program Files\Common Files\Microsoft Shared\Web Server Extensions\14\TEMPLATE\ CONTROLTEMPLATES\DefaultTemplates.ascx) and ensure you have copied all of the SharePoint control references to the top of your **ASCX** custom control. Your custom control **ASCX** file will look similar to this:

LISTING 3-3

```
<%@ Assembly Name="$SharePoint.Project.AssemblyFullName$" %>

<%@ Control Language="C#" AutoEventWireup="true"
CodeBehind="MyTemplate.ascx.cs" Inherits="MySolution.
Platform.CONTROLTEMPLATES.MyTemplate" %>

<%@Assembly Name="Microsoft.SharePoint, Version=14.0.0.0,
Culture=neutral, PublicKeyToken=71e9bce111e9429c" %>

<%@Register TagPrefix="SharePoint" Assembly="Microsoft.
SharePoint, Version=14.0.0.0, Culture=neutral, PublicKey
Token=71e9bce111e9429c" namespace="Microsoft.SharePoint.
WebControls"%>

<%@Register TagPrefix="ApplicationPages" Assembly="Microsoft.
SharePoint, Version=14.0.0.0, Culture=neutral, PublicKey
```

```
Token=71e9bce111e9429c" namespace="Microsoft.SharePoint.
ApplicationPages.WebControls"%>

<%@Register TagPrefix="SPHttpUtility" Assembly="Microsoft.
SharePoint, Version=14.0.0.0, Culture=neutral, PublicKey
Token=71e9bce111e9429c" namespace="Microsoft.SharePoint.
Utilities"%>

<%@ Register TagPrefix="wssuc" TagName="ToolBar" src="~/_
controltemplates/ToolBar.ascx" %>

<%@ Register TagPrefix="wssuc" TagName="ToolBarButton"
src="~/_controltemplates/ToolBarButton.ascx" %>
```

6. Next, we're going to copy the SharePoint default rendering template for list items. Find the following line of code in your **DefaultTemplates.ascx**:

   <SharePoint:RenderingTemplate id="ListForm" runat="server">

7. Copy the entire content of the control definition including the definition to your own **ASCX** custom list item definition.

8. Replace the value of the **ID** initlally set to **ListForm** to our custom name you defined earlier in content type: **MyTemplate**

What we have now is a custom rendering template that mimics an out-of-the-box list form template with out-of-the-box controls, fields, and buttons. Almost all of the controls you see in the template are built right in the **DefaultTemplates.ascx** file, and you can explore their structure.

Locate the following line of code if your **ASCX** file: *<SharePoint:ListFieldIterator runat="server"/>*, which represents a control that will go through each of the fields in a list and display them as a proper control in a proper state (read only, edit).

Let's add a piece if text right before the iterator control: **"This is my custom form:"**. Now let's deploy our Visual Studio solution; when you open the list instance on your site and try to edit, view, or create a new item, you will be presented with the message you placed.

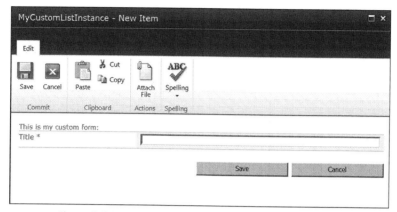

Figure 3-1 Custom List Item form with sample text added

Although it's a nice touch, the real business value of this comes from adding your own custom controls to the form and defining their behavior based on business rules surrounding the form context, which we discuss next.

Field Level Security in Your SharePoint List Forms

As you can see adding your context to the list item forms brings a lot of value to the table. One of the examples we will look at is how you can display or hide a control based on the security context of currently logged-in users. SharePoint has a notion of **Composite Field**, which is a rendering template that will render an **ASPX** control that depends on the type of the field in the current mode (read, edit). We will extend the behavior of current **Composite Field** to also render the field if the current user has required permissions to see it.

We will start by creating a custom control in our Visual Studio solution structure.

1. Locate the **Controls** folder in your Visual Studio structure and right click to **Add -> Class**.

2. Let's call the class **SecurityAwareCompositeField**.

3. Add the following namespace references to your class:

■ *using Microsoft.SharePoint.WebControls;*

■ *using Microsoft.SharePoint;*

4. Replace the class definition with the following code:

LISTING 3-4

```
public class SecurityAwareCompositeField : CompositeField
{
public string RequiredGroup
{ get; set; }
protected override void CreateChildControls()
{
base.CreateChildControls();
int groupID = SPContext.Current.Web.Groups[RequiredGroup].ID;
if (SPContext.Current.Web.IsCurrentUserMemberOfGroup(groupID))
{
        base.Visible = true;
}
else
{
        base.Visible = false;
}
}}
```

Above, we get a hold of the group that will be passed in our rendering template and determine whether current user belongs to the group. If a user doesn't belong to the group, we hide the new control; otherwise, we show it.

5. Now, we'll add the reference to our new control from the rendering template you created earlier. Add the following item to the header of your **ASCX**:

LISTING 3-5

```
<%@ Register
TagPrefix="mycontrols"
```

```
Assembly="MySolution.Platform, Version=1.0.0.0,
Culture=neutral, PublicKeyToken=2652984327752174"

Namespace="MySolution.Platform.Controls" %>
```

Here **mycontrols** is an arbitrary name and assembly name, and the rest of the assembly information is taken from *[Drive]:\windows\ assembly*, the properties of your assembly.

6. Add the instance of your custom control to the rendering template replacing the *<SharePoint:ListFieldIterator runat="server"/>*.

LISTING 3-6

```
<tr>

<mycontrols:SecurityAwareCompositeField ID="TitleField"

RequiredGroup="Viewers" runat="server" FieldName="Title" />

</tr>
```

By replacing the field control iterator, you set your own logic for iterating your fields. In here, we create an instance of the control and assign it to use **Title** field and our **Required Group** is **Viewers**. Meaning that whoever does not belong to the **Viewers** group will not see the title control, even if you have the site collection administrator logged in.

Your user control will end up with the following rendering template code:

LISTING 3-7

```
<SharePoint:RenderingTemplate id="MyTemplate" runat="server">

<Template>

<span id='part1'>

<SharePoint:InformationBar runat="server"/>

<div id="listFormToolBarTop">

<wssuc:ToolBar CssClass="ms-formtoolbar" id="toolBarTbltop"
RightButtonSeparator=" " runat="server">

<Template_RightButtons>

<SharePoint:NextPageButton runat="server"/>
```

```
<SharePoint:SaveButton runat="server"/>

<SharePoint:GoBackButton runat="server"/>

</Template_RightButtons>

</wssuc:ToolBar>

</div>

<SharePoint:FormToolBar runat="server"/>

<SharePoint:ItemValidationFailedMessage runat="server"/>

<table class="ms-formtable" border="0" width="100%">

<SharePoint:ChangeContentType runat="server"/>

<SharePoint:FolderFormFields runat="server"/>

<tr>

<mycontrols:SecurityAwareCompositeField ID="TitleField"

RequiredGroup="Viewers" runat="server" FieldName="Title" />

</tr>

This is my custom form:

<SharePoint:ApprovalStatus runat="server"/>

<SharePoint:FormComponent TemplateName="AttachmentRows"
runat="server"/>

</table>

<table cellpadding="0" cellspacing="0" width="100%">

<tr><td class="ms-formline">

<img src="/_layouts/images/blank.gif" width='1' height='1'
alt="" /></td></tr>

</table>

<table cellpadding="0" cellspacing="0" width="100%"
style="padding-top: 7px"><tr><td width="100%">

<SharePoint:ItemHiddenVersion runat="server"/>

<SharePoint:ParentInformationField runat="server"/>

<SharePoint:InitContentType runat="server"/>

<wssuc:ToolBar CssClass="ms-formtoolbar" id="toolBarTbl"
```

```
RightButtonSeparator=" " runat="server">

<Template_Buttons>

<SharePoint:CreatedModifiedInfo runat="server"/>

</Template_Buttons>

<Template_RightButtons>

<SharePoint:SaveButton runat="server"/>

<SharePoint:GoBackButton runat="server"/>

</Template_RightButtons>

</wssuc:ToolBar>

</td></tr></table>

</span>

<SharePoint:AttachmentUpload runat="server"/>

</Template>

</SharePoint:RenderingTemplate>
```

To test the logic, deploy your solution and navigate to the list instance based on a custom content type we used in last sample. When you choose to add a new item, you will see that no fields are rendered, though there is only one anyway. Add your username to the **Viewers** group on a portal.

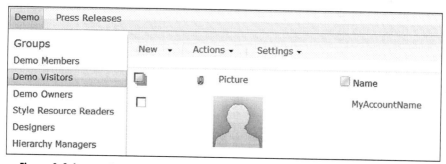

Figure 3-2 Account name added to the group required by the security aware field

Now, when you try adding new item, you will be recognized as a valid use by the control and the field will be rendered.

This simple example shows that it's pretty easy to define your custom look and field on item detail forms and you can piggyback on SharePoint list forms to implement your custom and complex functionality.

Manage Behavior of SharePoint 2010 Composite Fields

Continuing on the theme of adding your custom fields and controls on the SharePoint list item template, next we'll take a look at how you can define your own custom action buttons. Despite the fact that you can define **ASPX** button on your form, there is a real benefit in some scenarios to use out-of-the-box SharePoint item form buttons. SharePoint out-of-the-box item form buttons include **Save, Publish, Go Back**, and few others. In this example, we're going to create an instance of our own **Save** button. The button will inherit its parent functions allowing us to save the item and also add our own logic in the mean time.

We will reuse the same rendering template, custom list definition, and content type that we used in the last sample. Let's continue on with creating a new custom control.

1. In Visual Studio Server Explorer, locate the **Controls** folder and add a new class.

2. Let's call the class **MySaveButton**.

3. Add the following namespace reference:

■ using Microsoft.SharePoint.WebControls;

4. Replace the class definition with the following code:

LISTING 3-8

```
public class MySaveButton : SaveButton

{

protected override void CreateChildControls()

{

base.CreateChildControls();

this.Text = "My Custom Save";

switch (ControlMode)
```

```
{
case SPControlMode.Edit:
{
CompositeField bodyField =
        ((CompositeField)this.Parent.Parent.Parent.
        FindControl("Title"));
if (bodyField != null)
{
        bodyField.ControlMode = SPControlMode.Display;
}
}
break;
// handle any other template modes such as New etc.
default:
Visible = false;
break;
}
}}
```

In here, we're setting the text of our newly created button to be **My Custom Save**. Also we get a hold of the **Title** field we have defined on a form. If our form is an **Edit** form—in other words, we're editing an item—the button sets the **Title** field to be read only. If the form is anything other than edit, the button is not displayed and the current rendering on the **Title** control remains the same.

5. Since we already have a reference to custom control namespace in our custom rendering template, we just need to define a button in a bottom button container along with other buttons. Below is the section outputting other out-of-the-box buttons with our custom button highlighted:

LISTING 3-9

```
<wssuc:ToolBar CssClass="ms-formtoolbar" id="toolBarTbl" Righ
tButtonSeparator=" " runat="server">
```

```
<Template_Buttons>

<SharePoint:CreatedModifiedInfo runat="server"/>

</Template_Buttons>

<Template_RightButtons>

<SharePoint:SaveButton runat="server"/>

<SharePoint:GoBackButton runat="server"/>

<mycontrols:MySaveButton runat="server"/>

</Template_RightButtons>

</wssuc:ToolBar>
```

6. In your rendering template file **MyRenderingTemplate.ascx**
   locate the following field definition we used in the last sample:

   <mycontrols:SecurityAwareCompositeField ID="TitleField"

   RequiredGroup="Viewers" runat="server" FieldName="Title" />

7. Replace the code above with:

   <SharePoint:CompositeField ID="Title" runat="server"
   FieldName="Title"/>

This definition will ensure only title field is rendered on the form.

After you deploy your solution, navigate to the list we used for testing
and click **Add new item**. You will see that nothing has changed on the
form. It's only when you create an item and try to edit it that you will
see a new button displayed on the form, like this:

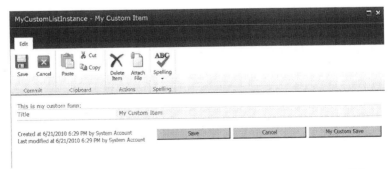

Figure 3-3 Custom Save Item button displayed on the item detail edit form

You will also see that the **Title** field appears to be read only despite the fact that this is an edit form. If we had more fields on a form – they would all be editable except our **Title** field.

Similar to how you can manage what is displayed on a form, by extending SharePoint **Save** Web control, you can choose to add custom logic before the item is saved to the list. This provides alternative logic flow for your users to choose. For example, if a standard SharePoint list item save button will just save an item, with your custom button, you can trigger an alert or some additional action. Here is the example of the code you can embed in your **MySaveButton** class from Step 4 to append arbitrary string to the title of the item that has been saved with a custom save button as opposed to a default save button:

LISTING 3-10

```
protected override bool SaveItem()

{

base.ListItem["Title"] += " - Saved with my custom button";

return base.SaveItem();

}
```

To see the new save logic in action, deploy the solution and see the difference when you save with out-of-the-box save button versus your custom save button. One point to add is that if you like, you can disable the out-of-the-box button by getting a hold of it just as we got a hold of the title control in Step 4 above.

Dynamically Changing SharePoint 2010 List Form Rendering Templates

If you've noticed, every time we performed the replacement of our rendering template of a list, it resulted in solution deployment and complete loss of any test data we had in the list. It's not a problem when it happens in your development environment, but what if you want to implement a new rendering template on a production environment. You may have already deployed your custom rendering template, but it's the list schema where you need to call it. I doubt anyone will let you kill the list instance and create a new one with all of the data lost. Fortunately, there is a solution where you can assign a new rendering template, providing it has been deployed to the server. Having a rendering template on a server is as simple as copying it to the **ControlTemplates** folder.

In this example, we will be using SharePoint Designer 2010, which is a free download, so if you don't have it installed, go ahead and download it. You're not required to have SharePoint Designer installed on the server computer. As long as you have it installed on a client computer and have sufficient username and password credentials to edit your site – you will have no problem going through this walkthrough.

Here is how to assign the template to your custom list.

1. Open SharePoint Designer and open the URL of the site where your target list instance is located.

2. Once the site is open, on the right hand side of the SharePoint Designer navigation, select **Lists and Libraries**.

3. Select the list where you would like to change the rendering template for; the list information page will open in the main window.

4. Locate the **Forms** section in the main area of the SharePoint Designer and click on the name of the form for which you would like to change the rendering template. If you like to change it for all **New/View/Edit** forms, you will have to perform a switch on each form individually.

5. The Designer will load the selected view and the item detail view that is currently used. At the bottom of SharePoint Designer window, locate three display options: **Design**, **Split**, and **Code**. Click the **Split** option.

6. SharePoint Designer will split the screen, part of it being code and part of it being a user interface with your form. Click anywhere on the form view that is currently used.

7. In the code view, you will see a part of the code highlighted; that's the area that represents current list view form. Scroll down

to the bottom of the highlighted code until you locate the **TemplateName** node.

8. The default value of the **TemplateName** is **ListForm**. Replace the **ListForm** with the rendering template name that you provisioned earlier to the **ControlTemplates** folder.

9. This concludes the switch. Press the save button to save your changed form. The form will be swapped for everyone else using it after you save it. Now you can repeat the steps starting with Step 4 to make changes to the remaining forms if required.

SharePoint Designer is quite a powerful tool. We're not going to explore all of its strengths here, mainly because it's not considered a developer tool that allows you to produce solutions. However, you should take a look at some of the capabilities of SharePoint Designer to make recommendations to your users when situations similar to this occur. In some cases, small changes on the portal can save the day while you prepare for a proper upgrade or deployment.

Making Changes to List View and List Item Detail View Using XSL

So far, we have looked at how you can modify the look and feel of the default list item detail template and customize it to render your own controls and even execute custom actions. SharePoint uses the notion of views and templates in many other scenarios—for example, a list view. The difference between the list item detail view rendering template we discussed in last example is that the list view rendering in driven by an XSL template. Every time you access the list view or create your own view in the list with any parameters you wish, the data is loaded and its look transformed with XSL.

To better understand how far you can go with extending the list view, let's take a look at out-of-the-box **Blog** template.

1. Navigate to the root of your site you use for debugging and testing of your applications.

2. Click **Site Actions -> New Site**.

3. From the list of site templates, locate **Blog**.

4. Provide the title of the site and URL and click **Create**.

Once the site has been created, you will be taken right to the list view of the blog post page. Click on the title **Welcome to your Blog** and you will see a list item detail view for post list items. The Web Part in the center is a view of list item detail page transformed with an XSL. To verify that, click **Site Actions -> Edit Page**. From the edit page, click **Edit Web Part** as shown on the screenshot below.

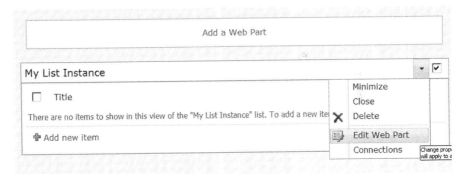

Figure 3-4 Editing Web Part properties

One of the great new features available in SharePoint is the ability easily assign a new XSL rendering template to the **List View** Web Part that hosts all of the views in SharePoint. Scroll down to the bottom of your Web Part properties window on the right of the screen and locate the **Miscellaneous** section. Expand the section and locate the **XSL link** field. This field allows you to specify the location of the XSL that will transform the look of the rendering template for this view.

As you can imagine, there this particular list view already has its own custom template defined somewhere in the list schema. In fact, we will be using this very template to make a copy of it to build up our own modification. First, let's take a look at how we can make ad-hoc modification through the **Miscellaneous** Web Part property.

1. Open the following folder in your SharePoint root: *[Drive]:\ Program Files\Common Files\Microsoft Shared\Web Server Extensions\14\TEMPLATE\LAYOUTS\XSL*.

This is where SharePoint keeps all of its XSL templates.

2. Open **blog.xsl** in a Notepad and copy its entire content to the clipboard.

3. Go back to your Visual Studio solution structure we've been using all along and locate the **Layouts** mapped folder.

4. Right click on the folder and create a new subfolder in it called **XSL**.

5. Right click on the XSL folder to add a new item. The item will be located under the **Data** category; the template will be called **XSLT file**. Give your new file a name like **MyXSLSheet.xsl**.

6. Open the newly created **MyXSLSheet.xsl** and paste the contents of the clipboard you have copied from **blog.xsl**.

7. You will see a lot of transformation code since this template holds the code for several lists and item detail pages for the **Blog** site template. To make it easier in your Visual Studio, you can collapse the code into nodes by hitting **CTRL+M +L** and expanding the root node.

8. Search for the following string in the file:

   <!-- BaseViewID='0' and TemplateType='301' is Home Page view for Blog's posts list -->

   The comment above suggests that we're working with the template for blog posts. However, there is a more certain way to find out which exact template we're working with—we'll take a look at it further down.

9. Expand the structure under the comment in the above step and locate the following comment:

   <!-- Posts.aspx and the home page should show the body of the post -->.

   Place the following text right after the comment: "**This is my sample text –**".

10. Save the file and deploy your solution from Visual Studio.

11. Go back to your site and click **Site Actions -> Edit Page** to open the **Edit Web Part** panel.

12. Scroll down to the **Miscellaneous** section and enter the following relative URL in the **XSL link** property: /_layouts/xsl/MyXSLSheet.xsl.

13. Click OK on the **Edit Web Part** panel and the **Stop Editing** button on the ribbon.

You will see that the text you placed in the XML configuration file will be rendered on the page. This essentially means that you can add any markup to the existing XSL view and not disturb the behavior of the other items that belong to the blog post template. The same approach can be applied to any list view in SharePoint since all **ListView** Web Parts support custom XSL transformations.

Defining List View Look and Feel in Your Custom List Schema

In the last example, we looked at how you can define the look of your list view using the XSL of the blog post template. In this example, we'll take a look at how you can take any list you create from the custom list definition in Visual Studio and make it render however you want with custom XSL.

Let's start with creating a custom list definition in Visual Studio.

1. Locate the **ListDefinitions** folder in your Visual Studio structure and add a new **List Definition** item in it.

2. The type of list definition we will be inheriting is a **Custom List**.

3. Let's also choose to create a list instance with our list definition.

Once the list definition is created, open the **schema.xml** file, the file has very basic markup and we have only two views:

LISTING 3-11

```
<View BaseViewID="0" Type="HTML"
        MobileView="TRUE" TabularView="FALSE">
```

and

LISTING 3-12

```
<View BaseViewID="1" Type="HTML"
WebPartZoneID="Main"
```

```
CssStyleSheet="blog.css"
DisplayName="$Resources:core,objectiv_schema_mwsidcamlidC24;"
DefaultView="TRUE"
MobileView="TRUE"
MobileDefaultView="TRUE"
SetupPath="pages\viewpage.aspx"
ImageUrl="/_layouts/images/generic.png"
Url="AllItems.aspx">
```

You will also notice that one of the properties in the view is the **XSL link** you're familiar from the last example; the value of it is **main.xsl**: *<XslLink Default="TRUE">main.xsl</XslLink>*.

You guessed right, there is a **main.xsl** in *[Drive]:\Program Files\ Common Files\Microsoft Shared\Web Server Extensions\14\ TEMPLATE\LAYOUTS\XSL* defining how your list items are going to look.

Next, let's create a new XSL file for this list to inherit the look from.

1. Navigate to the **Layouts** folder in your Visual Studio solution and create an **XSL** folder in it.

2. Add an **XSLT** type of a document from the **Data** category just like in the last example; let's call it **MyXSLSheet.xsl.**

3. Replace the content of the newly created **MyXSLSheet.xsl** with the following code:

LISTING 3-13

```
<xsl:stylesheet xmlns:x="http://www.w3.org/2001/XMLSchema"
xmlns:d="http://schemas.microsoft.com/sharepoint/dsp"

version="1.0" exclude-result-prefixes="xsl msxsl ddwrt"
xmlns:ddwrt="http://schemas.microsoft.com/Web Parts/v2/
DataView/runtime" xmlns:asp="http://schemas.microsoft.com/
ASPNET/20" xmlns:__designer="http://schemas.microsoft.com/
Web Parts/v2/DataView/designer" xmlns:xsl="http://www.
w3.org/1999/XSL/Transform"

xmlns:msxsl="urn:schemas-microsoft-com:xslt"
xmlns:SharePoint="Microsoft.SharePoint.WebControls"

xmlns:ddwrt2="urn:frontpage:internal" ddwrt:oob="true">

<xsl:import href="/_layouts/xsl/main.xsl"/>
```

```
<xsl:output method="html" indent="no"/>

<xsl:param name="NoAJAX" select="1"/>

<xsl:template mode="Item" match="Row[../../@BaseViewID='1']">

<xsl:param name="Fields" select="."/>

<xsl:param name="Collapse" select="."/>

<xsl:param name="Position" select="1"/>

<xsl:param name="Last" select="1"/>

<xsl:variable name="thisNode" select="."/>

<table width="100%" border="0" cellspacing="0"
cellpadding="0" dir="None">

<tr>

<td width="690">

<h4>

<xsl:apply-templates select="$Fields[@Name='LinkTitle']"
mode="PrintField">

<xsl:with-param name="thisNode" select="."/>

<xsl:with-param name="Position" select="$Position"/>

</xsl:apply-templates>

</h4>

</td>

<xsl:if test="($thisNode/../@value.listpermission.
EditListItems = '1') and

        ($thisNode/../@value.listpermission.ManageLists =
        '1') ">

<td align="right" class="ms-blogedit">

<a href="javascript:"

        onclick='ShowPopupDialog("{$HttpVDir}/Lists/Platform-
        ListInstance1/EditForm.aspx?ID={$thisNode/@ID}&amp;

        Source={$HttpVDir}/Lists/PlatformListInstance1/

        EditItem.aspx?ID={$thisNode/@ID}");return false;'>
```

```
        Edit Item
</a>
</td>
</xsl:if>
</tr>
</table>
<div class="ms-CommentBody">
<div dir="">
If you had more than one field - this is where you could
output them.
</div>
</div>
</xsl:template>
</xsl:stylesheet>
```

The above **TemplateType='10000'** will depend on the **Template ID** you have assigned in your list definition **Elements.xml** file. Also, references to **/Lists/Platform-ListInstance1** will depend on the URL attribute in the **Elements.xml** of your list definition. Take a look at the template to see how the logic is constructed; we'll see how it works in a moment.

4. Navigate to your list definition schema.xml file, and for the **BaseViewID="1"** set the value of the **XSL link** to be the following: *<XslLink Default="TRUE">MyXSLSheet.xsl</XslLink>*.

5. Deploy the solution from Visual Studio and navigate to the root URL of your test site.

6. Create a new item or two in the newly create list instance and observe the look of how those items are placed in the list view.

The XSL template we defined above will render the title of the item and a link to its edit form if the user has permissions to edit items in a list. Also, if we had any other fields in our list, we could render them just like the title field, but instead we just display a hardcoded message. Here is how my list is going to look after I add a few items into it:

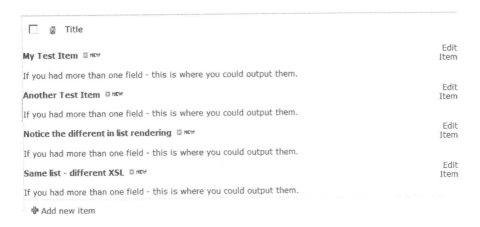

Figure 3-5 Custom list with few items in it, rendered with custom XSL

As you can see, we have completely transformed what out-of-the-box list view looks like. Those changes are local changes only; none of the other lists will be affected. Customizations like the same above can really make a difference when you're considering changes to your user interface. After all, you could have created a custom Web Part and performed queries on the list to display them with the desired template. The approach in this sample demonstrated how you could use extension points to make desired changes without rewriting the out-of-the-box functionality that exists in SharePoint already. The only barrier of this approach is that XSL is something that not too many .NET developers are familiar with, but as this sample demonstrated, valuable piece of knowledge to have.

Adding Web Parts to Item Detail View Form

We have looked at how you can create your own rendering template to place custom controls on the form. However, in some cases all you may ever want is to add a Web Part or two on the form and leave the rest of the form as is. There is an out-of-the-box site template that has a similar scenario implemented, and again it's a blog template. In blog template, we have a post item view form, which is a read only representation of a post, which in turn has a **New Item** form for comments. The comments and posts are linked together by a list relationship we discussed in the last chapter.

In this example, we'll take a look at how you can provision custom forms to an existing item detail form in your custom list based on a custom definition we've been using all along.

Let's start with provisioning custom content editor Web Part to the page.

1. In your Visual Studio solution, locate the **Pages** folder and right click on it to create a new item of type **Module**. Give your module any name you prefer.

2. The module will come with a sample text file; delete the sample file. Right click on the module folder name to add an existing item from the following location: *[Drive]:\Program Files\Common Files\Microsoft Shared\Web Server Extensions\14\TEMPLATE\ Pages*.

   The file name you're adding is a **form.aspx**. This file is a generic template for all of the item detail forms in SharePoint.

3. Let's open the **Elements.xml** in your module and replace its content with the following:

LISTING 3-14

```
<?xml version="1.0" encoding="utf-8"?>
<Elements xmlns="http://schemas.microsoft.com/sharepoint/">
<Module Name="FormPage"
        Url="Lists/Platform-ListInstance1"
        Path="Module1">
<File Url="DispForm.aspx"
        IgnoreIfAlreadyExists="TRUE"
        Path="form.aspx">
<AllUsersWebPart WebPartZoneID="Left" WebPartOrder="3">
<![CDATA[
```

```xml
<?xml version="1.0" encoding="utf-8"?>
<WebPart xmlns:xsi="http://www.w3.org/2001/XMLSchema-
instance"
xmlns:xsd="http://www.w3.org/2001/XMLSchema"
xmlns="http://schemas.microsoft.com/WebPart/v2">
<Title>Content Editor</Title>
<FrameType>Default</FrameType>
<Description>Allows authors to enter rich text content.</
Description>
<IsIncluded>true</IsIncluded>
<ZoneID>Main</ZoneID>
<PartOrder>0</PartOrder>
<FrameState>Normal</FrameState>
<Height />
<Width />
<AllowRemove>true</AllowRemove>
<AllowZoneChange>true</AllowZoneChange>
<AllowMinimize>true</AllowMinimize>
<AllowConnect>true</AllowConnect>
<AllowEdit>true</AllowEdit>
<AllowHide>true</AllowHide>
<IsVisible>true</IsVisible>
<DetailLink />
<HelpLink />
<HelpMode>Modeless</HelpMode>
<Dir>Default</Dir>
<PartImageSmall />
<MissingAssembly>Cannot import this Web Part.</MissingAssembly>
<PartImageLarge>/_layouts/images/mscontl.gif</PartImageLarge>
<IsIncludedFilter />
```

```
<Assembly>Microsoft.SharePoint, Version=14.0.0.0,
Culture=neutral, PublicKeyToken=71e9bce111e9429c</Assembly>

<TypeName>Microsoft.SharePoint.WebPartPages.
ContentEditorWebPart</TypeName>

<ContentLink xmlns="http://schemas.microsoft.com/WebPart/v2/
ContentEditor"/>

<Content xmlns="http://schemas.microsoft.com/WebPart/v2/
ContentEditor">

This is a sample content</Content>

<PartStorage xmlns="http://schemas.microsoft.com/WebPart/v2/
ContentEditor"/>

</WebPart>]]>

</AllUsersWebPart>

</File>

</Module>

</Elements>
```

4. In the pasted code from above, ensure the module definition, *<Module Name="FormPage" Url="Lists/Platform-ListInstance1" Path="Module1">*

   URL attribute is valid parameter of the custom list **Elements.xml** file we've been using all along in our earlier samples. The **Path** attribute will contain the name you gave to the module when you created one.

5. The next line of code right below the module definition, *<File Url="DispForm.aspx" IgnoreIfAlreadyExists="TRUE" Path="form. aspx">*, defines that we will be placing our custom content editor Web Part containing text into the **display** form and not the **new** or **edit** form. The **Path** attribute will specify that we will be using our **form.aspx** template file we copied earlier.

6. Deploy the solution with Visual Studio and navigate to your test site.

If you were using the test list we created a definition and instance for in last few samples, you will have to create a list item first. Once the item is created—since we have modified a **display** form template—open a **display** form of the item. Right below the item columns you will see a text that we coded into the Web Part "**This is a sample content**". Since content editor Web Part is just as any other Web Part including custom ones, using this technique you can inject any content into forms, even the ones that will be interacting with the rest of the fields.

NOTE:

If you thought that typing that entire content editor Web Part XML was a cruel move on my part, I will show you a little shortcut that you can use to extract any Web Part XML.

1. Navigate to any page on the site that has Web Part zones on it, for example a home page.

2. Click **Site Actions-> Edit Page.**

3. Pick any Web Part zone and click **Add a Web Part**. Pick any Web Part for which you would like to have a definition XML.

4. Click the Web Part menu (an arrow down on the right hand side corner of the Web Part instance) and click **Export**. If you can't find **Export**, proceed to the next step.

5. Click Web Part menu (an arrow down on the right hand side corner of the Web Part instance) and select **Edit Web Part**.

6. On the Web Part editing panel, expand the **Advanced** category and from the **Export Mode** drop down and pick **Export All Data**. Click OK, and the **Export** menu will appear.

7. Save the file that you're offered—which is your XML that is ready to paste into your Visual Studio.

Just as we are able to add a common Web Part to the display form of the list item detail page, we can add the not so common Web Parts, such as the **List View** of another list. This approach will make it possible to edit the item in another list while viewing current list item. This is the exact approach that the blog item display form uses to allow users to enter comments on a blog. Here is how such Web Part can be defined:

LISTING 3-15

```
<AllUsersWebPart WebPartZoneID="Left" WebPartOrder="3">
<![CDATA[
<WebPart xmlns="http://schemas.microsoft.com/WebPart/
v2" xmlns:lfwp="http://schemas.microsoft.com/WebPart/v2/
ListForm">
<Assembly>Microsoft.SharePoint, Version=14.0.0.0,
Culture=neutral, PublicKeyToken=71e9bce111e9429c</Assembly>
<TypeName>Microsoft.SharePoint.WebPartPages.ListFormWebPart</
TypeName>
<Title>My Title</Title>
<Description></Description>
<FrameType>Default</FrameType>
<lfwp:TemplateName>ListForm</lfwp:TemplateName>
<lfwp:ListTitle>Tasks</lfwp:ListTitle>
<lfwp:ControlMode>New</lfwp:ControlMode>
<lfwp:HideIfNoPermissions>true</lfwp:HideIfNoPermissions>
<lfwp:DisableInitialFocus>true</lfwp:DisableInitialFocus>
</WebPart>]]>
</AllUsersWebPart>
```

Deploy the solution using Visual Studio and navigate to the list instance we have been working in this sample. Create a new item and save it; remember our form will de added to display form only. When your item is ready open it and you will see a New Item form right below the rest of the content on the form.

Over the last few samples shown in this chapter, we went over several approaches of how you can extend SharePoint capabilities that handle list forms and list item detail forms. The main business value for those approaches is that you no longer need to build custom forms from the ground up or try to wire related logic to save items in a list or perform other functions that are part of the platform and have been well tested. The question is not how much testing did out-of-the-box component get versus your own, as significant as it is, but how supported will your customization be by the product in a future. If you rely on extending existing functionality, chances are you have more support and a better migration story when a new version comes out as opposed to a solution that has been built independently.

CHAPTER 4

Using External Data with SharePoint 2010 Out-of-the-Box Components and Custom Features

As repetitive as I may sound, SharePoint has some great features, allowing working with external data. Mainly, Business Connectivity Services (BSC) is a new service application running in SharePoint that allows connecting to external data sources and retrieving data from those sources for consumption by portal users in a list-like user interface. The main advantage to having your external data exposed as a list is the decrease in training that is required for users to catch up with the new user interface. Since lists are used extensively in SharePoint, it's easy for users to understand features and developers to interact with the object model.

In this chapter, we're going to take a look at how you establish connection with your external data source, build your data connection, and use that data connection to retrieve data into the external list.

Connecting to SQL Server Data Source

SQL Server data source is probably the most common data source that you will be connecting to with BCS tools. After all, it's deployed in multiple environments and there are many custom tools and applications that use SQL databases. The scenario of connecting to the SQL server data source is so common that SharePoint Designer, a free tool we looked in the previous chapter, has a built in mechanism to connect to the SQL server data store. In this particular scenario, we're using SharePoint Designer to connect to the data source and create methods to extract data from it.

First, let's download a demo database, the **Adventure Works 2008**. The database can be currently located at this URL: http://msftdbprodsamples.codeplex.com and if it changes, you can always find it by searching **adventure works database download**. After you downloaded and extracted the database, you can attach it to the local SQL server (I assume you'll be using local SQL server on the same server as your SharePoint install); here is how:

1. Open SQL Server Management Studio and connect with an account privileged to attach new databases.

2. Expand the **server** node and right click on **Databases**. Select **Attach** from the menu.

3. In the **Databases to attach** section click the **Add** button and locate the folder to which you have extracted your sample database.

4. Click OK and your database will be located in the **Object Explorer** node structure.

Now that we have our sample database, ensure you have installed the SharePoint Designer 2010.

Now, let's create a new **External** content type with SharePoint Designer.

1. Open SharePoint Designer and click **Open Site**.

2. Specify the URL of your site and click Open. The default site panel details will open.

3. On the **Site Objects** left navigation area whether you have any existing content types already or not, click **External Content Type** on the ribbon.

4. On the **New external content type** form that will open, specify
   the following values:

■ Name: **MyExternalContentType**

■ Namespace: Leave as-is

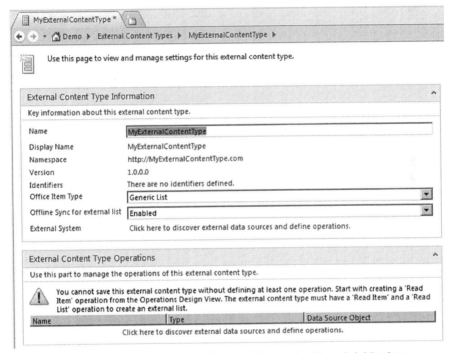

Figure 4-1 Adding a new External Content Type using SharePoint Designer

5. On the same section in front of **External System** click the link that
   says **Click here to discover external data sources and define
   operations**.

6. On this page click **Add Connection** and pick **SQL Server** from the
   dropdown box offered.

7. You will be prompted to enter the following:

■ Database Server: **[your database server name]**.

■ Database name: **AdventureWorksLT2008** (or any other name
   that you have your sample database under).

■   Identity option: **Connect with User's identity** is the easiest choice
    but you have to run your SharePoint Designer under the same
    domain you're currently logged in.

8. Click **OK** and allow SharePoint Designer to take it's time to load
    the database objects.

Next, we will be creating what's known as **operations** in SharePoint
designer. Operations are essentially means for SharePoint to **Create/
Read/Edit/Delete** data in the external system. After all, all of the
custom user interface that will be given to the user to play with will
be translated into the commands issued on the data source. Once
the list has loaded, you will be able to drill down the structure and
pick stored procedures and functions that will perform the function
of operations in SharePoint Designer. You can always choose to
generate new operation, which is what we will choose below.
When you create new operations, those will not be stored in the
database and your structure will not be altered. The operations will
be defined in the XML schema of the SharePoint designer and the
underlying SQL commands will be recorded to drive the operation
(**Create**, **View** etc).

9. Once SharePoint Designer establishes a successful connection
    with the data source, you will see a database name in the **Data
    Source Explorer.**

10. Drill down the structure of **Table -> Customer**.

11. Right click on the **Customer** table name and select **Create
    All Operations** which will take care of creating queries
    responsible for:

■   Reading the list.

■   Reading an individual item by selected ID.

■   Create a new item.

■   Editing of individual item by ID.

■   Deleting selected item.

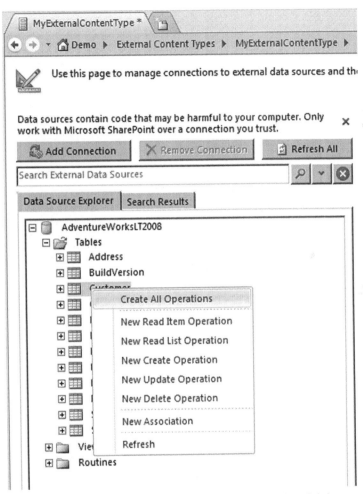

Figure 4-2 Creating operations based on the entity in the database

12. Click Next in **Operation Properties** step.

13. Under **Parameters Configuration**, leave all of the parameters as
    suggested. Take a look at some of the available features, such
    as whether some fields must be required or whether there is a
    foreign key relationship between fields. You can also uncheck
    fields you don't want to be returned, for example password
    information.

14. Under **Filter Parameters**, choose to add a new parameter and accept default. SharePoint Designer will pick **CustomerID** as a parameter.

15. Click **Finish** and **Save** the results.

After you finish configuring the connection, SharePoint Designer will generate a report of new BDC Model and associated operations as shown below:

External Content Type Operations		▲
Use this part to manage the operations of this external content type.		
✓ This external content type has read, write, and search capabilities. You may associate it with other external content types by creating an Association operation from the Operations Design View.		

Name	Type	Data Source Object
Create	Create	Customer
Read Item	Read Item	Customer
Update	Update	Customer
Delete	Delete	Customer
Read List	Read List	Customer

Figure 4-3 SharePoint Designer completed configuration of the BDC Model and operations

Once you click **Save** on the resulting screen, SharePoint Designer will deploy your newly created configuration as a BDC Model. Your model will become available for use and you can create new external lists that will interact with it.

Let's create an external list.

1. In SharePoint Designer's left hand side navigation for – **Site Objects**, locate and click **Lists and Libraries**.

2. On the ribbon, click **External List** and pick your newly created external content type.

3. Provide the name of the external list.

4. Navigate to the root of your SharePoint test site and open an external list, which should be located on the left hand side navigation menu.

If you have received an **Access Denied** message, it's mainly because of the account you are accessing the list with has not been added to the appropriate collection of users able to make BDC Model changes or even access it.

To resolve the permission issue do the following:

1. Navigate to the Central Administration of your SharePoint site.

2. Under the **Application Management**, click **Manage Service Applications**.

3. Select (do not click link) **Business Data Connectivity Service**.

4. On the ribbon, click **Administrators** and ensure administrator name has been added. You will probably want to add a site collection administrator and the account you used to run SharePoint installation Wizard with to this section.

5. Now click on the **Business Data Connectivity Service**.

6. Locate the **External Content Type** name we have just deployed and put a check mark beside it.

7. Click **Set Metadata Store Permissions** button and add the groups and appropriate level of their access to the metadata store.

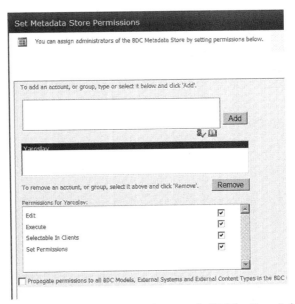

Figure 4-4 Setting appropriate level of access to BDC for SharePoint users

8.   Now, click **Set Object Permissions** and add groups and the appropriate level of permissions that those groups will have in terms of accessing data from your **BDC Model**.

You should be all set up now. Navigate to the root of the SharePoint test site, locate your external list, and open it.

As you can see, the **External list** loaded a limited number of items on the page and the overall look and feel is just like any other SharePoint list. There are few functional limitations, but the main functionality is the same. You can create new items, edit them, and update items, all depending on the permissions that can be defined more granularly.

A few of the missing features include:

- **Workflow capabilities** – workflows rely on state of the items in the data store. Since SharePoint doesn't have complete access to the information to determine the state of the item, this feature is not available.

- **Alert capabilities** – SharePoint cannot monitor external data stores and pick up information required by an alert framework to send alerts to users.

- **RSS feed** – same reasoning.

- **Edit in datasheet** – purely due to performance impact of loading all of the items into an edit mode.

- **Tagging an item** – since item is an external system item, tagging may have not been accurate depending on whether the item has been deleted without proper monitoring.

- **Attaching files to an item** – for obvious reasons of not being able to modify the external data schema to store files.

Creating External Content Types with Visual Studio

In the last sample, we looked at how easy it is to connect to external data that reside in an SQL Server, and in many cases, this is all you need. In some other not so easy cases, where you data reside in proprietary databases or databases not supported in SharePoint Designer, you have an option to create a data connection model in Visual Studio.

Let's create a sample business connectivity model.

1. In the root of your Visual Studio project solution structure, create a new folder called **BCS**.

2. Right click on the newly created folder to add a new item of type: **Business Data Connectivity Model**, further called **BDC model**. Give your model a desired name.

3. You will be presented with the model diagram. From the View menu in Visual Studio, click **Other Windows -> BDC Explorer**. Also, add **Other Windows -> BDC Method Details**. Those two windows will make it easier to navigate your model and make changes.

4. Back in your Solution Explorer, under the newly created **BDC model**, you will see two code files:

■   **Entity1.cs** - an object representing the entity and its fields.

■   **Entity1Service.cs** – a service class that will define operation such as **create/edit/delete/view**.

Let's put this model to some use and add our custom functionality to it.

1. In your **Entity1.cs**, rename the class name to **Customer**, and change the name of the CS file from **Entity1.cs** to **Customer.cs**. Visual Studio will offer to rename all of the references; click **Yes**.

2. Define your newly renamed **Customer** class with the following fields:

LISTING 4-1

```
public partial class Customer

{

public string CustomerID { get; set; }

public string Name { get; set; }

public string Address { get; set; }

}
```

3. In your **Entity1Service.cs**, rename the class name to **CustomerService**, and change the name of the CS file from **Entity1Service.cs** to **CustomerService.cs**.

4. Define your newly renamed **CustomerService** with the following
    methods:

LISTING 4-2

```
public class CustomerService

{

        public static Customer ReadItem(string id)

        {

        Customer customer = new Customer();

        customer.CustomerID = id;

        switch (id)

        {

            case "0" :

            customer.Name = "Yaroslav Pentsarskyy";

            customer.Address = "555 Yaroslav's Way";

            break;

            case "1":

            customer.Name = "Jim Pentsarskyy";

            customer.Address = "555 Jim's Way";

            break;

            default: break;

        }

        return customer;

        }


        public static IEnumerable<Customer> ReadList()

        {

        Customer[] customerList = new Customer[2];

        Customer customer = new Customer();

        customer.CustomerID = "0";
```

```
customer.Name = "Yaroslav Pentsarskyy";

customer.Address = "555 Yaroslav's Way";

customerList[0] = customer;

Customer customer1 = new Customer();

customer1.CustomerID = "1";

customer1.Name = "Jim Pentsarskyy";

customer1.Address = "555 Jim's Way";

customerList[1] = customer1;

return customerList;

}

}
```

There is nothing too complex here, just some demo data being returned. First is the method that returns one item by ID, which is used in **View Item** list form. The **ReadList** method will return the contents of the list in a list view.

5. Let's now open the model view by double clicking the **BDCM** file, in my case called **BdcModel1.bdcm** and ensure you have the BDC Explorer window opened.

6. Expand the model nodes until you see the entity name **Entity1**. Right click on the entity name to select properties and rename the **Name** value to **Customer**.

7. In your model view, right click on the identifier property **Identifier1** and select **Properties**. Change the name of **Identifier1** to **CustomerID**.

8. In your BDC Explorer window expand all of the BDC nodes and rename property fields following the same rules:

■ **Identifier1** -> CustomerID

■ **Message** -> Name

■ **Entity1** -> Customer

■ **EntityList** -> CustomerList

9. To add a new descriptor, right click on the entity (Customer) and select **Add Type Descriptor**, then rename the standard name of **TypeDescriptor** to **Address** using nthe properties window of the descriptor.

10. Save your model.

After the rename and changing of properties, your model structure in BDC Explorer will look like this:

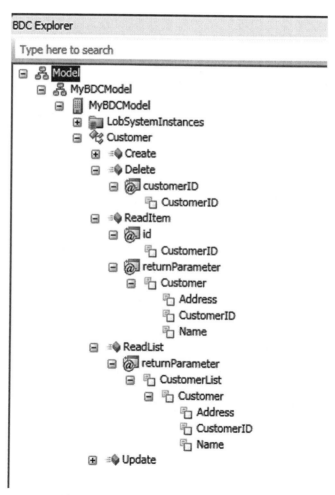

Figure 4-5 BDC Explorer – model structure

You will notice that in your Visual Studio structure in the Features
folder, you will have another feature created. It will have a **Scope**
value set to **Farm** since all BDC models will have to be deployed to
the server farm and, thus, be accessible to anyone with the right
access.

Let's take a look at the current functionality of what we have built.

1. Deploy the **Platform** project of the solution using Visual Studio
   and after the successful deployment, navigate to the root of
   your portal.

2. Click **Site Actions -> More Options**.

3. On the left menu bar, select **List -> External List**, and click **Create**.

4. Give your list a name and in the **External Content Type** box, use a
   picker to select a newly provisioned model.

5. Click **Create** when ready.

Look at that ... looks just like any SharePoint list, but we well know it
isn't just a list. When you click on the item drop down menu, the only
option you will see there is View Item, which in turn when clicked will
display the item details as we specified them. If you think about it, we
haven't delivered any business value here in terms of functionality
of data returned. However, had we a Web service on the other end
returning data from an external system or a proprietary database, the
value will become more apparent.

Let's go back to our Visual Studio and add few more methods to
see how you can incorporate **Edit** and **Delete** options in the list item
dropdown menu.

1. Open your **BDCM** file and ensure you have the BDC Method
   Details window opened too.

2. At the very bottom of the BDC Method Details window, you will
   see an option to **<Add a Method>**.

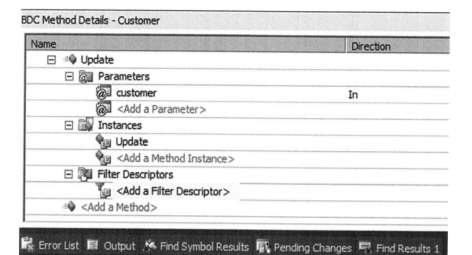

Figure 4-6 Option to Add a Method in Method Details window

3. Click on the dropdown and select **Creator**. The new method will be created. Repeat this step to also create:

■ **Deleter Method** – to handle delete operations.

■ **Updater Method** – to update the contents of the editing item.

4. Switch back to Solution Explorer and open **CustomerService.cs**. You will notice three methods added to the class. Visual Studio was even nice enough to pass in the proper parameters and assign all of the appropriate descriptors to handle the operation.

LISTING 4-3

```
public static Customer Create(Customer newCustomer)

{

throw new System.NotImplementedException();

}


public static void Delete(string customerID)

{

throw new System.NotImplementedException();

}
```

```
public static void Update(Customer customer)

{

throw new System.NotImplementedException();

}
```

I won't implement the logic for those demo methods here because I doubt you want to see any more variation of my name spelled in this book.

However, I hope this illustrates that you can take it from here and save or update the data, either from the file or any other database or Web service. To test our new functionality, deploy your solution with Visual Studio and simply refresh the external list you have created before. The external list will pick up new changes and display new **New/Edit/Delete** options. Note that the **New** option will be available in the ribbon section on the **Items** tab.

LEARN MORE:

Video screencast: Creating BDC model in Visual Studio 2010.

http://vimeo.com/7874711

Exporting and Importing Your BDC Model

As you have seen in the previous example, once you have your BDC Model defined in Visual Studio, it's easy to deploy it to the server using Visual Studio tools. Let's now take a look at how you can export a BDC model from one environment and import it to another environment.

We'll start with export of the existing model.

1. Navigate to the Central Administration of your SharePoint site.

2. Under **Application Management** category, select **Manage Service Applications**.

3. Locate and click **Business Data Connectivity Service**.

4. On the ribbon in the edit tab locate the **View** section; you should see a dropdown with **External Content Types** selected in it. Select **BDC Models**.

5. Now check the model we have created in the first sample in this chapter using SharePoint Designer. You will recognize it by BDC Model Name atrtribute containing to **SharePointDesigner-AdventureWorksLT2008** followed by an automaticly generated ID.

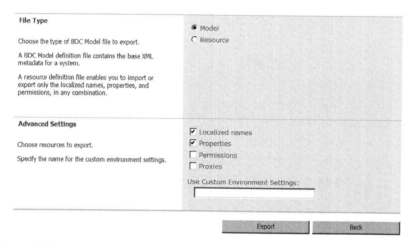

Figure 4-7 Model created in SharePoint Designer available to export from SharePoint Central Administration

6. Use the **Export** button on the ribbon.

7. On the export options page, you will be asked whether you want to export additional details about your model, such as permissions. Unless you're exporting the model that will run in exactly the same configured environment, leave all of the default options and click Export.

8. You will be offered a **BDCM** file to download, which contains the XML definition of the model and all of its assessors and descriptors.

Now let's see how we go about importing the same model to the new environment.

1. Navigate to the Central Administration of your SharePoint site.

2. Under the **Application Management** category, select **Manage Service Applications**.

3. Locate and click **Business Data Connectivity Service**.

4. On the ribbon, click the **Import** button.

5. Click Browse to locate your **BDCM** file. You can keep all of the options as default unless you checked additional options during the export.

6. When ready, click **Import**.

7. Verify that the model was imported by selecting the **BDC Models** option on the ribbon **View** section where **External Content Types** is selected by default.

The same operation can be executed by a PowerShell commands that look like this:

LISTING 4-4

```
Add-PSSnapin "Microsoft.SharePoint.Powershell"


$SiteUrl=$("http://localhost")


$serviceContext = Get-SPSiteAdministration -Identity $SiteUrl


Write-Host "Connecting to DBC"


$bdc = Get-SPBusinessDataCatalogMetadataObject -BdcObjectType
Catalog -ServiceContext $serviceContext


Write-Host "Importing ..."


Import-SPBusinessDataCatalogModel -Identity $bdc -Path ".\
BdcModel1.bdcm" -force -ModelsIncluded -PropertiesIncluded
-PermissionsIncluded -Verbose -ErrorAction Stop
-ErrorVariable $err
```

You will notice that we passed additional parameters to **Import-SPBusinessDataCatalogModel** command, such as –

PermissionsIncluded, this is the same **Permission Import** parameter as you would specify in the Central Administration user interface, if required.

Importing BDC Models into Visual Studio

At the beginning of this chapter, we talked about creating BDC Models with SharePoint Designer. For simple scenarios like accessing external SQL data and not making additional calls and transactions, SharePoint Designer is a perfect tool to create a BDC model quickly. However, you probably want to use that model in your Visual Studio solution so that it can be deployed with the rest of the solution. For cases like these, we will look at how you can export the model from SharePoint Designer and Import it into your Visual Studio solution.

Let's start with Export.

1. Open your SharePoint Designer and the SharePoint site URL.

2. On the Site Objects explorer, on the left hand side, click **External Content Types**.

3. On the main editing panel, select your BDC Model. If you've created one in the previous example, it will be called **Customer**.

4. On the SharePoint Designer ribbon, click Export BDC Model and give it a name.

5. Click OK, and save the **BDCM** file to a chosen location a disk.

Now to the Visual Studio Import steps.

1. In your Visual Studio solution structure, ensure you have a folder called BCS.

2. Add a new item to the BCS folder of type: **Business Data Connectivity Model**.

3. Locate the **BDCM** file in your Solution Explorer, right click on it, and select **Open With**.

4. Select **XML (Text) Editor** from the list; you may be asked if you want to close the editing class view of the model, click **Yes**.

5. Open the model XML file you have saved from SharePoint Designer in the previous import steps.

6. Copy the content of the SharePoint Designer generated XML to your Visual Studio model XML file.

7. Save the file, and in your solution, double click the model **BDCM** file again to load it in class view.

8. Located and delete files:

- **Entity1.cs**
- **Entity1Service.cs**

Those are not going to be used since all of the operations will be defined in the XML you have exported, since those are just calls to SQL statements and stored procedures.

9. You will notice that Visual Studio created another **Farm** scoped feature in your solution. All of the BDC models have to be deployed by separate features. You can technically add more than one model to the feature but you will get an error during the deployment.

Figure 4-8 BDC Model successfully imported in Visual Studio

You can now deploy your solution from Visual Studio, navigate to
the root of your SharePoint site, and see that you can create a new
External List instance of it.

You can see how this approach is really saving time in terms of you not
having to define your schema in Visual Studio for such a simple model.
You also saved time required for an administrator to import your model
manually.

Provisioning SharePoint External List Schema Programmatically

No matter how easy and convenient it is to create an external list
using SharePoint Designer or SharePoint user interface, when it has
to be part of the solution it has to be provisioned with the solution. In
here, we'll take a look at how external lists can be provisioned in your
site using schema or feature receiver.

Let's create a new list definition for our external list:

1. In your Visual Studio solution structure, locate the **Lists** folder and
    add a new item of type **List instance**.

2. On the next page, define all of the desired values except the
    type of the definition you want to instantiate; this one should be
    set to **External List**. At the time of writing this sample, I could not
    find the **External List** definition, which should be really available.
    If that's the case for you, create an instance of **Custom list** and
    follow to the next step. Otherwise, proceed to Step 5.

3. In the newly created list instance, open **Elements.xml** and
    rename the following attributes of ListInstance:

-   TemplateType: 600

-   FeatureId: "00BFEA71-9549-43f8-B978-E47E54A10600"

4. The above parameters can be obtained from the External
    List template definition located here: *[Drive]:\Program Files\
    Common Files\Microsoft Shared\Web Server Extensions\14\
    TEMPLATE\FEATURES\ExternalList.*

    The **FeatureId** is located in **Feature.xml** and the **TemplateType** is
    located in *ListTemplates\ExternalList.xml.*

5. Now that you have an external list instance set, insert the following code into the list definition XML right before **</ListInstance>**:

LISTING 4-5

```
<DataSource>

     <Property Name="LobSystemInstance" Value="Your
     instance" />

     <Property Name="EntityNamespace" Value="NamespaceName.
     EntityName" />

     <Property Name="Entity" Value="EntityName" />

     <Property Name="SpecificFinder"
     Value="ViewMethodNameItem" />

</DataSource>
```

For each of the property values from the code above, you need to replace the following values with the values of the external content type we created in the previous sample.

To locate the details of your external system, follow the steps below.

1. Navigate to the Central Administration for your SharePoint site.

2. Under the **Application Management** category, click **Manage Service Applications**.

3. Locate and click **Business Data Connectivity Service**.

4. If you have successfully deployed the BDC Model from the last sample, you will see its details here. Here are the values you will need to transfer to your external list definition:

■ LobSystemInstance: **BdcModel1**

■ EntityNamespace: **MySolution.Platform.BCS.BdcModel1**

■ Entity: **Customer**

■ SpecificFinder: **ReadItem**

Once you have transferred all of the values to your list definition, perform the **deploy** from within Visual Studio. Navigate to the root of your portal and you will see the list provisioned with all of the values and functions that you defined before in your BDC Model. If you're not

too happy hardcoding your list settings into XML file, there is another
method to create an external list, using a feature receiver or an
executable application.

Let's see how we can provision the same external list with a feature
receiver.

1. First, delete an existing list instance so that the newly created
   one doesn't cause a conflict during the deployment.

2. In the **Features** folder of your Solution Explorer, locate the feature
   that has a scope value set to **Web**.

3. Right click on the feature name and select **Add Event Receiver**,
   and open a newly created receiver handler file.

4. Uncomment the **FeatureActivated** method and replace the
   feature activation method code with the following:

LISTING 4-6

```
public override void FeatureActivated(SPFeatureReceiverProper
ties properties)

{

SPWeb rootWeb = properties.Feature.Parent as SPWeb;

if (rootWeb.Lists["MyExternalList"] == null)

{

        SPListDataSource ds = new SPListDataSource();

        ds.SetProperty(SPListDataSource.BDCProperties.
        LobSystemInstance,

            "BdcModel1");

        ds.SetProperty(SPListDataSource.BDCProperties.
        EntityNamespace,

            "MySolution.Platform.BCS.BdcModel1");

        ds.SetProperty(SPListDataSource.BDCProperties.Entity,

            "Customer");

        ds.SetProperty(SPListDataSource.BDCProperties.
        SpecificFinder,

            "ReadItem");
```

```
rootWeb.Lists.Add("MyExternalList", "", "Lists/
MyExternalList", ds);
}

}
```

5. Now, build the solution and deploy it to the site using Visual Studio. If you don't see the list provisioned to your site, it's because it is not on the Quick Launch of the left navigation menu. Once you click View Site Content, you can find it there.

Executing Queries on External Lists

Once the external list is provisioned and connected to the BDC Model, you would expect the same behavior in terms of querying the list as when you do for a native SharePoint list, and you're right. In this example, we'll take a look at how you can query an external list and some of the nuances to be aware of. One of the most common behaviors you will notice is that SharePoint external list query will execute longer, which is an inherent problem with any external content—it's not local, so it takes time to run external queries and receive results.

Another behavior is when your external data is not available; you will get an error, because as far as SharePoint is concerned, communication has failed and no reasonable result can be retrieved.

Lastly, due to the fact that loading a SharePoint external list takes time, SharePoint has a default threshold on how many items are returned per view. Mainly, because the last thing you need is a long running query occupying your server network and processing resources, resulting in your company's intranet to perform below the standard.

Now that you know some of the known external list behaviors, let's go ahead and create a query that will retrieve results from an external list we have created using an event receiver in our last example:

1. Locate the **WebParts** folder in your Visual Studio structure and right click on it to create a new item of the type: **Visual Web Part**.

2. Give your Web Part a desired name and create it.

3. Open Web Part **ASCX** file, in my case **VisualWebPart1UserControl.
   ascx**, and paste the following code right after the *<%@ Control
   Language="C#"* definition.

LISTING 4-7

```
<asp:repeater runat="server" ID="MyTable">

<ItemTemplate>

        <asp:Label ID="Name" runat="server" Text='<%#
        Eval("Name") %>' />

        <br/>

        <asp:Label ID="Address" runat="server" Text='<%#
        Eval("Address") %>' />

        <br/><br/>

</ItemTemplate>

</asp:repeater>
```

All we're doing above is creating a Repeater control and outputting
the name and address of the Customer object in our external data
system.

4. Now, let's open the CS file of the visual Web Part, in my case
   VisualWebPart1UserControl.ascx.cs, and namespace references
   below:

■ *using Microsoft.SharePoint;*

■ *using System.Data;*

5. Paste the code below to replace page load method in your
   class:

LISTING 4-8

```
protected void Page_Load(object sender, EventArgs e)

{

SPQuery query = new SPQuery();

query.Query = string.Empty;

query.ViewFields = "<FieldRef Name='Name'/><FieldRef
Name='Address'/>";
```

```
SPList list = SPContext.Current.Web.Lists["MyExternalList"];

DataTable table = GetData(SPContext.Current.Web, list,
query);

MyTable.DataSource = table;

MyTable.DataBind();

}


private DataTable GetData(SPWeb web, SPList list, SPQuery
query)

{

DataTable resultTable = null;

resultTable = list.GetItems(query).GetDataTable();

return resultTable;

}
```

Above in the **Page_Load** method, we created an instance of an **SPQuery** object, which will not have any query defined; in other words it will return all elements. The important part is that the Query property of the object cannot be **null**, but can be empty. Our **ViewFields** has to call fields we would like to render in our **ASCX** file. If you call something that doesn't exist in the object, you will receive an exception. Once we have all of the data required, we call our helper method to perform a query and return results in a table.

Deploy your application from within Visual Studio and navigate to the root of your portal. Add a Web Part to the page from the **Custom** category. The Web Part will display output similar to this:

LISTING 4-9

```
Yaroslav Pentsarskyy

555 Yaroslav's Way

Jim Pentsarskyy

555 Jim's Way
```

When we talked about performing a query on lists a few chapters ago, we used the **CrossListQueryCache** object which could pull data

not only from a give list but from anywhere on the site. The method
we used from this object was **GetSiteData**, which implied that the
data should be a site or Web data. Since external lists are not part of
the site—at least their data isn't—those cannot be queried using this
handy method. One drawback from querying all external lists to find
results of your criteria is also the performance of the execution; as you
can imagine, it will deteriorate if we have a large number of external
lists.

SharePoint External List Item Throttling and Limits

We discussed application performance quite a bit in this chapter, so
it's no surprise we'll dive a bit deeper on some of the mechanisms
SharePoint gives you control over how you want to limit the number of
items being returned in your query.

In this example, we'll be using Power Shell script to perform the setting
change. It's always good to know what your external item query
threshold is before SharePoint cuts it off, but in either case, you will know
when you hit the limit. You will receive an error message similar to below:

LISTING 4-10

```
Microsoft.BusinessData.Runtime.ExceededLimitException:
Database Connector has throttled the response.

The response from database contains more than '100' rows.

The maximum number of rows that can be read through Database
Connector is '100'.

The limit can be changed via the 'Set-SPBusinessDataCatalogTh
rottleConfig' cmdlet
```

As the message suggests, by using the Set-SPBusinessDataCatalogTh
rottleConfig command, we can make things right again. Here is the
exact sequence of commands to be executed from your PowerShell
environment:

LISTING 4-11

```
Add-PSSnapin "Microsoft.SharePoint.Powershell"

$bdcProxy = Get-SPServiceApplicationProxy |

        where {$_.GetType().FullName
```

```
     -eq ('Microsoft.SharePoint.BusinessData.SharedService.'

   + 'BdcServiceApplicationProxy')}
$dbRule = Get-SPBusinessDataCatalogThrottleConfig
     -Scope Database -ThrottleType Items
     -ServiceApplicationProxy $bdcProxy
Set-SPBusinessDataCatalogThrottleConfig
     -Identity $dbRule -Maximum 10000 -Default 10000
```

Another way to access throttle configuration is using Central Administration user interface.

1. Navigate to the Central Administration.

2. Under **Application Management**, click **Manage Web Applications**.

3. Select the **Web Application** you're working with—by default it's **SharePoint - 80**.

4. On the ribbon, click the **General Settings** button and select the **Resource Throttling** option.

In here, you will be able to manage some of the following throttling parameters:

- **List View Threshold** – the maximum number of items that a database operation can involve at one time for a list view

- **List View Threshold for Auditors and Administrators** – same as above but for administrators and auditors

- **List View Lookup Threshold** – defines the maximum number of Lookup, Person/Group, or workflow status fields for a list view

- **List Unique Permissions Threshold** – if you have unique permissions defined in your list, this value specifies the maximum number of unique permissions that a list can have at one time

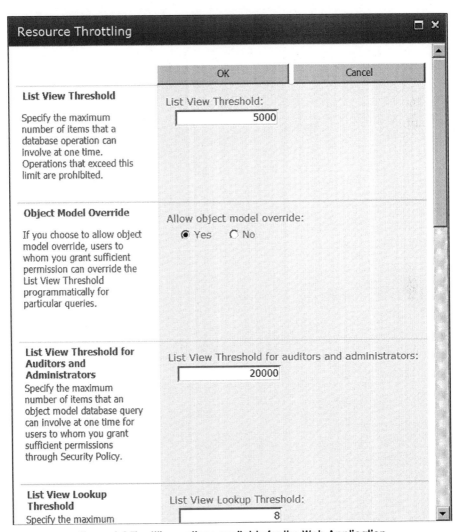

Figure 4-9 Throttling options available for the Web Application

Those settings are going to be applied on a database level not only to limit the rendering of items in the browser when they exceed the limit, but to also to limit the network traffic associated with pulling large numbers from the database.

CHAPTER 5

Process Automation and Scheduling Long Running Operations

In the last few chapters, I mentioned about Service Jobs at least once. Service Jobs in SharePoint are scheduled pieces of functionality running on a background. Usually you would create a service job to perform functions that take time ordinarily and can't be executed in a real time while a user waits for the page to refresh. Service Jobs are better than batch files because they are running within SharePoint and can be administered within SharePoint too, with the user interface part being taken care of.

To access all of the Service Job definitions follow this.

1. Navigate to the Central Administration of your SharePoint site.

2. Select **Monitoring** link of the left part of your side bar.

3. Under **Time Jobs** category, click **Review Job Definitions**.

Just as many other components in SharePoint, your time job will be provisioned using a feature. Basic requirement to provision a Service Job is pretty simple. Let's go ahead to see how we create one:

1. In your Visual Studio solution structure, locate the **Features** folder and create a new feature in it.

2. Ensure your feature is scoped to **Web Application**.

3. Right click on the name of the newly created feature and select **Add Event Receiver**.

4. Switch to the code of your newly created event receiver.

5. Add the following namespace references into the appropriate section:

■ *using Microsoft.SharePoint.Administration;*

■ *using System.Diagnostics;*

6. Locate your **FeatureActivated** method and place the following code in it:

LISTING 5-1

```
public override void FeatureActivated(SPFeatureReceiverProper
ties properties)
{
SPWebApplication webApplication = (SPWebApplication)
properties.Feature.Parent;
SPJobDefinition jobDefinition =
        webApplication.JobDefinitions["My Service Job Name"];
if (jobDefinition!=null)
{
        jobDefinition.Delete();
}
try
{
        MyJobDefinition myJobDefinition =
            new MyJobDefinition("MyServiceJobId",
            webApplication);
        SPMinuteSchedule minuteSchedule = new
        SPMinuteSchedule();
        minuteSchedule.BeginSecond = 1;
        minuteSchedule.EndSecond = 59;
```

```
        minuteSchedule.Interval = 1;

        myJobDefinition.Schedule = minuteSchedule;

        myJobDefinition.Update();

}

catch (Exception ex)

{

        Debug.Write("Exception in Feature Activated
        occurred: " +

        ex.Message);

}

}
```

In the code above, first we delete an existing instance of our job definition if, for whatever reason, it is still there when we activate the feature. We use **webApplication.JobDefinitions** to enumerate our job definitions. Then, we create an instance of our custom job definition **MyJobDefinition**, which we're about to add below. Our job will run every one minute as per schedule that was created.

7. Before creating our job class, we'll take care of deleting our job definition when the provisioning feature **FeatureDeactivating** is deactivated.

LISTING 5-2

```
public override void FeatureDeactivating(SPFeatureReceiverPro
perties properties)

{

SPWebApplication webApplication =
        (SPWebApplication)properties.Feature.Parent;

SPJobDefinition jobDefinition =
        webApplication.JobDefinitions["My Service Job Name"];

if (jobDefinition!=null)

{

        jobDefinition.Delete();
```

```
}
```

```
}
```

8. Now, let's add a custom job definition class. Create a new folder under the root of your Visual Studio solution called **ServiceJobs**.

9. Add a new **Class** to the folder called **MyJobDefinition.cs**, and open the code of the newly create class.

10. Ensure you have added the following namespace references:

■   *using Microsoft.SharePoint.Administration;*

■   *using System.Diagnostics;*

11. Replace the default definition of the class with the following code:

LISTING 5-3

```
public class MyJobDefinition : SPJobDefinition
{
        public MyJobDefinition() : base()
        {
        }


        public MyJobDefinition(string jobName, SPWebApplication
        webApplication)
        : base(jobName, webApplication, null, SPJobLockType.
        Job)
        {
        this.Title = "My Service Job Name";
        }


        public override void Execute(Guid targetInstanceId)
        {
        try
        {
```

```
    SPWebApplication webApplication = this.Parent as
    SPWebApplication;

    // TODO: your custom execution goes here

}

catch (Exception ex)

{

    Debug.Write("Problem during service job execution:
    " + ex.Message)

}

}

}
```

Above our class will have only one method **Execute** performing the execution of the custom code that will run as a part of the scheduled process.

12. Remember to reference the namespace from your job definition class in your feature receiver. Once that's done, all of the dependencies should be resolved and your solution should be ready to deploy.

So how do you test that your custom Service Jobs really works?

First, you can navigate to the **Central Administration -> Monitoring -> Review Job Definitions** and see if **My Service Job Name** is in the list. When you locate it and click the link, you should see the schedule that was set up for your job.

Job Title

My Service Job Name

Job Description

Job Properties

This section lists the properties for this job.

Web application: SharePoint - 80

Last run time: N/A

Recurring Schedule

Use this section to modify the schedule specifying when the timer job will run. Daily, weekly, and monthly schedules also include a window of execution. The timer service will pick a random time within this interval to begin executing the job on each applicable server. This feature is appropriate for high-load jobs which run on multiple servers on the farm. Running this type of job on all the servers simultaneously might place an unreasonable load on the farm. To specify an exact starting time, set the beginning and ending times of the interval to the same value.

This timer job is scheduled to run:

○ Minutes   Every [1]   minute(s)
○ Hourly
○ Daily
○ Weekly
○ Monthly

Run Now   Disable   OK   Cancel

Figure 5-1 Custom service job schedule

As you can see, you don't really have to worry about hardcoding your time job schedule. You can set initial parameters and let the administrator modify the schedule using the Central Administration user interface.

The tricky part with Service Jobs is that there isn't an easy error reporting mechanism for the code to give you immediate feedback that your custom code worked or not. Here is the way to debug your Service Job execution:

1. Open your **MyJobDefinition.cs** custom job definition class and place a breakpoint where you want to start debugging.

2. From the Visual Studio **Debug** menu select **Attach to Process**.

3. From the list of available processes, select **OWSTIMER.exe**. Note that you may have to select **Show processes from all users** and **Show processes in all sessions** to see the **OWSTIMER.exe** in the list.

4. Once ready, click **Attach** and wait for the time job to trigger. Once the time job has triggered according to your schedule, you will be taken to the Visual Studio breakpoint you have selected.

CHAPTER 6

Metadata, Tags, Rating: Working with and Extending Social Features of SharePoint 2010

Metadata related service is one of the greatest improvements in the new version of SharePoint and has many applications in existing site components. In this chapter, we will take a look at a few major pieces of the User Profile Service application, which leverages major social data features in SharePoint.

For the samples below, we will need to ensure that with SharePoint installation you have enable User Profile Service Application. Here are the steps:

1. Navigate to SharePoint Central Administration, and under **Application Management**, click **Manage Service Applications.**

2. Scroll through the list and locate **User Profile Service Application.** If you can find it, you're set and don't need to proceed further.

3. If you can't find the User Profile Service Application, click **Configuration Wizards** on the left hand side navigation, and then click **Launch the Farm Configuration Wizard.**

4. On the new page, click **Start the Wizard.**

5. Under services, ensure you have checked User Profile Service Application and click **Next**.

6. Wait for SharePoint to configure necessary components for the service application; you should be all set. Ignore the page offering you to create a new site collection if you already have one.

The User Profile Service Application mainly works with user profiles and their properties. User profiles and properties are all stored in the same database separate from other repositories in SharePoint, just like any other **Service Application.**

Let's take a look at the existing **User Properties.**

1. Assuming you are logged into SharePoint Central Administration, under **Application Management**, click **Manage Service Applications.**

2. In the list, click **User Profile Service Application**, and under the **People** category, click **Manage User Properties.**

Use this page to add, edit, organize, delete or map user profile properties. Profile properties can be mapped to Active Directory or LDA Data Connectivity.

New Property   New Section   Manage Sub-types   Select a sub-type to filter the list of properties:

Property Name	Change Order	Property Type
> Basic Information	⌄	Section
Id	⌃⌄	unique identifier
SID	⌃⌄	binary
Active Directory Id	⌃⌄	binary
Account name	⌃⌄	Person
First name	⌃⌄	string (Single Value)
Phonetic First Name	⌃⌄	string (Single Value)
Last name	⌃⌄	string (Single Value)
Phonetic Last Name	⌃⌄	string (Single Value)
Name	⌃⌄	string (Single Value)
Phonetic Display Name	⌃⌄	string (Single Value)
Work phone	⌃⌄	string (Single Value)
Department	⌃⌄	string (Single Value)

Figure 6-1 List of available User Properties

You will see a list of all the available properties and their types. You'll notice—depending on the type you will have access to—different parameters within the property configuration page. For example, let's take a look at the **About Me** property. Hover over the property and access the **Edit** menu. Check out some of the values and compare them with another property in the list: **Interests**.

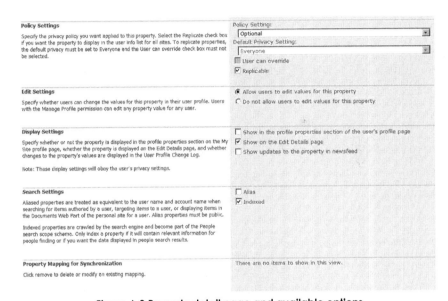

Figure 6-2 Property detail page and available options

You will notice that the first property is a simple text property, where **Interests** has additional options since this property saves metadata type of information where users can type one or more interests that will be stored in the metadata store for functionalities such as tag clouds.

Creating Your Own User Profile Properties

Extending existing properties is a task that will come in handy when you need to store more information about a user than SharePoint provides, for example, company specific project information. You can create additional properties, either through a user interface, or, if you like, you can make your changes deployable using a solution—you would create them as a part of a feature receiver.

Let's take a look at how we can provision custom property using a feature receiver:

1. Locate the **Features** folder in your Visual Studio solution structure and create a new feature scoped to a site.

2. Add a new feature receiver to your feature and open the newly created **CS file**.

3. In the namespace reference section of your file paste the following items:

- using Microsoft.Office.Server.UserProfiles;

- *using Microsoft.SharePoint;*

- *using Microsoft.SharePoint.Taxonomy;*

- *using System.Web;*

- *using Microsoft.SharePoint.WebControls;*

- *using System.Web.Profile;*

- *using Microsoft.SharePoint.Portal.WebControls;*

- *using System.Collections.Generic;*

- *using System.Diagnostics;*

4. You will notice that few references were highlighted; we're missing assembly references. Right click on the references of your project and add the following references:

- *Microsoft.Office.Server.UserProfiles*

- *Microsoft.SharePoint.Taxonomy* —you might see two of them there. Pick the one with the DLL name: *Microsoft.SharePoint. Taxonomy.dll*

- *Microsoft.sharepoint.portal.dll* located here: *[Drive]:\ Program Files\Common Files\Microsoft Shared\Web Server Extensions\14\ISAPI*

- *Microsoft.Office.Server*

- *System.Web*

5. Paste the following code instead of commented **FeatureActivated** method:

LISTING 6-1

```
public override void FeatureActivated(SPFeatureReceiverProper
ties properties)

{

SPSite siteColl = properties.Feature.Parent as SPSite;

SPServiceContext serviceContext = SPServiceContext.
GetContext(siteColl);

UserProfileConfigManager profileConfigManager =

        new UserProfileConfigManager(serviceContext);

CorePropertyManager coreProperties =

        profileConfigManager.ProfilePropertyManager.
        GetCoreProperties();


if (coreProperties.GetSectionByName("MyCustomPropertySecti
on") == null)

{

        CoreProperty MySection = coreProperties.Create(true);

        MySection.Name = "MyCustomPropertySection";

        MySection.DisplayName = "My Section Display Name";

        coreProperties.Add(MySection);

}


try

{

List<string> MyCustomProperties = new List<string>();

MyCustomProperties.Add("MyCustomPropertyName");

ProfilePropertyManager propertyManager =

profileConfigManager.ProfilePropertyManager;


foreach (string profileProperty in MyCustomProperties)

{
```

```
if (coreProperties.GetPropertyByName(profileProperty) == null)

{

        CoreProperty propertyInstance = coreProperties.
        Create(false);

        propertyInstance.Name = profileProperty.Replace(" ",
        string.Empty);

        propertyInstance.Type = "string";

        propertyInstance.Length = 50;

        propertyInstance.Separator = MultiValueSeparator.
        Semicolon;

        propertyInstance.DisplayName = profileProperty;

        propertyInstance.Description = profileProperty;

        propertyInstance.IsAlias = false;

        propertyInstance.IsSearchable = true;

        propertyInstance.Commit();


        ProfileTypeProperty profileTypeProperty =

        propertyManager.GetProfileTypeProperties(ProfileType.
        User)

            .Create(propertyInstance);

        profileConfigManager.ProfilePropertyManager

            .GetCoreProperties().Add(propertyInstance);

        propertyManager.GetProfileTypeProperties(ProfileType.
        User)

            .Add(profileTypeProperty);

    }

}

}

catch (DuplicateEntryException exception)

{

        Debug.Write(exception.Message);
```

```
    }
}
```

The logic is as follows:

1. Get a hold of the **UserProfileConfigManager** to add a new property section.

2. Create a list of properties you need to provision—in our case just one: **MyCustomPropertyName**.

3. Create a new **CoreProperty** in the **ProfilePropertyManager** instance and commit the property to the database.

4. In case the property already exists, you will get a **DuplicateEntryException** exception.

Let's deploy the solution with Visual Studio and create our custom properties. Next on the list is to make use of our properties in user profiles.

Creating SharePoint User Profiles Programmatically

Properties we created in our last sample are just definitions. In order to hold values, those properties need to be instantiated in objects — user profiles. A user profile is a collection of records in the User Profile Service Application database. In this sample, we will take a look at how you can create new user profiles.

Let's look at how we create a user profile using the Central Administration user interface.

1. Assuming you are logged into SharePoint Central Administration, under **Application Management**, click **Manage Service Applications**.

2. In the list, click **User Profile Service Application**, and under the **People** category, click **Manage User Profiles**.

3. Click the **new** profile button.

4. One of the first required fields is the account name, which has to be a legitimate name that exists in the Active Directory or your local development machine.

5. Fill out the rest of the fields—at least required ones—and click **Save and Close**.

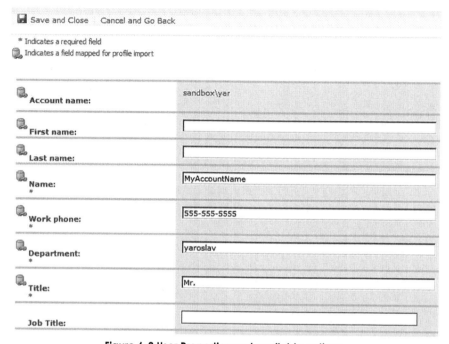

Figure 6-3 User Properties and available options

Now, let's take at look how we can create a user profile programmatically.

1. In your Visual Studio solution structure, let's create a new feature with an event receiver just like we have created in a previous sample to provision user properties.

2. Set the scope of the feature to Site.

3. Ensure your namespace reference section contains the following items:

■ *using Microsoft.Office.Server.UserProfiles;*

■ *using Microsoft.SharePoint;*

■ *using Microsoft.SharePoint.Taxonomy;*

■ *using System.Web;*

- *using Microsoft.SharePoint.WebControls;*
- *using System.Web.Profile;*
- *using Microsoft.SharePoint.Portal.WebControls;*

4. Replace the **FeatureActivated** method of the receiver with the following code:

LISTING 6-2

```
public override void FeatureActivated(SPFeatureReceiverProper
ties properties)

{

SPSite siteColl = properties.Feature.Parent as SPSite;

SPServiceContext serviceContext = SPServiceContext.
GetContext(siteColl);

UserProfileManager userProfileManager =
        new UserProfileManager(serviceContext);

UserProfile newProfile =
        userProfileManager.CreateUserProfile(AccountName,
        AccountName);


newProfile[PropertyConstants.WorkPhone].Add(WorkPhone);

newProfile[PropertyConstants.Department].Add(Department);

newProfile[PropertyConstants.Title].Add(Title);

newProfile[PropertyConstants.DistinguishedName].
Add(AccountName);

newProfile[PropertyConstants.Office].Add(Office);

newProfile.Commit();

}
```

In the above code, ensure you have replaced the placeholder values for user property values with the actual data. You will notice how I defined properties that happen to be required on the screen. As it turns out, the only field that you are required to enter for the user profile database, to access your changes is the user account name. Not all of the other properties, though required to be filled through a user interface, are required to be entered using an object model in the feature receiver.

Let's deploy our Visual Studio solution to see whether our new profile gets provisioned.

You may encounter that your user profile already exists, especially after testing this code a few times. You can either remove the user profile from the profile management interface or include the following code before creating an account:

LISTING 6-3

```
UserProfile existingProfile = userProfileManager.
GetUserProfile(@"domain\username");

if (existingProfile!=null)

{

        userProfileManager.RemoveUserProfile(existingProfile.ID);

}
```

Assuming you are logged into SharePoint Central Administration, under **Application Management**, click **Manage Service Applications**. In the list, click User Profile Service Application, and under the **People** category click **Manage User Profiles**. In here, you can search for a profile name; once you get a result, you can edit the item using the user interface.

Add New Terms to SharePoint User Profile Properties

In last two examples, we looked at how we can create new text property and create user profiles. Now let's take a look at how to work with more complex properties driven by metadata.

Open the user profile you created in the previous example, or any other existing user profile you're willing to test. Scroll down to the bottom until you find the **Skills** property.

The difference between this property and other properties is that when you start typing in the text box, it will start to autocomplete on your keyword depending on the tags and other metadata currently available in the metadata store. In this example, we'll take a look at how you can retrieve complex metadata driven property values like **Skills**, property and how to write your own values.

Let's start with a solution allowing you to add new terms.

1. In your Visual Studio, create a new feature with and add an event receiver to it just like we used in previous examples to create new user profiles.

2. Verify that the scope of the feature is set to Site.

3. Ensure you have the following namespace reference defined:

■ *Microsoft.Office.Server.UserProfiles;*

4. Replace the existing **FeatureActivated** code with the following listing:

LISTING 6-4

```
public override void FeatureActivated(SPFeatureReceiverProper
ties properties)
{
SPSite siteColl = properties.Feature.Parent as SPSite;
SPServiceContext serviceContext = SPServiceContext.
GetContext(siteColl);
UserProfileManager userProfileManager =
        new UserProfileManager(serviceContext);
UserProfile userProfile =
        userProfileManager.GetUserProfile(@"domain\username");
if (userProfile !=null && userProfile[PropertyConstants.Skills]
!= null)
{
        userProfile[PropertyConstants.Skills].Add("Javascript");
        SPContext.Current.Web.AllowUnsafeUpdates = true;
        // or userProfile[PropertyConstants.Skills].
        AddTaxonomyTerm( … );
        userProfile.Commit();
}
}
```

The above code gets a hold of the user profile specified as **domain\ username**. In some cases, you may need to get a hold of a currently logged in user. The profile of a currently logged in user is generally not available during solution being deployed since the deployment is happening user a system account. You can however access the profile of a currently logged in user when it's available by using the following line of code: *ProfileLoader.GetProfileLoader(). GetUserProfile();*

Next, access one of the existing constants that denote different property values. The easiest way to find other property values available is to search MSDN with the keyword **PropertyConstants**. If you have an existing taxonomy term object available or have created one, you can pass it over to the **AddTaxonomyTerm** method. If you're just like me, trying to add a text value, you can pass a string value to the user profile **Add** method and it will handle converting this text string to a taxonomy term.

If you followed last two samples in this chapter, you have a feature that provisions new user profile and deletes its current version. In this case you need to ensure that the current feature has a dependency on the profile provisioning feature. Otherwise your profile may not exist at the time of this feature being activated. Open profile provisioning feature page in Visual Studio and scroll to **Feature Activation Dependenices** to add a dependency on profile provisioning feature.

Let's deploy our solution using Visual Studio.

If you used **ProfileLoader** object to get a context of a current user in your feature instead of specifying the user name explicitly you will get an error due to system not being able to retrieve current user profile:

Error occurred in deployment step 'Activate Features': Value cannot be null.

Parameter name: serviceContext

The feature, however, has been deployed to the site and you can activate in manually.

1. Navigate to the root of your test SharePoint site.

2. Click **Site Actions -> Site Settings**.

3. Click **Site collection features**.

4. Locate the feature name where you defined your event receiver; click **Activate**.

Now, let's access the user profile page of our test user. The value of **Skills** property now should have new skills filled in.

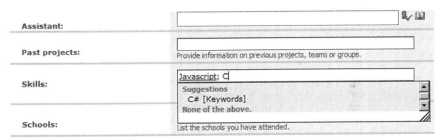

Figure 6-4 Details of User Profile metadata field

Retrieving Taxonomy Types Properties from SharePoint User Profile

In our last sample, we looked at how we can assign new value to the user property. In this sample, to make things a little different, we will create a visual Web Part that will retrieve user property values —of the **Skills** property—and render the returned value text.

Let's create a visual Web Part solution.

1. Locate the **WebParts** folder in your Visual Studio solution structure and add a new item of type: **Visual Web Part**.

2. In the newly creates Web Part **ASCX** file, locate the code behind the **CS file** and add the following namespace references:

■ *Microsoft.Office.Server.UserProfiles;*

■ *System.Collections.Generic;*

■ *Microsoft.SharePoint;*

■ *Microsoft.SharePoint.Taxonomy;*

3. Add the following code to your class replacing **Page_Load** method as well.

LISTING 6-5

```
protected void Page_Load(object sender, EventArgs e)

{

MyTable.DataSource = GetSkills();

MyTable.DataBind();

}


public List<string> GetSkills()

{

string socialDataStatsSite = SPContext.Current.Site.Url;

List<string> myskills = null;

using (SPSite siteColl = new SPSite(socialDataStatsSite))

{

SPServiceContext serviceContext = SPServiceContext.
GetContext(siteColl);


UserProfile userProfile = ProfileLoader.GetProfileLoader().
GetUserProfile();

if (userProfile[PropertyConstants.Skills] != null)

{

        myskills = new List<string>();

        Term[] skillTerms =

        userProfile[PropertyConstants.Skills].
        GetTaxonomyTerms();

        if (skillTerms != null)

        {

            foreach (Term term in skillTerms)

            {
```

```
        if (term != null)

        {

            myskills.Add(term.Name);

        }

      }

    }

}

}

return myskills;

}
```

The above code performs pretty much the same function as in the last example. The only difference is that after getting a hold of the user profile we access the taxonomy terms, of the **Skills** property (**GetTaxonomyTerms**) and save it in our list of terms, which is displayed later in a grid view.

4.   Open the **ASCX** file of your Visual Web Part and enter the following code right after control definition:

LISTING 6-6

```
<asp:gridview runat="server" ID="MyTable"
AutoGenerateColumns="True">

</asp:gridview>
```

Next, deploy your solution using Visual Studio and open the root of your SharePoint test site. Add a newly provisioned Web Part to the page and you will see many values that have been extracted from the taxonomy property field.

```
Top
─────────────────────────────────────────────────────────────────────

┌───────────────────────────────────────────────────────────────────┐
│                                                                     │
│                                                                     │
└───────────────────────────────────────────────────────────────────┘

  RetrieveProfilePropertyValues
  ┌─────────────────────────────┐
  │            Item             │
  ├─────────────────────────────┤
  Javascript
  C#
  Other Programming Languages

  Press Releases

  This query has returned no items. To configure the query for this Web Part, open the tool pane.
```

Figure 6-5 Web Part accessing User Profile properties

This particular sample gives you enough information to get started with writing custom Web Parts that interact with the profile service. The main idea behind the profile service is to allow developers to store non-overwhelming, specific user information that will be traveling with them and be easily accessible right from the context of the user profile.

User Profile Integration with Out-of-the-Box Features: Update MySite Status Message Programmatically

If you think that user profile data is stored just for a profile sheet to be filled out, you will be surprised to know that profile data is used pretty much everywhere in SharePoint. In this example, we will create our custom Web Part that will access user profile service to read and modify user status messages.

Usually, to get to your own status message you would do the following:

1. Navigate to the root of your test SharePoint site.

2. On the top right hand side corner, click on your username and select **MySite**.

3. When the MySite opens, click on **MyProfile** and you will be on the page where you can modify your status message.

As an example here, we will create a Web Part that allows up to update the message but a Web Part can be placed anywhere and, therefore, users can update their status at a project site or wherever.

Follow the steps below to get started.

1. Locate the **WebParts** folder in your Visual Studio structure and add a new item of type: **Visual Web Part**.

2. Switch to your Web Part **ASCX** code behind file and ensure you have the following two namespace references defined:

- *using Microsoft.SharePoint;*

- *using Microsoft.Office.Server.UserProfiles;*

3. Now paste the listing below right below the **Page_Load** method in your code.

LISTING 6-7

```
public static string GetStatus()

{

string statusMessage = string.Empty;

string socialDataStatsSite = SPContext.Current.Site.Url;

using (SPSite siteColl = new SPSite(socialDataStatsSite))

{

        SPServiceContext serviceContext = SPServiceContext.
        GetContext(siteColl);


        UserProfile userProfile = ProfileLoader.GetProfileLoader().
        GetUserProfile();

        SPContext.Current.Web.AllowUnsafeUpdates = true;


        if (userProfile[PropertyConstants.StatusNotes] != null

        && userProfile[PropertyConstants.StatusNotes].
        Value!=null)

        {

            statusMessage =
```

```
userProfile[PropertyConstants.StatusNotes].Value.
ToString();
        }
    }
    return statusMessage;
}
```

Just as in the previous sample, we will get a hold of one of the properties of **ProfileLoader** and our status message will be in the **PropertyConstants.StatusNotes** property.

4. In a similar way, we're going to set the status message. Add a helper function into your **CS file** right below **GetStatus**:

LISTING 6-8

```
public static void SetStatus(string statusMessage)

{

string socialDataStatsSite = SPContext.Current.Site.Url;

using (SPSite siteColl = new SPSite(socialDataStatsSite))

{

        SPServiceContext serviceContext = SPServiceContext.
        GetContext(siteColl);


        UserProfile userProfile = ProfileLoader.GetProfileLoader().
        GetUserProfile();

        SPContext.Current.Web.AllowUnsafeUpdates = true;


        userProfile[PropertyConstants.StatusNotes].
        Add(statusMessage);

        userProfile.Commit();

}

}
```

5. While in the same spot, we're going to add populate the status message in our user control by adding the following line of code into **Page_Load**:

lblCurrentStatus.Text =GetStatus();

6. Also right below **Page_Load**, we're going to add a handler for a button click event created next.

LISTING 6-9

```
protected void btnUpdateStatus_Click(object sender, EventArgs e)

{

SetStatus(txtNewStatus.Text);

}
```

7. Now let's switch to **ASCX** control view and add the following code:

LISTING 6-10

```
<%@ Register

Tagprefix="SPSWC" Namespace="Microsoft.SharePoint.Portal.
WebControls" Assembly="Microsoft.SharePoint.Portal,
Version=14.0.0.0, Culture=neutral, PublicKeyToken=71e9bce111e
9429c" %>


<SPSWC:ProfilePropertyImage

PropertyName="PictureUrl"

RenderWrapTable="False" ShowPlaceholder="true"

id="PictureUrlImage" ImageSize="Large"

CenterVertically="true" runat="server" />


<asp:Label ID="lblUserName" runat="server"></asp:Label>

<br />

<asp:TextBox ID="txtNewStatus" runat="server"
TextMode="MultiLine">

</asp:TextBox>

<br/>

<asp:Button ID="btnUpdateStatus" runat="server"

Text="Update Status" onclick="btnUpdateStatus_Click" />
```

```
<br/>

Current Status

<br/>

<asp:Label ID="lblCurrentStatus" runat="server">

</asp:Label>

<br/>

<asp:Label ID="lblLastUpdated" runat="server">

</asp:Label>

<End formatting>
```

The first line of code will register a SharePoint control that will render the user's picture, whatever it happens to be. The picture can be uploaded using an upload mechanism on the profile editing page. The rest of the code is a markup to render buttons and labels that will render the beautiful user interface shown below.

To provision the Web Part, execute deploy using Visual Studio, and then add the Web Part anywhere on the page where you can see it.

Figure 6-6 Custom status message Web Part added to the page

If you think that the User Profile Service Application holds your **Department name**, **Interests** and other details, you will be surprised to know that there is way more to it. The User Profile Service Application database holds rating and other social data, which we're going to discuss next.

Getting Started with SharePoint Social Rating Feature

One of the new things in the latest release of SharePoint is a Social Rating service. The social rating feature allows enabling asynchronous ratings on document libraries and list items. This means that you can have a document in the document library and at any given time, users can cast their votes for it; the rating service will pick up the votes once every so often and calculate the average rating. The result is a nice looking user interface, displaying ratings of each item. Rating can be enabled per document library or list and is turned on for all items in that list.

Here is how to enable rating from the document library:

1. Navigate to the library of your choice; on the ribbon, select the **Library** tab.

2. Click the **Library settings** button located in the **Settings** group.

3. Click the **Rating settings** link and select **Yes** to enable rating on the library.

If you navigate back to the library, you will see the rating control available, which you can click on to set rating.

Here is something to keep in mind. All of your ratings will be stored in the rating container in a different database from the content database. One benefit of this is that if the site is a high traffic site—if you have many users casting ratings on the same items—the ratings will be transitionally saved in a database. Based on the defined frequency, which we discuss next, all of the ratings will be calculated into an average. At the time of average being calculated, the rating value will be rounded up and recorded in the content database for everyone to see.

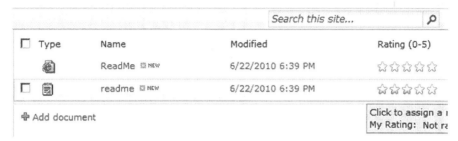

Figure 6-7 Rating controls in SharePoint library

One take away from this is that ratings will not be averaged immediately and you may want to make your users aware of this. Also, if you have any custom workflows or event receivers that run on library items, when the rating average column gets updated on the list, the update events will be fired and your workflow or event receiver might be fired too.

Changing Update Frequency of SharePoint Rating and Social Data Synchronization

As you already know, you rely on SharePoint synchronization to take care of the **Average** calculation on the list items. Rating average synchronization is a performance intensive operation. After all, we might have thousands of rating records per list and we might have many lists on our site too. Because of that reason, rating synchronization happens on a defined schedule. At the time of average rating calculation, the result is also recorded into the content database, to be shown in the average column of your list.

Let's take a look at how we can adjust the schedule to meet our own needs.

1. Navigate to your Central Administration.

2. Select **Monitoring** on the left hand side menu.

3. Under **Timer Jobs** category, click on **Review Job Definitions**.

4. Locate and click **User Profile Service Application - Social Rating Synchronization Job**.

5. Next, locate and click **User Profile Service Application - User Profile to SharePoint Full Synchronization**. This job ensures the rating is synchronized from user profile database to SharePoint content database.

6. Take a look at the synchronization schedule. For your test environment only, select the update schedule to be every minute.

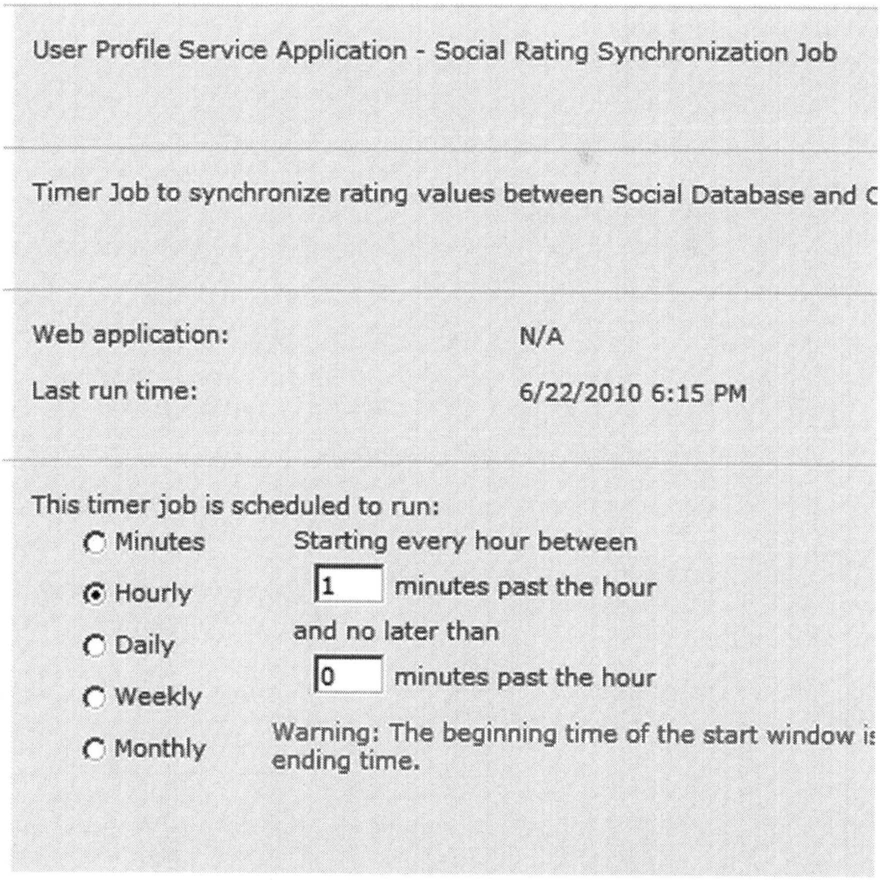

User Profile Service Application - Social Rating Synchronization Job

Timer Job to synchronize rating values between Social Database and C

Web application: N/A

Last run time: 6/22/2010 6:15 PM

This timer job is scheduled to run:
- ○ Minutes   Starting every hour between
- ◉ Hourly   `1`   minutes past the hour
- ○ Daily   and no later than
- ○ Weekly   `0`   minutes past the hour
- ○ Monthly   Warning: The beginning time of the start window is ending time.

Figure 6-8 Rating synchronization job definitions

Keep in mind that the setting of one minute is an intensive operation and only recommended on your development environment where you will be creating a few items and testing synchronization on it. You can also choose to click **Run Now** to run the synchronization in on-demand fashion.

To test this setting, navigate to the root of your test SharePoint site and the library you have enabled ratings and cast a rating. In about a minute, you should see an average being calculated and an average column being updated for the list.

Programmatically Enable Rating on SharePoint Lists and Libraries

If you see the value in the SharePoint rating system for your solutions, you probably will end up using it in your solutions. For your solutions, you will have to enable rating service automatically on the lists and libraries you are interested in. One other reason to programmatically provision the rating feature on lists is when you'd like your users to create new libraries and lists with ratings already configured on the service so they don't have to go through the motion of enabling it.

As unbelievable as it sounds, to enable the rating feature in the list or library you simply need to provision two fields into the list: **Rating (0-5)** and **Average**. SharePoint will take care of all the rendering on the client user interface and display the rating JavaScript.

Let's go ahead and create a feature that will provision the rating fields into our list.

1. Locate the **Features** folder in your solution structure and add a new feature.

2. Ensure the scope of the feature is **Web**.

3. Add an **Event Receiver** to our feature.

4. Open the code of the feature receiver and ensure you have added the following reference into the namespace reference section:

■ *using Microsoft.Office.Server.SocialData;*

5. To enable rating on a **Tasks** list uncomment the **Feature_ Activated** method and add the following code into it:

LISTING 6-11

```
public override void FeatureActivated(SPFeatureReceiverProper
ties properties)
{
string listName = string.Empty;

string averageRatingId = string.Empty;

string ratingCountId = string.Empty;


try
{
// use any list name here that you want to enable rating on
listName = "Tasks";
// those are reserved column IDs
averageRatingId = "5a14d1ab-1513-48c7-97b3-657a5ba6c742";
ratingCountId = "b1996002-9167-45e5-a4df-b2c41c6723c7";
SPList list = ((SPWeb)properties.Feature.Parent).
Lists[listName];
SPField fieldByField =
        GetFieldById(new Guid(averageRatingId),
list.ParentWeb.AvailableFields);
if (fieldByField != null &&
        !list.Fields.ContainsField(fieldByField.StaticName))
{
list.Fields.AddFieldAsXml(fieldByField.SchemaXml, true,
        SPAddFieldOptions.AddFieldToDefaultView |
        SPAddFieldOptions.AddToAllContentTypes);
}
SPField ratingCountField =
        GetFieldById(new Guid(ratingCountId),
list.ParentWeb.AvailableFields);
```

```
if (ratingCountField != null &&

!list.Fields.ContainsField(ratingCountField.StaticName))

{

        list.Fields.AddFieldAsXml(ratingCountField.SchemaXml,

        false, SPAddFieldOptions.AddToAllContentTypes);

}

list.Update();

Repropagate(list);

}

catch { }

}
```

You might be wondering what those two GUID-like strings are in my code, those are reserved fields denoting:

- Average Rating column ID:

    5a14d1ab-1513-48c7-97b3-657a5ba6c742

- Rating count column ID:

    b1996002-9167-45e5-a4df-b2c41c6723c7

As you can imagine, those two columns IDs can be picked from *[Drive]:\Program Files\Common Files\Microsoft Shared\Web Server Extensions\14\TEMPLATE\FEATURES\Ratings.*

> You will find the **ratingsfields.xml** file in this folder, where you can see the exact definitions of the columns.

6. By now you will notice that there are two methods that cannot be resolved:

- **GetFieldById** – helper method which will get a field name by GUID passed; those are special rating field IDs we're passing.

- **Repropagate** – will propagate rating functionality to list items that have been created before the feature has been activated (otherwise they won't get rating stars user interface beside them). This scenario rarely happens if you provision a list and activate feature with the solution deployment—but let's be safe.

7. Enter the following code right below the **FeatureActivated** definition:

LISTING 6-12

```
private static void Repropagate(SPList list)

{

SocialRatingManager ratingManager =

        new SocialRatingManager(SPServiceContext.Current);

string baseUrl = list.ParentWeb.Url;

if (baseUrl.EndsWith("/", StringComparison.
OrdinalIgnoreCase))

{

        baseUrl = baseUrl.TrimEnd(new char[] { '/' });

}

foreach (SPListItem item in list.Items)

{

string itemUrl = item.Url;

if (itemUrl.StartsWith("/", StringComparison.
OrdinalIgnoreCase))

{

        itemUrl = itemUrl.TrimStart(new char[] { '/' });

}

SPSecurity.RunWithElevatedPrivileges(delegate

{

        ratingManager.PropagateRating(new Uri(baseUrl + "/" +
        itemUrl));

});

}

}

private static SPField GetFieldById(Guid id,
SPFieldCollection fieldArray)

{
```

```
    try
    {
        return fieldArray[id];
    }
    catch
    {
        return null;
    }
}
```

Now that all of the references are resolved, let's deploy this solution in Visual Studio and navigate to the root of your test SharePoint site to check out the **Tasks** list to see if it has the rating feature enabled.

Once enabled, you should be able to vote and see the average calculated in about a minute, if you have completed the sample before and decreased the synchronization interval.

Adding Item Rating Control to Your Custom List Forms

Although we went over the creation of custom list forms and placing controls on them in earlier chapters, it's appropriate to mention the method of adding custom rating control here due to its special nature.

The rating control, or as I will refer to it as rating stars, is as any other control in SharePoint—automatically rendered depending on the type of the field in the list or library. It's very much bound to the data in the list item and cannot function on its own. In other words, I can't rip out the control and place it somewhere on a Web Part or a custom **ASPX** page; otherwise, it will lose a context of the item it's bound to and won't function properly.

Let's take a look at the scenario where we have a custom list on a site where look is defined though XSL; we'll go ahead and add our custom control to XSL and see how it renders on the page.

1. Locate the **Layouts** folder in your Visual Studio solution, and ensure you have an **XSL** folder within it.

2. Add a new item to the root of the **XSL** folder of type: **XSLT** located in the **Data** tab in the **Add New Item** prompt.

3. Give the file a name: **MyXSLSheet.xsl** or any other name, as long as you keep the **XSL** as an extension.

4. Open the file and replace its contents with the following code:

LISTING 6-13

```
<xsl:stylesheet xmlns:x="http://www.w3.org/2001/XMLSchema"
xmlns:d="http://schemas.microsoft.com/sharepoint/dsp"

version="1.0" exclude-result-prefixes="xsl msxsl ddwrt"
xmlns:ddwrt="http://schemas.microsoft.com/WebParts/v2/
DataView/runtime" xmlns:asp="http://schemas.microsoft.com/
ASPNET/20" xmlns:__designer="http://schemas.microsoft.
com/WebParts/v2/DataView/designer" xmlns:xsl="http://www.
w3.org/1999/XSL/Transform"

xmlns:msxsl="urn:schemas-microsoft-com:xslt"
xmlns:SharePoint="Microsoft.SharePoint.WebControls">

<xsl:import href="/_layouts/xsl/main.xsl"/>

<xsl:output method="html" indent="no"/>

<xsl:param name="NoAJAX" select="1"/>

<xsl:template mode="Item" match="Row[../../@
TemplateType='100']">

<xsl:param name="Fields" select="."/>

<xsl:param name="Collapse" select="."/>

<xsl:param name="Position" select="1"/>

<xsl:param name="Last" select="1"/>

<xsl:variable name="thisNode" select="."/>

<table width="100%" border="0" cellspacing="0"
cellpadding="0" dir="None">

<tr>

<td width="690">

<h4>

<xsl:apply-templates select="$Fields[@Name='LinkTitle']"
mode="PrintField">
```

```
<xsl:with-param name="thisNode" select="."/>

<xsl:with-param name="Position" select="$Position"/>

</xsl:apply-templates>

<xsl:apply-templates select="$Fields[@Name='RatingCount']"
mode="PrintField">

<xsl:with-param name="thisNode" select="."/>

<xsl:with-param name="Position" select="$Position"/>

</xsl:apply-templates>

<xsl:apply-templates select="$Fields[@Name='AverageRating']"
mode="PrintField">

<xsl:with-param name="thisNode" select="."/>

<xsl:with-param name="Position" select="$Position"/>

</xsl:apply-templates>

</h4>

</td>

</tr>

</table>

</xsl:template>

</xsl:stylesheet>
```

Above, we have defined a typical item rendering XSL template that we looked at in an earlier chapter. This template verifies that the type of list it will be applied to is a custom list (we know that by the **Template ID = 100**):

<xsl:template mode="Item" match="Row[../../@ TemplateType='100']">.

Depending on your list, you may have a different template ID, which can always be looked up. To look up a template ID of the list, open the following folder: *[Drive]:\Program Files\Common Files\Microsoft Shared\Web Server Extensions\14\TEMPLATE\ FEATURES*, where you will find the name of the feature representing the list you're interested in, for example: **CustomList**. The list will contain a definition folder with the definition XML file in it that will contain a template type attribute called **Type**. The **ID** of the type is something you would use in your template to ensure it's being applied to a correct list type. In case you're applying a template to just one list or library, you may consider not verifying the **Template ID** since none of the other instances of lists or libraries will be using it.

The section that actually renders the average field and rating count field is this:

LISTING 6-14

```
<xsl:apply-templates select="$Fields[@Name='RatingCount']"
mode="PrintField">

<xsl:with-param name="thisNode" select="."/>

<xsl:with-param name="Position" select="$Position"/>

</xsl:apply-templates>
```

Above, the names of the fields are rendered on a page.

Let's now apply the template to our list.

1. Navigate to the root of your test SharePoint site.

2. Create a custom list on the site.

3. Click on the link that will take you to the **All Items** view of the list.

4. Click **Site Actions -> Edit Page**.

5. Access the Web Part properties window of the list view.

6. In **Miscellaneous** section, locate the **XSL** link property and set its value to /_layouts/XSL/MyXSLSheet.xsl.

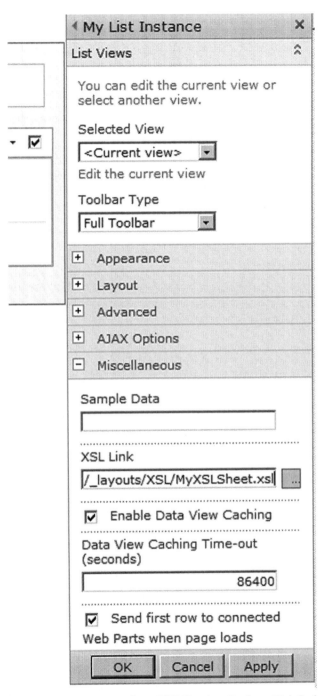

Figure 6-9 Setting the value of XSL Sheet on the form Web Part

7. Click **OK**, and your list should render again with the rating field displayed.

When working with social rating feature in SharePoint, eventually you will want to know how you can get rid of the old entries in the rating system. Unlike many other polling systems, social rating feature in SharePoint will store associated user ratings in the database along with the user name who casted the rating and the URL on which it was casted. That's right; the social rating feature uses the URL as an identifier for items. One benefit of it is that you can cast ratings on items that are external URLs. The bad news is that when you create a document library, enable rating on it, and set a rating score—even when you delete it—when creating a new document library with the same name and enable rating on it, the items that have never been seen by anyone before will have ratings assigned to them. This is unfortunate and, hopefully, we will see some improvements to prevent situations like this from happening. At the present moment, it's important to be aware of the issue.

There are also no supported methods to purge the rating data from the database, which again seems like a good idea to implement in the future.

Working with Managed Metadata Service and Tagging Features

One of the next new features we will be discussing in this chapter is **Managed Metadata** service application and a group of features that are associated with it. In SharePoint, metadata is a piece of content that is assigned to lists and libraries, and describes the item. Before latest release of SharePoint, metadata fields could be assigned only on an individual library or a site column and could be used in document libraries or lists. In the latest release, the metadata concept is taken to the next level, providing users fill in metadata either from an existing centralized metadata store or propose new metadata for everyone to use providing users have permissions to do so.

Metadata service has a few new features associated with it, such as ribbon tagging buttons, list item form autocomplete for metadata terms, etc.

To get started with metadata feature you will need to enable it and assign permissions on the metadata store.

1. Navigate to the Central Administration of your test SharePoint site.

2. Under **Application Management**, click **Manage Service Applications**.

3. Locate **Managed Metadata Service** from the list below and click on it. If you cannot find this option, click on the **Configuration Wizards** link on the left hand side navigation and launch a configuration wizard to activate **Managed Metadata Service**.

4. On the next page, **Term Store Management Tool**, ensure your user name is entered in the **Term Store Administrators**.

On the left hand side of the page, in the **Taxonomy Term Store**, you will see a tree-like hierarchy of terms. If you have gone through some of the samples in the previous chapter, you will have a few terms added in there. Here is how your **Term Store** may look on the figure below.

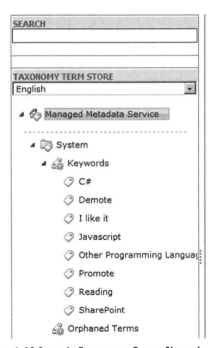

Figure 6-10 Sample Taxonomy Terms Store structure

When you add new terms to the terms store, SharePoint gradually synchronizes the data in the respective stores to make it available for use in sites. Similar to what we had in the **Social Ratings** service, the Managed Metadata Service Application has a scheduled job to perform the propagation of its settings.

Ensure the schedule of the scheduled job is appropriate to test your changes.

1. Navigate to the root of the Central Administration site.

2. Click on **Monitoring**, and under the **Timer Jobs** category, click **Review Job Definitions**.

3. Locate and click **User Profile Service Application - Social Data Maintenance Job**.

4. Specify an adequate interval for your testing, or run the job on-demand from this window.

The reason why we have a separate synchronization job is due to possible large volumes of metadata transactions. As you will see next, **Managed Metadata Service** is able to calculate the terms and tags throughout the site on various URLs, and in case the SharePoint site has high traffic, there might be a delay in operation if all the features and calculations happened in real time.

Tagging Content Programmatically with Managed Metadata Service

You have probably seen two ribbon buttons on the home page of your SharePoint test site allowing you to tag pages with selected tags or custom tags. In many cases, your solution might need to perform tagging on users' behalf. For example, we can use tagging to express if a user supports the content that has been recently published and perform a count of the total supported versus not supported articles that a user has tagged. Let's take a look at how we can use metadata service and its functions programmatically.

Let's start with creating a Web Part to tag existing content.

1. In your Visual Studio solution structure, locate the **WebParts** folder.

2. Add a new item to the folder of type: **Visual Web Part**, and provide an appropriate name for the Web Part.

3. Switch to the **ASCX** viewof the control and add the following markup under the **control** definition of your Web Part control:

LISTING 6-15

```
Enter tag:

<br/>

<asp:textbox ID="newTag" runat="server"></asp:textbox>

<br/>

<asp:linkbutton ID="tagPage" runat="server" onclick="tagPage_
Click">

Tag current page</asp:linkbutton> OR

<asp:linkbutton ID="tagCount" runat="server"
onclick="tagCount_Click">

Get tag count</asp:linkbutton>

<br/>

Tag Count: <asp:label ID="rank" runat="server" text="None">

</asp:label>
```

This user interface is going to display a text box where users enter the tag name and then press either a **Tag Page** button or **Get Tag Count**, which will either create a new tag for the page or get the count of how many times this page has been tagged with this tag.

4. Switch to the **CS**, code behind view of your control and add the following namespace references:

■ using Microsoft.SharePoint;

■ using Microsoft.Office.Server.SocialData;

■ using System.Collections.Generic;

■ using Microsoft.SharePoint.Taxonomy;

■ using System.Web;

■ using System.Linq;

5. Add the following code to the body of your code right below the **Page_Load** definition:

LISTING 6-16

```csharp
protected void tagCount_Click(object sender, EventArgs e)

{

SPSite siteColl = SPContext.Current.Site;

SPServiceContext serviceContext = SPServiceContext.
GetContext(siteColl);

SocialTagManager mySocialTagManager =

        new SocialTagManager(serviceContext);


SocialTerm[] socTerms = mySocialTagManager.GetAllTerms();
IEnumerable<SocialTerm> termQuery =

        socTerms.Where(socTerm =>

            (

            socTerm.Term.Name.Equals(newTag.Text)

            ));


int promoted = 0;

int index = 0;

Term[] taxTerms = new Term[1];


foreach (SocialTerm aTerm in termQuery)

{

        taxTerms[index++] = aTerm.Term;

}

IEnumerable<SocialTag> tagQuery =

        mySocialTagManager.GetTags(HttpContext.Current.Request.
        Url);

foreach (SocialTag tag in tagQuery)
```

```
{

    string termName = tag.Term.Name;

    if (termName.Equals(newTag.Text))

    {

        promoted++;

    }

}

rank.Text = Convert.ToString(promoted);

}
```

In here, we're getting a hold of the **SocialTagManager** and requesting to get all of the terms from the terms store. We can then get all of the tags for the current URL and ensure they filter out everything except the ones that we have had users enter into a text box.

6. Now, let's add the part that will tag the content with the keyword provided; paste the code below to the newly created **tagCount_Click**:

LISTING 6-17

```
private static void TagResource(string tag)

{

SPSite siteColl = SPContext.Current.Site;

SPServiceContext serviceContext = SPServiceContext.
GetContext(siteColl);

SocialTagManager mySocialTagManager =

        new SocialTagManager(serviceContext);

SocialTerm[] socTerms = mySocialTagManager.GetAllTerms();


IEnumerable<SocialTerm> termQuery =

        socTerms.Where(socTerm =>

        (

        socTerm.Term.Name.Equals(tag)
```

```
    ));

foreach (SocialTerm aTerm in termQuery)
{
        string termName = aTerm.Term.Name;
        if (termName.Equals(tag.ToString()))
        {
            mySocialTagManager
                .AddTag(HttpContext.Current.Request.Url, aTerm.
                Term,
                aTerm.Term.Name);
            break;
        }
}
}


protected void tagPage_Click(object sender, EventArgs e)
{
TagResource(newTag.Text);
}
```

In the code above, we retrieve the collection of tags from existing terms defined in our term store. If the name passed in a text box by our user matches the name of the existing tag in a term store, we add a new tag record with the current page URL.

7. Now, we can deploy our Web Part using Visual Studio and navigate to the root of our test SharePoint site.

8. On the site, add a new Web Part to the page and get a count of terms that you have in the term store in your Central Administration. Then, tag a page with the same term and get the count again. You should see an increase in the count of your tags.

The scenario above may not match your business requirements, but the goal here is to show you the flexibility with the object model enough to work with most scenarios.

CHAPTER 7

Creating SharePoint 2010 Ribbon Components and Managing Existing Ribbon Elements

SharePoint ribbon interface is probably one of the biggest changes to user interface that was released in this version. Although ribbon has been implemented in past versions of other Microsoft applications, we can really see now that with SharePoint, the ribbon is here to stay. It's definitely user interface that will require some getting used to. Many users perceive the SharePoint site as a website–type solution, and ribbon definitely does not fit into that image. On the other hand, if you think about SharePoint as a Web application extending client application capabilities to the Web, the ribbon is very appropriate to manage all sorts of functionalities. In this chapter, we'll take a detailed look at how to create your own custom ribbon controls under various conditions.

Creating Basic SharePoint Ribbon Controls

By now, you probably had many chances to take a look at the ribbon; after all, you have to use it every time you need to call up any function in SharePoint. At the time of writing this chapter, there were no publicly accessible tools that would let you generate ribbon markup on the fly by dragging and dropping controls. That is not to say that something like this won't be released soon. Maybe you're thinking about it as you reading this chapter. Despite all of the complexities that might be involved in ribbon authoring, you will be able to create any control that you see on the out-of-the-box ribbon.

Another important part of the ribbon architecture is that its controls, such as buttons, dropdown boxes, and other, reside in the context of the current page or element that has a ribbon context. This means that if you want to add a new button to the ribbon, you have to specify whether that button will appear in the document library, and if so, what type of library. Along with the library, you will have to specify what tab the ribbon appears on and in what group.

The easiest way to get started with this concept is to create a sample, so let's go ahead and create a ribbon button that will reside in the **Shared Documents** library on your team site. I assume you have a team site already created as a root of your site collection.

1. In your Visual Studio project structure, create a new folder in the root of the solution called Ribbon.

2. Click on the folder to add a new item of type: **Empty Element**, and give the instance a name **RibbonButton**

3. Open the **Elements.xml** file you have just created and replace the contents of it with the following code:

LISTING 7-1

```xml
<?xml version="1.0" encoding="utf-8"?>
<Elements xmlns="http://schemas.microsoft.com/sharepoint/">
<CustomAction
        Id="Ribbon.Library.Share.ButtonSample"
        Location="CommandUI.Ribbon"
        RegistrationId="101"
        RegistrationType="List"
        Title="Using Button">
<CommandUIExtension>
<CommandUIDefinitions>
```

```
<CommandUIDefinition
        Location="Ribbon.Library.Share.Controls._children">
<Button
        Id="Ribbon.Library.Share.Button"
        Sequence="20"
        LabelText="My Button"
        Image16by16="/_layouts/images/QuickTagILikeIt_16.png"
        TemplateAlias="o1"
        Command="NewRibbonButtonCommand" />
</CommandUIDefinition>
</CommandUIDefinitions>
<CommandUIHandlers>
<CommandUIHandler
        Command="NewRibbonButtonCommand"
        CommandAction="javascript:alert('Button clicked');" />
</CommandUIHandlers>
</CommandUIExtension>
</CustomAction>
</Elements>
```

I should mention few things about the code above:

1. The **ID** of the custom action can be user defined.

2. The **Location** attribute has to match a subset of defined locations in this case.

3. **Registration ID** and **Registration type** are optional attributes and are required only if you plan on attaching the ribbon button to the list or library. In our case, we want to attach our button to the list with the template number **101**, which is a document library. To find out what other registration type IDs are available, refer to the features folder and extract the template ID from the respective feature. For example, the custom list feature is located here: [Drive]:\Program Files\Common Files\Microsoft

Shared\Web Server Extensions\14\TEMPLATE\FEATURES\ CustomList. The **ID** of the list is specified in here: *ListTemplates\ CustomList.xml*, as a **Type** attribute.

4. The remaining required structure defines the nested nature of ribbon where we specify our custom control **<Button/>**.

5. Besides attributes that define the style of the button, there is an attribute that defines action when the button is clicked: **NewRibbonButtonCommand**.

Now let's deploy the solution using Visual Studio and open a **Shared Documents** library on the root of your team site site. Make sure that you click on the **Library** tab since that's where we defined our button in the **Location** attribute: *Ribbon.Library.Share.Controls*.

If your deployment succeeded, you should see a ribbon button as shown below.

Figure 7-1 Sample ribbon button in Shared Document library

Now that we know how to create the simplest version of a control, let's go ahead and try creating something more complex.

Creating a Fly Out Anchor on Your Ribbon

A fly out anchor is a type of a button, except when you click on it, it shows additional options as buttons. Fly out anchors are used frequently in SharePoint—for example, in the document library workflow options.

Let's reuse the same Visual Studio item we used in the previous example, but this time, replace the **<Button>** control in the **Elemnets. xml** structure with the **<FlyoutAnchor>**.

1. Open the **Elements.xml** in your ribbon elements file you created in the last sample.

2. Locate the section where you defined button controls.

LISTING 7-2

```
<Button

        Id="Ribbon.Library.Share.Button"

        Sequence="20"

        LabelText="My Button"

        Image16by16="/_layouts/images/QuickTagILikeIt_16.png"

        TemplateAlias="o1"

        Command="NewRibbonButtonCommand"/>
```

3. Replace the button definition from Step 2 with the following code of the fly out anchor:

LISTING 7-3

```
<FlyoutAnchor

        Id="Ribbon.Library.Share.FlyoutAnchor"

        Sequence="20"

        LabelText="My Flyout Anchor"

        Image16by16="/_layouts/images/QuickTagILikeIt_16.png"

        TemplateAlias="o1">
```

```xml
<Menu Id="Ribbon.Library.Share.FlyoutAnchor.Menu">

<MenuSection Id="Ribbon.Library.Share.FlyoutAnchor.Menu.
MenuSection"

        Sequence="10" DisplayMode="Menu16">

<Controls Id="Ribbon.Library.Share.FlyoutAnchor.Menu.
MenuSection.Controls">

<Button

        Id="Ribbon.Library.Share.FlyoutAnchor.Menu.MenuSection.
        MyButton"

        Sequence="10"

        Command="NewRibbonButtonCommand"

        LabelText="MyButton"

        Image16by16="/_layouts/images/QuickTagILikeIt_16.png"

        TemplateAlias="o2" />

</Controls>

</MenuSection>

<MenuSection Id="Ribbon.Library.Share.FlyoutAnchor.Menu.
MenuSection1"

        Sequence="20" DisplayMode="Menu16">

<Controls Id="Ribbon.Library.FlyoutAnchor.Menu.MenuSection1.
Controls">

<Button

        Id="Ribbon.Library.FlyoutAnchor.Menu.MenuSection1.
        MyButton1"

        Sequence="10"

        Command="NewRibbonButtonCommand"

        LabelText="MyButton1"

        Image16by16="/_layouts/images/QuickTagILikeIt_16.png"

        TemplateAlias="o3"

        />
```

```
</Controls>

</MenuSection>

</Menu>

</FlyoutAnchor>
```

One difference you will notice is that the fly out anchor defines its own structure of controls, which in our case are buttons just like from the previous sample. Also, a fly out anchor doesn't have a Java Script handler to handle clicks since it has a default one that unfolds dependent buttons. Since our buttons all reference the same Java Script function, the message that we will get when any of them is clicked will be the same.

4. Let's deploy our solution and navigate to the same **Shared Documents** library we used in the previous example.

    If your ribbon got deployed with no problems, you will see two buttons when clicking on the dropdown-looking button in the Shared section of the document library.

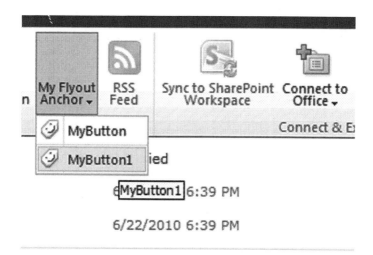

Figure 7-2 Fly out anchor on the SharePoint ribbon

What If Your Ribbon Java Script Is Too Large for One File

In the last two examples, our Java Script was a one-line piece of code, and in reality, your Java Script, whatever you end up doing with it, will be larger.

One of the approaches to creating ribbon items using a large piece of Java Script is to define it in a separate **CustomAction**. You have already seen how our entire ribbon is defined in **CustomAction**, but you can also define any helper elements or other ribbon elements all in one **Elements.xml** file.

Let's take a look at the last example, where we provisioned a fly out anchor; but this time, the Java Script will be defined with our new method.

1.   Locate the **Elements.xml** file you have been using to define your custom ribbons.

2.   Open the file and replace the contents of it with the following code:

LISTING 7-4

```
<?xml version="1.0" encoding="utf-8"?>

<Elements xmlns="http://schemas.microsoft.com/sharepoint/">

<CustomAction

        Id="Ribbon.Library.Share.ButtonSample"

        Location="CommandUI.Ribbon"

        RegistrationId="101"

        RegistrationType="List"

        Title="Using Button">

<CommandUIExtension>

<CommandUIDefinitions>

<CommandUIDefinition

        Location="Ribbon.Library.Share.Controls._children">

<FlyoutAnchor

        Id="Ribbon.Library.Share.FlyoutAnchor"

        Sequence="20"
```

```
        LabelText="My Flyout Anchor"

        Image16by16="/_layouts/images/QuickTagILikeIt_16.png"

        TemplateAlias="o1">

<Menu Id="Ribbon.Library.Share.FlyoutAnchor.Menu">

<MenuSection Id="Ribbon.Library.Share.FlyoutAnchor.Menu.
MenuSection"

Sequence="10" DisplayMode="Menu16">

<Controls Id="Ribbon.Library.Share.FlyoutAnchor.Menu.
MenuSection.Controls">

<Button

        Id="Ribbon.Library.Share.FlyoutAnchor.Menu.MenuSection.
        MyButton"

        Sequence="10"

        Command="NewRibbonButtonCommand"

        LabelText="MyButton"

        Image16by16="/_layouts/images/QuickTagILikeIt_16.png"

        TemplateAlias="o2" />

</Controls>

</MenuSection>

<MenuSection Id="Ribbon.Library.Share.FlyoutAnchor.Menu.
MenuSection1"

        Sequence="20" DisplayMode="Menu16">

<Controls Id="Ribbon.Library.FlyoutAnchor.Menu.MenuSection1.
Controls">

<Button

        Id="Ribbon.Library.FlyoutAnchor.Menu.MenuSection1.
        MyButton1"

        Sequence="10"

        Command="NewRibbonButtonCommand"

        LabelText="MyButton1"

        Image16by16="/_layouts/images/QuickTagILikeIt_16.png"
```

```
            TemplateAlias="o3"

            />

    </Controls>

    </MenuSection>

    </Menu>

    </FlyoutAnchor>

    </CommandUIDefinition>

    </CommandUIDefinitions>

    <CommandUIHandlers>

    <CommandUIHandler

            Command="NewRibbonButtonCommand"

            CommandAction="javascript:HelloRibbon();" />

    </CommandUIHandlers>

    </CommandUIExtension>

    </CustomAction>

    <CustomAction Id="Ribbon.Library.Share.FlyoutAnchorSample.
    Script"

            Location="ScriptLink"

            ScriptBlock="

            function HelloRibbon()

            {

            alert('Hello there, Ribbon!');

            }" />

    </Elements>
```

3. Now, deploy the solution with Visual Studio and take a look at
    the results.

You will see a different message indicating that a different Java Script
function was called.

In simple cases, this might address the problem. In cases where you
create a large ribbon library with multiple controls to handle your

custom application built on SharePoint, you will probably have user interaction developers giving you a large file or a few where all of the Java Script is stored.

In the scenario described above, you can use our **CustomAction** to reference a Java Script file like this:

LISTING 7-5

```
<CustomAction
Id="Ribbon.Library.Share.FlyoutAnchorSample.Script"

Location="ScriptLink"

ScriptSrc="/_layouts/SharePointProject1/RibbonActions.js" />
```

Assuming you're using our solution structure and have a mapped **Layouts** folder in your solution, that's where you would place your custom Java Script file, which will be deployed to the SharePoint root once the solution is deployed.

All of the functions defined in the external Java Script file will be available to ribbon control if the file is referenced with the method above.

Working with Ribbon Groups and Tabs

So far, we've been looking at how to create buttons and few other controls and how to handle actions when those controls are clicked. Now is the time to take a look at how you can position your controls in the different containers available, such as groups and tabs.

In last few samples, we created a button in the **Share** group of a **Library** tab. Let's now create a new tab and group similar to **Share**, and place a simple button in it.

1. Locate the **Elements.xml** you've been using to make changes to your ribbon.

2. Replace the code in the **Elements.xml** with the following:

LISTING 7-6

```
<?xml version="1.0" encoding="utf-8"?>

<Elements xmlns="http://schemas.microsoft.com/sharepoint/">
```

```xml
<CustomAction
        Id="MyProject.RibbonButton"
        Location="CommandUI.Ribbon.ListView"
        RegistrationId="101"
        RegistrationType="List">
<CommandUIExtension>
<CommandUIDefinitions>
<CommandUIDefinition
        Location="Ribbon.Tabs._children">
<Tab
        Id="MyProject.Ribbon.HelloTab"
        Title="Custom Tab Title">
<Scaling
        Id="MyProject.Ribbon.HelloTab.Scaling">
<MaxSize
        Id="MyProject.Ribbon.HelloTab.MaxSize"
        GroupId="MyProject.Ribbon.HelloTab.HelloGroup"
        Size="OneLargeButton"/>
<Scale
        Id="MyProject.Ribbon.HelloTab.Scaling.TabScaling"
        GroupId="MyProject.Ribbon.HelloTab.HelloGroup"
        Size="OneLargeButton" />
</Scaling>
<Groups Id="MyProject.Ribbon.HelloTab.Groups">
<Group
        Id="MyProject.Ribbon.HelloTab.HelloGroup"
        Title="Custom Group Title"
        Template="MyProject.Ribbon.Templates.HelloTemplate">
<Controls Id="MyProject.Ribbon.HelloTab.HelloGroup.Controls">
```

```xml
<Button
        Id="MyProject.Ribbon.HelloTab.HelloGroup.HelloButton"
        Command="MyProject.Scripts.HelloCommand"
        LabelText="Button Text!"
        TemplateAlias="CutomHelloTemplate"/>
</Controls>
</Group>
</Groups>
</Tab>
</CommandUIDefinition>
<CommandUIDefinition Location="Ribbon.Templates._children">
<GroupTemplate Id="MyProject.Ribbon.Templates.HelloTemplate">
<Layout
        Title="OneLargeButton"
        LayoutTitle="OneLargeButton">
<Section Alignment="Top" Type="OneRow">
<Row>
<ControlRef DisplayMode="Large" TemplateAlias="CutomHelloTemp
late" />
</Row>
</Section>
</Layout>
</GroupTemplate>
</CommandUIDefinition>
</CommandUIDefinitions>
<CommandUIHandlers>
<CommandUIHandler
        Command="MyProject.Scripts.HelloCommand"
        CommandAction="javascript:alert('New button
        clicked!');" />
```

```
</CommandUIHandlers>

</CommandUIExtension>

</CustomAction>

</Elements>
```

\<End formatting\>

Above, we used the following new definitions:

■ **\<Tab\>** - to define a tab.

■ **\<Scaling\>** - to define how your control will render, depending if the page is resized; in our example, we use the same size. This definition is optional.

■ **\<Groups\>** - defines groups under the **\<Tab\>**; purely a container.

■ **\<Group\>** - defines individual group under **\<Groups\>**. **Template** attribute inside your **\<Group\>** - will define how your group is displayed. The definition is in **\<GroupTemplate\>**.

■ **\<Controls\>** - will contain your controls; in our case, we just use **\<Button\>**.

■ Command inside your **\<Button\>** will carry the name of the command that will execute when the button is clicked—defined in **\<CommandUIHandler\>**.

■ **TemplateAlias** - contains the name of the template according to which your button will be displayed.

3. Deploy the solution and if the deployment was successful, you will see your custom tab and button rendered as shown below.

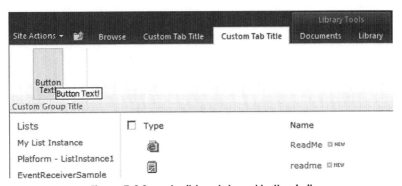

Figure 7-3 Sample ribbon tab and button in it

Creating Site Level Ribbon Tabs

Until now, we looked at how to create ribbon buttons that are bound to a particular list type's context. In other words, we created ribbon buttons and tabs that will show up only when you navigate to the library of your choice. In this sample, we'll take a look at how to create ribbon tabs that will be displayed on a site level ribbon.

Remember at the beginning of this chapter, I mentioned how ribbon is contextual and doesn't float around by itself. In this sample, in order for our ribbon tab to work, we not only will need to provision the XML markup for its structure elements, we will also need to activate the tab. Since SharePoint doesn't have enough information on the context of our tab—because we won't supply it—it will be hidden until instructed to show up.

Let's start with defining our ribbon elements.

1. In your Visual Studio, locate the **Ribbon** folder we created earlier and add a new item of type: **Empty Element**.

2. Open the **Element.xml** file and replace the contents of it with the following code:

LISTING 7-7

```xml
<?xml version="1.0" encoding="utf-8"?>
<Elements xmlns="http://schemas.microsoft.com/sharepoint/">
<CustomAction
        Id="MyProject.RibbonButton"
        Location="CommandUI.Ribbon">
<CommandUIExtension>
<CommandUIDefinitions>
<CommandUIDefinition
        Location="Ribbon.Tabs._children">
<Tab
        Id="MyProject.Ribbon.HelloTab"
        Title="Custom Tab Title">
```

```
<Scaling Id="Ribbon.Read.Scaling">
</Scaling>
<Groups Id="Ribbon.Read.Groups">
<Group
      Id="MyProject.Ribbon.HelloTab.HelloGroup"
      Title="Custom Group Title"
      Template="MyProject.Ribbon.Templates.HelloTemplate">
<Controls Id="MyProject.Ribbon.HelloTab.HelloGroup.Controls">
<Button
      Id="MyProject.Ribbon.HelloTab.HelloGroup.HelloButton"
      Command="MyProject.Scripts.HelloCommand"
      LabelText="Button Text!"
      TemplateAlias="CutomHelloTemplate"/>
</Controls>
</Group>
</Groups>
</Tab>
</CommandUIDefinition>
<CommandUIDefinition Location="Ribbon.Templates._children">
<GroupTemplate Id="MyProject.Ribbon.Templates.HelloTemplate">
<Layout
      Title="OneLargeButton"
      LayoutTitle="OneLargeButton">
<Section Alignment="Top" Type="OneRow">
<Row>
<ControlRef DisplayMode="Large" TemplateAlias="CutomHelloTemp
late" />
</Row>
</Section>
</Layout>
```

```
</GroupTemplate>

</CommandUIDefinition>

</CommandUIDefinitions>

<CommandUIHandlers>

<CommandUIHandler

      Command="MyProject.Scripts.HelloCommand"

      CommandAction="javascript:alert('New button
      clicked!');" />

</CommandUIHandlers>

</CommandUIExtension>

</CustomAction>

</Elements>
```

Above, we define our **CommandUIExtension** to be referenced the following location attribute **Ribbon.Tabs._children**, meaning that we place a new tab right in the root of the ribbon structure. The rest of the structure, such as groups and buttons is similar to what we have used in the previous example.

3. Now that we have our structure defined, we need to activate the ribbon on the context where we need it. Remember, just because you defined the structure of the ribbon, that doesn't mean the ribbon knows when to activate itself. The activation is done using a .NET code and, therefore, can be defined in the user control that later is referenced in your Master Page or in any other .NET components such as a Web Part. By definition, your ribbon activation code in a Web Part will be responsible for ensuring your Web Part is placed on a page you need and runs; otherwise, users won't see your custom tab activated.

4. Locate the **WebParts** folder in your Visual Studio solution structure and add a new **Visual Web Part**.

5. In your project references, add a new referenced DLL located here:

    [Drive]:\Program Files\Common Files\Microsoft Shared\Web Server Extensions\14\ISAPI Microsoft.Web.CommandUI.dll

6. Switch to code behind file of your **ASCX** control.

7. Add the following namespace reference in to your code:

■ *using Microsoft.SharePoint.WebControls;*

8. Replace the **Page_Load** method in your code with the following:

LISTING 7-8

```
protected void Page_Load(object sender, EventArgs e)

{

SPRibbon.GetCurrent(this.Page)

        .MakeTabAvailable("MyProject.Ribbon.HelloTab");

}
```

In here, we activate the tab by the **ID** we have defined in the **Elements.xml** file.

9. Deploy the solution and navigate to the root of your SharePoint test site.

10. You will not see a ribbon tab on the page; you will need to edit the page and add a new custom Web Part you have just created. As soon as the Web Part is added to the page, the custom ribbon tab will appear. You can save the page and click on the tab to test the button functionality.

Determining the State of Ribbon Tabs and Hiding Ribbon

Assuming your SharePoint test site is of a **Team Site** template, you see the ribbon all the time. Since Team Site is a collaboration site template, just like most site templates in SharePoint, it will include the ribbon by default. Publishing site template doesn't show the ribbon by default. After all, you don't want your public site users be able to see a ribbon; this will remind them of Microsoft Word too much. You can turn the ribbon on and off when you're working with publishing site template.

In this sample, we will take a look at how you can turn off ribbon on any site you're working with, as well as check the status of individual tabs on the ribbon and turn them off too.

Similar to the previous example, where we created new site level ribbon tabs, the state of tabs and the entire ribbon is a contextual property depending on where you are on the site. This means that you will have to run .NET code to determine the state of the ribbon at that particular state and see whether you still need to perform ribbon action.

As a suggestion, I recommend not turning off ribbon for the entire site by default, even when you think it's not necessary. If you need to turn off ribbon user interface, ensure that in your code you verify if the current user is an administrator. A lot of administrative functions are available through the ribbon, and if you remove it for everyone, your administrators will lose a lot of good functionality—for example, functionality to add new users to the site.

In fact, let's create a piece of functionality that verifies if the user is a site administrator and disables the ribbon if not.

Let's reuse the same Web Part you have created in the previous sample.

1. Locate the Web Part you have created in the last sample and switch to the code behind of the **ASCX** control of the **Visual Web Part**.

2. Add the following namespace reference to your **Visual Web Part** code:

■ *using Microsoft.SharePoint;*

3. Replace the **Page_Load** method content with the following code:

LISTING 7-9

```
protected void Page_Load(object sender, EventArgs e)

{

if (!SPContext.Current.Web.UserIsSiteAdmin)

{

SPRibbon.GetCurrent(this.Page).CommandUIVisible = false;

}

}
```

This code will verify whether the current user is an administrator and turn off the ribbon if the user isn't.

4. Deploy the solution and navigate to the root of your SharePoint test site. If you reused the Web Part from the last sample, it will be already added to the page, but the ribbon still shows up. Chances are that you run as an administrator, and to test the scenario when you're not an administrator, you will need to log in with a user that has lower privileges. Alternatively, you can remove the administrator privileges checking in the **Page_Load** method of the code behind in your Web Part.

Where is SharePoint Out-of-the-box Ribbon Defined?

From the moment we started experimenting with ribbon and adding buttons to tabs, you probably began wondering how nice it would be to be able to have a sample for each individual ribbon control that SharePoint uses for its own out-of-the-box ribbon control rendering. After all, by having access to out-of-the-box functionality and definitions, you would be able to build your own definitions much easier. Also, you would be able to define ribbon buttons and other controls not just within lists and libraries, but also in other types of containers that we didn't cover here.

Well, here is where you can find SharePoint ribbon definitions: *[Drive]:\Program Files\Common Files\Microsoft Shared\Web Server Extensions\14\TEMPLATE\GLOBAL\XML\ CMDUI.XML*

The file is quite large but if you open it in Visual Studio and collapse all outlining **(CTRL+M+L)**, you will see how groups, tabs, and controls are structured. You will also see the default templates for controls, which you can use in your code. Also, check out this video below as a bonus guide to starting your ribbon development.

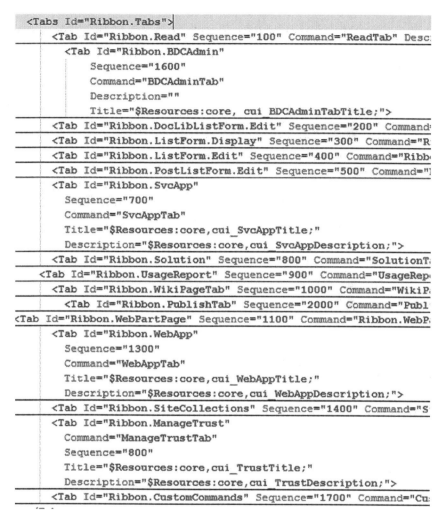

```
<Tabs Id="Ribbon.Tabs">
    <Tab Id="Ribbon.Read" Sequence="100" Command="ReadTab" Desc:
        <Tab Id="Ribbon.BDCAdmin"
            Sequence="1600"
            Command="BDCAdminTab"
            Description=""
            Title="$Resources:core, cui BDCAdminTabTitle;">
    <Tab Id="Ribbon.DocLibListForm.Edit" Sequence="200" Command
    <Tab Id="Ribbon.ListForm.Display" Sequence="300" Command="R
    <Tab Id="Ribbon.ListForm.Edit" Sequence="400" Command="Ribb
    <Tab Id="Ribbon.PostListForm.Edit" Sequence="500" Command="
    <Tab Id="Ribbon.SvcApp"
        Sequence="700"
        Command="SvcAppTab"
        Title="$Resources:core,cui_SvcAppTitle;"
        Description="$Resources:core,cui_SvcAppDescription;">
    <Tab Id="Ribbon.Solution" Sequence="800" Command="SolutionT:
    <Tab Id="Ribbon.UsageReport" Sequence="900" Command="UsageRep
    <Tab Id="Ribbon.WikiPageTab" Sequence="1000" Command="WikiP
        <Tab Id="Ribbon.PublishTab" Sequence="2000" Command="Publ
<Tab Id="Ribbon.WebPartPage" Sequence="1100" Command="Ribbon.WebP
    <Tab Id="Ribbon.WebApp"
        Sequence="1300"
        Command="WebAppTab"
        Title="$Resources:core,cui_WebAppTitle;"
        Description="$Resources:core,cui_WebAppDescription;">
    <Tab Id="Ribbon.SiteCollections" Sequence="1400" Command="S
    <Tab Id="Ribbon.ManageTrust"
        Command="ManageTrustTab"
        Sequence="800"
        Title="$Resources:core,cui_TrustTitle;"
        Description="$Resources:core,cui_TrustDescription;">
    <Tab Id="Ribbon.CustomCommands" Sequence="1700" Command="Cu:
```

Figure 7-4 Collapsed version of ribbon definitions

LEARN MORE:

Video screencast: Tips & Tricks: Creating Complex SharePoint 2010 Ribbon Elements

http://vimeo.com/10685740

Opening Modal Windows upon Ribbon Control Clicked

One of the most standard SharePoint out-of-the-box actions that happen when you click a ribbon button, for example, is opening a modal dialog. There are two components you will need to get your custom page opening upon ribbon button click: a ribbon definition and a page.

Let's go ahead and create sample that will open a custom page in a modal when the ribbon is clicked.

1. In your Visual Studio structure, create a new **Empty Element** typed item within the **Ribbon** folder.

2. Open the **Element.xml** file of the newly created element definition and replace the content of the file with the following code:

LISTING 7-10

```
<Elements xmlns="http://schemas.microsoft.com/sharepoint/">

<CustomAction

        Id="Ribbon.MyTab"

        Title="Adds a new Ribbon tab to Generic List"

        RegistrationType="List"

        RegistrationId="100" Location="CommandUI.Ribbon.
        ListView">

<CommandUIExtension>

<CommandUIDefinitions>

<CommandUIDefinition

        Location="Ribbon.Tabs._children">

<Tab Id="Ribbon.MyTab" Sequence="110" Title="My Tab Name">

<Scaling Id="Ribbon.MyTab.Scaling">

<MaxSize

        Id="Ribbon.MyTab.Scaling.MyGroup.MaxSize"

        Sequence="15" GroupId="Ribbon.MyTab.MyGroup"

        Size="LargeMedium"/>

</Scaling>

<Groups Id="Ribbon.MyTab.Groups">

<Group
```

```
        Id="Ribbon.MyTab.MyGroup"

        Sequence="15" Title="My Group Name"

        Template="Ribbon.Templates.MyTab.MyGroup.
        CustomTemplate">
<Controls Id="Ribbon.MyTab.MyGroup.Controls">
<Button

        Id="Ribbon.MyTab.MyGroup.Button"

        Alt="Ribbon.MyTab.MyGroup.Button"

        Command="Ribbon.MyTab.MyGroup.Button_CMD"

        Image16by16="/_layouts/images/siteIcon.png"

        Image32by32="/_layouts/images/siteIcon.png"

        LabelText="Button"

        Sequence="10" TemplateAlias="o1"

        ToolTipTitle="Button"

        ToolTipDescription="Shows a dialog" />
</Controls>
</Group>
</Groups>
</Tab>
</CommandUIDefinition>
<CommandUIDefinition

        Location="Ribbon.Templates._children">
<GroupTemplate Id="Ribbon.Templates.MyTab.MyGroup.
CustomTemplate">
<Layout Title="LargeMedium">
<OverflowSection Type="OneRow"

        TemplateAlias="o1" DisplayMode="Large"/>
<OverflowSection Type="ThreeRow"

        TemplateAlias="o2" DisplayMode="Medium"/>
</Layout>
```

```
</GroupTemplate>

</CommandUIDefinition>

</CommandUIDefinitions>

<CommandUIHandlers>

<CommandUIHandler

        Command="Ribbon.MyTab.MyGroup.Button_CMD"

        CommandAction="javascript:RibbonButtonHandler();" />

</CommandUIHandlers>

</CommandUIExtension>

</CustomAction>

<CustomAction Id="Ribbon.Library.Actions.Scripts"

        Location ="ScriptLink"

        ScriptSrc="/_layouts/Chapter7/RibbonActions.js" />

</Elements>
```

Here, our ribbon will be defined on the list view of a custom list with the list definition of type: **100**. Our ribbon tab and its button will call a script command, **RibbonButtonHandler** which is defined in an external file: **RibbonActions.js**. This file will be located in the **Layouts** mapped folder we're about to create next.

3. Locate the **Layouts** mapped folder in your solution and create a new folder within it called **Chapter7** just to keep things separate. If you name it some other name, remember to update the reference in the ribbon definition in Step 2.

4. Add a new item to the **Chapter7** folder of type **JScript File** from the Web category in Visual Studio dialog to add new item. Give your file the following name: **RibbonActions.js**

5. Open the newly created file and replace its content with the following code:

LISTING 7-11

```
function RibbonButtonHandler()

{
```

```
var options = {

url: "/_layouts/Chapter7/MyCustomPage.aspx",

width: 500,

height: 600

};


SP.UI.ModalDialog.showModalDialog(options);
}
```

Here we open a new modal dialog using the out-of-the-box command: *SP.UI.ModalDialog.showModalDialog*

6. Within the *Layouts/Chapter7* folder, add a new item of type: **Application Page**, and give it a name: **MyCustomPage.aspx.**

7. Open your newly created application page and locate the following code within its content:

LISTING 7-12

```
<asp:Content ID="Main" ContentPlaceHolderID="PlaceHolderMain"
runat="server">

</asp:Content>
```

8. Replace the content found in last step with the following:

LISTING 7-13

```
<asp:Content ID="Main" ContentPlaceHolderID="PlaceHolderMain"
runat="server">

This is the content of my custom page

</asp:Content>
```

9. Deploy your solution from Visual Studio and navigate to the root of your SharePoint test site. As you remember, our custom ribbon button is bound to a list view of a custom list. This means you need to create a custom list of your site and navigate to its view.

10. Locate and click our custom **My Tab Name** tab and click on the button there; you will see a dialog with the content of the page we created.

Although in this example we created our custom application page so that we could add new functionality to its code, you can reference any SharePoint page in your **RibbonActions.js** event if it's a complex page with Web Parts on it. Give it a try!

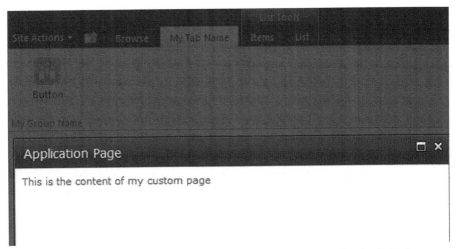

Figure 7-5 Modal window opened when custom ribbon button is clicked

Over the last few samples, you've been going through quite a lot that has to do with ribbon. You learned how to create simple and a bit more complex ribbon elements and how to find out the structure of out-of-the-box ribbon items to create your own. It's definitely a new approach to referencing your custom applications. Now you don't have to worry where to place buttons that call your custom functions; chances are, they're going to be in ribbon.

CHAPTER 8

Search: Extending Search Components and Incorporating Search Features in Your Portal

Search in SharePoint deserves separate attention since it's a separate, independent, and complete set of components. From an architectural point of view, search has components that have been standardized as a service application just like BCS and other service applications we talked about earlier. Customizations to search component may vary from light changes to how your users will see the search results to changes on how search ranks and performs its queries.

There are two types of search output features available in SharePoint.

When you create a team site, you automatically get a search box on the top of your site and this one lets you search for a term on a site and redirects you to a results page once you're done. This results page has some out-of-the-box capabilities such as RSS feed, alerts, and so on. If you try to edit this page, you won't be able to; it's a simplest result page that comes with SharePoint.

If you like to choose what will be displayed on your search page, just as you do on any other SharePoint pages, you're going to have to create a separate subsite for a search center.

Just like any other site, you have to create an instance of your new search center. In this chapter, I assume you will use the basic version of the search center unless stated otherwise.

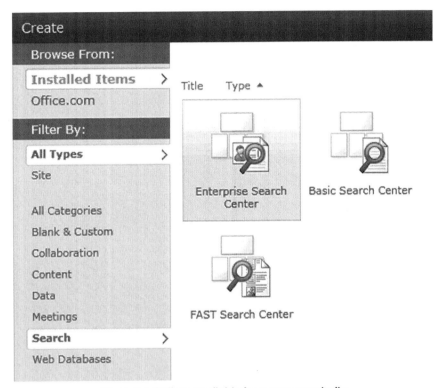

Figure 8-1 Options available for a new search site

Add Your Own Search Refinement Categories

If you haven't already, create an instance of your search site to use in this chapter.

1. Navigate to the root of your SharePoint site.

2. Click **Site Actions -> New Site**. From the Search category, select **Basic Search Center**.

3. After you give your site a name and it is successfully created, navigate to the root of your SharePoint test site again.

4. Click **Site Actions -> Site Settings**.

5. Under **Site Collection Administration**, click **Search Settings**.

6. For the **Site Collection Search Center** option, select **Enable** custom scopes and type the URL of your newly created search center site—in my case: http://localhost/search

7. Your **Site Collection Search Results Page** will be /search/results. aspx.

8. Click **OK**.

The above sequence not only created a site, but also linked the root of your SharePoint test site to a new search center. Now all of the search queries from the main site will be redirected to the search center rather than the default search page that's not editable.

One of the new features available in this release of SharePoint out-of-the-box is search refinements. **Refinements** Web Part is available on the left hand side of the search results page. If you're familiar with previous version of SharePoint, you will also know about Facetted Search Web Part, which was an add-on from CodePlex. In this version we have an out-of-the-box solution that has the same behavior and is also much more extensible than a free version from CodePlex.

Let's take a look at the **Refinements** Web Part configuration:

1. While on the search results page, click **Site Actions -> Edit Page**.

2. The page will switch into the edit mode. Locate the **Refinements** Web Part and choose to view Web Part properties by clicking **Edit Web Part**.

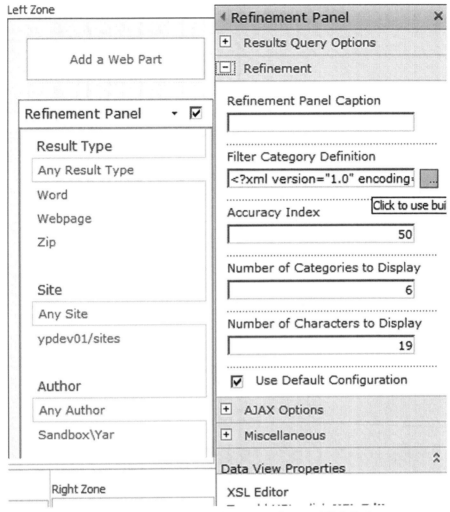

Figure 8-2 Web Part properties of the refinement Web Part

3. From the refinement panel, expand the refinement category and click on the ellipsis of the **Filter Category Definition** property.

4. You will be taken to the edit mode of the property. For a better view, copy the entire view of the XML in the dialog box to clipboard.

5. Switch to the Visual Studio solution we're using for testing and add a new item under any of the existing folders (say WebParts).

The item will be of type: **XML** under **Data** category of the **Add New Item** dialog.

6. Replace the contents of the newly created XML with the contents from clipboard.

7. Collapse all outlining of the pasted markup (**CTRL+M+L**) and expand the first node. Your markup will look similar to below:

LISTING 8-1

```xml
<?xml version="1.0" encoding="utf-8"?>
<FilterCategories>
<Category
        Title="Result Type"
        Description="The file extension of the item"
        Type="Microsoft.Office.Server.Search
            .WebControls.ManagedPropertyFilterGenerator"
        MetadataThreshold="5"
        NumberOfFiltersToDisplay="4"
        MaxNumberOfFilters="0"
        SortBy="Frequency"
        SortDirection="Descending"
        SortByForMoreFilters="Name"
        SortDirectionForMoreFilters="Ascending"
        ShowMoreLink="True"
        MappedProperty="FileExtension"
        MoreLinkText="show more"
        LessLinkText="show fewer"> ... </Category>
<Category
        Title="Site"
        Description="Which site this document is from"
        Type="Microsoft.Office.Server.Search
            .WebControls.ManagedPropertyFilterGenerator"
```

```
MetadataThreshold="5"

NumberOfFiltersToDisplay="4"

MaxNumberOfFilters="20"

SortBy="Frequency"

SortByForMoreFilters="Name"

SortDirection="Descending"

SortDirectionForMoreFilters="Ascending"

ShowMoreLink="True"

MappedProperty="SiteName"

MoreLinkText="show more"

LessLinkText="show fewer" />

...
```

```
</FilterCategories>
```

Examine the markup. Notice how each refinement category is defined with **<Category>** node. All of the attributes set in the node can be found by searching **FilterCategory Members** on MSDN. A few of the main ones are:

- **Title** – determines the name of the refinement as displayed to the user.

- **Type** – denotes the namespace that will provide refinements; for the most part, we will be using *Microsoft.Office.Server.Search. WebControls.ManagedPropertyFilterGenerator* to render values of managed properties that live in SharePoint.

- **MappedProperty** – defines the name of the managed property in SharePoint Search service application that will be displayed here as a refinement category; we will discuss how to create those and use existing managed properties.

Other properties are just accessories and can definitely be useful, depending on your scenario. That's why I recommend taking a look at them in MSDN by searching **FilterCategory Members**.

As the topic of this sample suggests, we're here to learn how you can add new and existing managed properties to search refinement categories. In essence, every item in SharePoint has columns, which are considered parts of item metadata. Each of the fields in metadata is picked up by search during the search crawl being executed. If we create a new field in a list and create an item that uses that field and stores data in our new field, our field automatically becomes a crawled property the next time our search crawl performs the crawl.

The crawled property will remain idle and unused unless you map it to a managed property. The reason why we have managed property is so that we can aggregate a few crawled properties that have been collected by the crawler and call them one name that can be used in search criteria. Let's create a new managed property.

1. Navigate to the root of your test SharePoint site.

2. Create a new **Custom List** on that site and give it any name.

3. Switch to the list settings of a newly created list and create a new column called **MyNewColumn**. Leave the type as **Single line of text** and click **OK**.

4. Create a new item in the list and give it any values for two of the columns that are there. Now that your new column contains data, it's a candidate for a new crawled property creation.

Let's initiate a new crawl in Central Administration to speed up the process.

1. Navigate to the Central Administration of your test SharePoint site.

2. Click on **Managed Service Applications** and click **Search Service Application** on the following screen.

3. On the left hand side navigation bar, under the **Crawling** category, click **Content Sources**.

4. On the default content source that usually is called **Local SharePoint sites**, from the context menu, click **Start Full Crawl** and ensure the crawl finishes and the status is set to **Idle**.

Now that we have crawled new content, let's create a new managed property that contains our new crawled property representing the field.

1. From the same page we left off in the last sequence, on the
   left hand side menu, under **Queries and Results** click **Metadata
   Properties**.

2. You will see a list of all of the managed properties that are
   available to be search. Click on the **New Managed Property** to
   create your own.

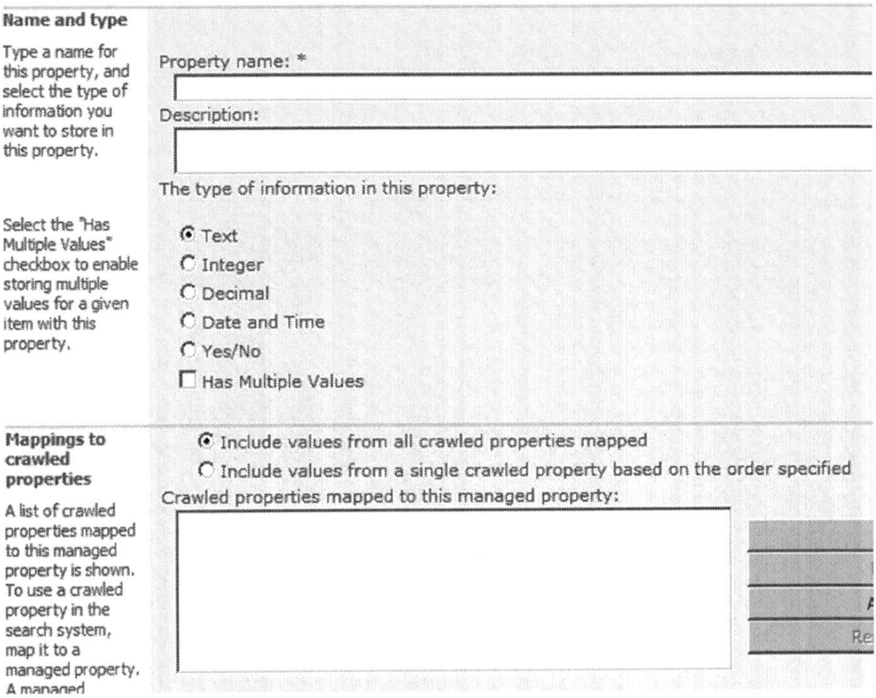

Name and type

Type a name for this property, and select the type of information you want to store in this property.

Property name: *

Description:

The type of information in this property:

Select the "Has Multiple Values" checkbox to enable storing multiple values for a given item with this property.

◉ Text
○ Integer
○ Decimal
○ Date and Time
○ Yes/No
☐ Has Multiple Values

Mappings to crawled properties

A list of crawled properties mapped to this managed property is shown. To use a crawled property in the search system, map it to a managed property. A managed

◉ Include values from all crawled properties mapped
○ Include values from a single crawled property based on the order specified

Crawled properties mapped to this managed property:

Figure 8-3 New Search Property detail

3. For property name, specify **MyManagedProperty**.

4. In the section called **Mappings to crawled properties** click the
   Add Mapping button, which will bring up a list of all of the new
   crawled properties.

5. In the **Crawled property selection** modal window, type in the
   name of your new column: **MyNewColumn** into the **Crawled
   property name** field and click **Find**.

6. Verify that you have received at least one result of
    MyNewColumn. Usually SharePoint crawler names crawled
    property with the name of the column with a prefix or suffix
    if there is more than one column with the same name. For
    example, *ows_ MyNewColumn(Text)*. **Text** defines the type of
    the field.

7. Select the name of the column and click **OK** to add it to the list.

8. Ensure the list of **MyNewColumnMappings to crawled properties**
    contains your new item and click **OK.**

9. Initiate a new crawl just as we did before for the search to
    update its records.

Now that you have created your new managed property
and performed a crawl, you can search content by your new
property or set refinements. To search by your new property, type
in the following in the search text box on your search center site:
MyManagedProperty:"New". This will search for all of the items on the
site that contain **New** in **MyManagedProperty** managed property.

Here is how to make your new property available in a refinement Web
Part.

1. Switch to the Visual Studio solution you opened and in which you
    created a new XML file at the beginning of this sample.

2. In your XML code, right after **<FilterCategories>** node, add a new
    category node that look like this:

LISTING 8-2

```
<Category

        Title="My Managed Property"

        Description="Allows refinement by My Managed Property"

        Type="Microsoft.Office.Server.Search

            .WebControls.ManagedPropertyFilterGenerator"

        MetadataThreshold="5"

        NumberOfFiltersToDisplay="4"

        MaxNumberOfFilters="20"
```

```
ShowMoreLink="True"

MappedProperty="MyManagedProperty"

MoreLinkText="show more"

LessLinkText="show fewer"/>
```

The node definition is pretty self-explanatory; essentially, we're only defining new managed property for our refinement category. Copy the entire content to the clipboard.

3. Access the **Refinement Panel** Web Part properties just as we did earlier in this sample and open the **Filter Category Definition** property under **Refinement** category.

4. Paste the contents of your clipboard to the definition property edit window and click **OK**.

5. Right below the property where you have pasted the custom XML, you will find the **Use Default Configuration** check box. Uncheck it to make sure your new changes are picked up.

6. Save the properties of the Web Part and exit the edit mode of the page.

To test the new refinement category, search for **new** or any other value that we have in our custom list item created in the custom list. The search will return possibly a few items or just one, depending on how much test data you have in your site. Whatever the number of results is, you will see the custom refinement item on the left hand side

Adding New Metadata to Your Search Results View

The central focus of any search page is a result section. After, all that's the whole reason your users will navigate to the search page. Depending on your scenario, some of your users may find more value if your search results look a certain way or contain more or less of a default subset of information. In this example, we'll take a look how you can remove some metadata from the search results and add new metadata property we created in the last sample.

Take a look at the default search result returned by SharePoint.

test	🔍	Preferences
		Advanced

1-10 of 17 results

📄 PerformancePoint® Capacity Planning
was used for each scenario. Detailed information such as **test** results and specific parameters ا
given in each of the **test** results sections later in this article. ...
Authors: Sandbox\Yar   Date: 4/1/2010   Size: 389KB
http://ypdev01/sites/DocID/Shared Documents/PerformancePointCapacityPlanningDoc.docx

📄 Estimate Performance and Capacity Requirements for Workflow in SharePoint
2010
was used for each scenario. Detailed information such as **test** results and specific parameters ا
given in each of the **test** results sections later in this article. ...
Authors: Sandbox\Yar   Date: 4/1/2010   Size: 1MB
http://ypdev01/sites/DocID/Shared Documents/WorkflowCapacityPlanningDoc.docx

📄 Estimate performance and capacity requirements for InfoPath Forms Services
This section defines the **test** scenarios and provides an overview of the **test** process that was ا
for each scenario. **Test** results are given in later
Authors: Sandbox\Yar   Date: 4/1/2010   Size: 21 [Estimate performance and capacity requirements for
http://ypdev01/sites/DocID/Shared Documents/In [InfoPath Forms Services 2010]

📄 Capacity Planning and Sizing for Microsoft SharePoint Server 2010 Based Divi
Portal
This document outlines the **test** methodology and results to provide guidance for capacity ... ad
to the server farm during multiple iterations of the **test** complies to the same specs. ...
Authors: Sandbox\Yar   Date: 2/1/2010   Size: 223KB
http://ypdev01/sites/DocID/Shared Documents/Divisional PortalCapacityPlanningDoc.docx

Figure 8-4 Default search result

As you can see, there are few key properties that are present and
some of them are more unusual than they may appear at first. We
have a link to our item, a date, a text with what seems like item
content, and the URL of the item. On the other hand, take a look at
the following item:

information such as test	🔍	Preferences
		Advanced

1-10 of 12 results

📄 Capacity Management and Sizing for Microsoft SharePoint Server
This document is provided **"as-is"**. **Information** and views expressed in this do
validate and tune your environment to achieve your performance and capacity ا
Authors: Sandbox\Yar   Date: 4/1/2010   Size: 1MB
http://ypdev01/sites/DocID/Shared Documents/SPServer2010CapacitySizingO

Figure 8-5 Search result of an item with a large body text

As you will see in a moment, SharePoint search uses a special calculated field to define what is going to show in an area where the item body is displayed. The property is called **HitHighlightedSummary** and it will change depending on your search keyword. The **HitHighlightedSummary** will display the area surrounding your search keyword in the body of an item. SharePoint already knows that the item has to be displayed because it contains the text or metadata you searched. Now, SharePoint will try to prove it to you that this search result is worth looking at because it contains a body that may be something that will help you identifying it. If you searched for a text that is contained in the metadata of the item, that metadata will show up. If your keyword is showing more in the body of the document, then this part of the body will be displayed in the **HitHighlightedSummary**. This is an important piece of functionality to understand, since you may want to customize your search results to hide certain pieces of metadata that will still show up in search results as a part of **HitHighlightedSummary** field.

Let's take a look at the default markup of the search results Web Part.

1. While on the search results page, click **Site Actions -> Edit Page**.

2. The page will switch into the edit mode. Locate the **Search Core Reults** Web Part and choose to view Web Part properties by clicking **Edit Web Part**.

3. From the Web Part editing panel, expand the **Core Results** category and then expand the **Default Properties** category.

4. Locate and uncheck the **Use Location Visualization** option and you will see **Fetched Properties** and **XSL editor** options become available.

5. Copy the contents of **Fetched Properties** to your clipboard.

6. Switch to the Visual Studio solution we're using for testing and add a new item under any of the existing folders (say WebParts). The item will be of type **XML**, under **Data** category of the **Add New Item** dialog.

7. Replace the contents of the newly created XML with the contents from the clipboard.

Your XML markup will look similar to below.

LISTING 8-3

```
<Columns>
        <Column Name="WorkId"/>
        <Column Name="Rank"/>
        <Column Name="Title"/>
        <Column Name="Author"/>
        <Column Name="Size"/>
        <Column Name="Path"/>
        <Column Name="Description"/>
        <Column Name="Write"/>
        <Column Name="SiteName"/>
        <Column Name="CollapsingStatus"/>
        <Column Name="HitHighlightedSummary"/>
        <Column Name="HitHighlightedProperties"/>
        <Column Name="ContentClass"/>
        <Column Name="IsDocument"/>
        <Column Name="PictureThumbnailURL"/>
        <Column Name="PopularSocialTags"/>
        <Column Name="PictureWidth"/>
        <Column Name="PictureHeight"/>
        <Column Name="DatePictureTaken"/>
        <Column Name="ServerRedirectedURL"/>
</Columns>
```

Those are all of the properties that SharePoint requests from each
search result. If search results don't have any of the property items,
nothing really happens; the field just gets ignored and it's not
rendered on a page.

Let's take a look at how the look and feel of the search results is built.

1. Assuming your search results page is still in edit mode and **Search Core Results** Web Part properties are opened, click on the **XSL Editor** button located in **Display Properties** category we looked at before.

2. Copy the contents of the editor dialog to the clipboard.

3. Switch to your Visual Studio and paste the contents of your clipboard to a new XML file similar to where we pasted search properties.

4. Collapse all markup outlining (**CTRL+M+L**) and expand the first node.

You will notice that most of the nodes are templates that define the rendering of various components displayed on the search page. The main part of the XSL style sheet is located at the very bottom of the style sheet and calls rendering of sub elements. Here is how this part looks:

LISTING 8-4

```
<!-- XSL transformation starts here -->
<xsl:template match="/">
<xsl:if test="$AlertMeLink">
        <input type="hidden" name="P_Query" />
        <input type="hidden" name="P_LastNotificationTime" />
</xsl:if>
<xsl:choose>
<xsl:when test="$IsNoKeyword = 'True'" >
        <xsl:call-template name="dvt_1.noKeyword" />
</xsl:when>
<xsl:when test="$ShowMessage = 'True'">
        <xsl:call-template name="dvt_1.empty" />
</xsl:when>
<xsl:otherwise>
        <xsl:call-template name="dvt_1.body"/>
```

```
</xsl:otherwise>

</xsl:choose>

</xsl:template>
```

In here, we verify that there is a search keyword entered in the body and start rendering content using the **dvt_1.body** template defined above in the XSL.

If you navigate the XSL structure, you will eventually find the template of your interest.

Let's remove the **HitHighlightedSummary** from the search result and place the value of our custom property we created earlier in the sample instead.

1. Assuming you're still in Visual Studio and you have the XSL of the search style sheet open, search for the following string *<div class="srch-Description2">*.

2. You will find the section similar to below.

LISTING 8-5

```
<div class="srch-Description2">

<xsl:choose>

<xsl:when test="hithighlightedsummary[. != '']">

        <xsl:call-template name="HitHighlighting">

        <xsl:with-param name="hh"
        select="hithighlightedsummary" />

</xsl:call-template>

</xsl:when>

<xsl:when test="description[. != '']">

        <xsl:value-of select="description"/>

</xsl:when>

<xsl:otherwise>

        <img alt="" src="/_layouts/images/blank.gif" height="0"
        width="0"/>

</xsl:otherwise>
```

```
</xsl:choose>

</div >
```

This section is responsible for showing the summary abstract of your search result, if applicable.

3.   Let's now add additional metadata to the file markup.

LISTING 8-6

```
<div class="srch-Description2">

<xsl:choose>

<xsl:when test="hithighlightedsummary[. != '']">

        <xsl:call-template name="HitHighlighting">

        <xsl:with-param name="hh"
        select="hithighlightedsummary" />

</xsl:call-template>

</xsl:when>

<xsl:when test="description[. != '']">

        <xsl:value-of select="description"/>

</xsl:when>

<xsl:otherwise>

        <img alt="" src="/_layouts/images/blank.gif" height="0"
        width="0"/>

</xsl:otherwise>

</xsl:choose>

<xsl:if test="string-length(MyManagedProperty) &gt; 0">

        The value of the MyManagedProperty is:

        <xsl:value-of select="MyManagedProperty"/>

</xsl:if>

</div >
```

Above, we added a comparison to see whether our new property has a value, and if so, we will output its value.

4. Copy a modified version of your XSL to the clipboard and replace the contents of **Search Core Results** XSL with it.

5. In your **Search Core Results Fetched Properties**, ensure you have added a new property to your XML right before the closing tag of columns definition **</Columns>**, the value of the column is *<Column Name="MyManagedProperty"/>*.

6. Save Web Part properties and stop page editing mode.

Launch another search and you will see all of your other search results returning item descriptions as usual. Your custom description will show up for the items you have created for your test list. If you can't find those items, ensure you searched for a keyword that you might have used in one of the item properties.

Adding Graphic Representation of Item Rating to Your Search Results

In the last sample, we looked at how to add a simple column to the search results. This time we'll add more functionality to our search results—a graphic rating. A few chapters ago, we looked at how rating can be enabled on the document library and content that's rated will show a nice graphical representation of the rating. In this sample we'll take a look at how we can display similar rating functionality on the search result. After all, it'd be nice if your users could see the rating of the item. At the end, our users won't be able to vote on the item, but they will see the rating stars.

First, we need to ensure rating is enabled on one of your document libraries and that there has been at least one rating posted to the library and average rating calculated. The reason for that is because we're going to create a new managed property that will pick up our rating column, and if there is no value in the rating column, the search will not create a new crawled property for it.

If you're sure that you have at least one item with column in the document library, perform a full crawl from Central Administration to make sure this value has been picked up. Below are the next steps:

1. Assuming you're still in Central Administration, click **Metadata Properties** on the left hand side of your search service application window.

2. Click **New Managed Property**.

3. For the name of the property, chose **Rating** of type **Decimal**, then click **Add Mapping**.

4. In the new modal box, search for **rating** and pick column named **ows_AverageRating(Decimal)**.

5. Click **OK** to add new managed property.

6. Navigate to the search results page and access the **Search Core Results** Web Part properties, as you did in the last sample.

7. Open the **Display Properties** category, and for **Fetched Properties**, add **Rating** as follows: <Column Name="Rating"/>.

8. Choose to edit your XSL and, using Visual Studio, locate the same section you've been working with before by searching <div class="srch-Description2">.

9. Replace the section with the code below.

LISTING 8-7

```
<div class="srch-Description2">

<xsl:choose>

<xsl:when test="hithighlightedsummary[. != '']">

        <xsl:call-template name="HitHighlighting">

        <xsl:with-param name="hh"
        select="hithighlightedsummary" />

</xsl:call-template>

</xsl:when>

<xsl:when test="description[. != '']">

        <xsl:value-of select="description"/>

</xsl:when>

<xsl:otherwise>
```

```xml
        <img alt="" src="/_layouts/images/blank.gif" height="0"
        width="0"/>
</xsl:otherwise>

</xsl:choose>

<xsl:choose>

<xsl:when test="rating > 0">

        <span>

        <xsl:attribute name="title">

        <xsl:value-of select="rating"/>

        </xsl:attribute>

        <xsl:call-template name="stars">

        <xsl:with-param name="starCount" select="rating"/>

        </xsl:call-template>

        <xsl:if test="round(rating) > rating">

        <img src="/_Layouts/Images/Ratings/RatingsNew.png"/>

        </xsl:if>

        </span>

        <br/>

</xsl:when>

<xsl:otherwise>

        <b>Not Rated</b>

        <br/>

</xsl:otherwise>

</xsl:choose>

</div >
```

Just as we did last time, this time we add logic to verify whether there is a rating for an item and if so, we call a template to render the output.

10. Now, add the template that we call from the previous steps, search for *<!-- XSL transformation starts here -->* and add code below right before this item.

LISTING 8-8

```
<xsl:template name="stars">
<xsl:param name="starCount"/>
<xsl:param name="value" select="1"/>
<xsl:if test="$value &lt;= $starCount">
        <img src="/_Layouts/Images/Ratings/RatingsNew.png"/>
        <xsl:call-template name="stars">
        <xsl:with-param name="starCount" select="$starCount"/>
        <xsl:with-param name="value" select="$value + 1"/>
        </xsl:call-template>
</xsl:if>
</xsl:template>
```

Above, we define a template that will receive an average rating and display appropriate value for graphical representation of that rating using *rating stars*.

11. Copy the contents of the file from Visual Studio and paste it into the **Edit XSL** of your **Search Core Results** Web Part.

12. Click **OK** to save the properties of the Web Part and exit the edit mode.

When you execute a search again, you will see that whatever items are not rated have received a *Not Rated* label, and the ones that are rated will have rating stars beside the summary of the search result.

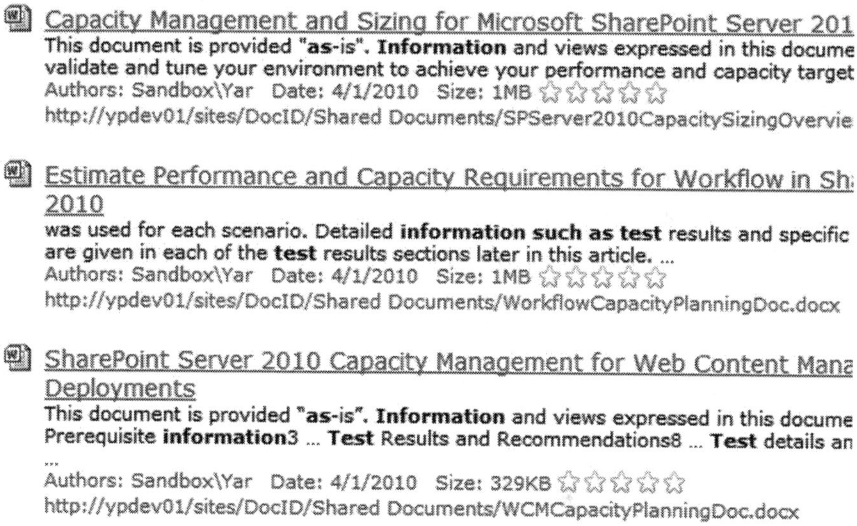

📄 Capacity Management and Sizing for Microsoft SharePoint Server 201
This document is provided "as-is". **Information** and views expressed in this docume
validate and tune your environment to achieve your performance and capacity target
Authors: Sandbox\Yar   Date: 4/1/2010   Size: 1MB ☆☆☆☆☆
http://ypdev01/sites/DocID/Shared Documents/SPServer2010CapacitySizingOvervie

📄 Estimate Performance and Capacity Requirements for Workflow in Sh:
2010
was used for each scenario. Detailed **information such as test** results and specific
are given in each of the **test** results sections later in this article. ...
Authors: Sandbox\Yar   Date: 4/1/2010   Size: 1MB ☆☆☆☆☆
http://ypdev01/sites/DocID/Shared Documents/WorkflowCapacityPlanningDoc.docx

📄 SharePoint Server 2010 Capacity Management for Web Content Mana
Deployments
This document is provided "as-is". **Information** and views expressed in this docume
Prerequisite **information**3 ... **Test** Results and Recommendations8 ... **Test** details an
...
Authors: Sandbox\Yar   Date: 4/1/2010   Size: 329KB ☆☆☆☆☆
http://ypdev01/sites/DocID/Shared Documents/WCMCapacityPlanningDoc.docx

Figure 8-6 Rating showing for the search results

Similar to this customization, you can leverage the XSL template to make many changes to the style and look and feel.

CHAPTER 9

Working with SharePoint 2010 Publishing and Custom Pages

Most of the SharePoint solutions are built around managing content and structure. Sites and their subsites, along with pages, make up a hierarchy that business users navigate through to access their data stored in lists, libraries, and other containers. One of the main features that are leveraged when building SharePoint solutions is pages. Pages are stored in page libraries just like documents are stored in in document libraries. Just like list items, pages can have a generic or specific content type, and you can treat them as list items. Pages can contain metadata properties that represent various values on a page, including a page's content. The look of the page is driven by what's known as the layout page. A layout page defines what Web Part zones your page will have. In some cases, you may want additional metadata to be captured from a user to represent a page. This additional metadata will have to be captured with appropriate controls (dropdown lists, text boxes) right on a page in page editing mode. The controls and their look and type will also be defined in page layout. In more complex solutions, chance are you will have at least a few layout pages that will represent a specific or generic look for many of your page instances.

Here is a scenario of how this all fits together.

Let's assume you want to have a unique section on your site dedicated to company news. You also want to be able to display the most recent news on a home page of your site. One way to approach this is to create a site that will host your news as a publishing site. Each page on the site will inherit from a custom content type for a news item. Your content type will define any additional metadata your page may include, such as the department this particular piece of news belongs to. Having a content type defined, we will define a page layout that drives rendering of your news page. Next, we define a generic page that will use a content type and a page layout to drive its structure and presentation. Once an instance of a news page is created, along with its custom content type, you can perform list query operations (discussed in a previous chapter) to filter out the items you care about and display them on a home page. In this chapter, we'll take a look at how you go about provisioning your pages and building your site structure with pages.

Getting Started with Creating Custom SharePoint Pages

Let's assume you have a section on your site just like in the example from above that will host company news. We want your users to be able to create news pages in a pages library. We also want to make sure your users will have an area to enter the piece of news they would like to post and choose a department from which the news is coming.

We will be using the same Visual Studio structure we've used all along to create our test solutions. Let's start with creating our custom page layout tied to a custom content type for our pages:

1.   First, ensure the debugging site you are using in your Visual Studio solution is a **Publishing Site** template. When you interact with Visual Studio item type wizard, it will pick up options only available on your debugging site. This means that if your debugging site is a **Team Site** template, you will not get an option to create a new content type inherited from a **Page** content type.

2. In your Visual Studio solution structure, locate a **ContentTypes** folder and add a new item to the folder of type: **Content Type**. Give it a name: **MyCustomPage**, and set it to inherit from **Page**. Click **Finish**.

3. The **Elements.xml** file of the newly created content type will open and you will get a chance to edit its title and other details. Take a note of the **ID** attribute of the content type, as you'll need it in later steps.

4. Now, locate the **PageLayouts** folder in your solution and add a new item of type **Module**. Give it a name: **LandingPage** and click **Finish**.

5. You will notice two files provisioned, one of which is a sample file. Delete the sample file.

6. Our newly created module will provision a page layout to the page layouts gallery, which is a special library that holds all the page layouts. The best starting point to creating a new page layout based of the existing page layout is to make a copy of existing page layout and modify it. Let's copy an existing page layout. In the publishing site you use for test click, **Site Actions -> Site Settings**.

7. Under the **Galleries** category, click **Master pages and page layouts**.

8. From the list of available files, select and download to disk **BlankWebPartPage.aspx**. If you want to learn more about different types of page layouts available out-of-the-box, create a new page on your publishing site by using the **Site Actions -> New Page** menu option. Once the page is created under the **Page** ribbon tab, click **Page Layout** to explore various layouts and how you could use one over another as a starting point.

9. Switch back to your Visual Studio and locate your **Landing Page** module that we created earlier. Add an existing item to your module, which is the **BlankWebPartPage.aspx** you saved to disk.

10. Rename the file to **LandingPage.aspx** just for consistency.

11. Open the **Elements.xml** file in your **LandingPage** module and replace its content with the following:

LISTING 9-1

```xml
<?xml version="1.0" encoding="utf-8"?>
<Elements xmlns="http://schemas.microsoft.com/sharepoint/">
<!-- page layouts -->
<Module Name="PageLayouts"
        Url="_catalogs/masterpage"
        Path="PageLayouts"
        RootWebOnly="TRUE">


<File Url="LandingPage.aspx"
        Type="GhostableInLibrary"
        Path=" LandingPage\LandingPage.aspx">
<Property Name="Title" Value="LandingPage Page Layout" />
<Property Name="MasterPageDescription" Value="LandingPage
Page Layout" />
<Property Name="ContentType" Value="MyCustomPage" />
<Property Name="PublishingAssociatedContentType"
Value=";# MyCustomPage;#0x010100C568DB52D9D0A14D9B2FDCC96666E
9F2007948130EC3DB064584E219954237AF3900bc25837a141242eabc35dc
6a382e3fd6;#" />
</File>
</Module>
</Elements>
```

Above, we provisioned the **ASPX** file representing your page layout to the gallery. The page layout is identical to one of the out-of-the-box layouts, but we will change that later. Another important property value in XML above is the **PublishingAssociatedContentType** representing the name and the **ID** attributes of the content type we created in Step 3 here. Make sure you copy those from your content type definition, called **MyCustomPage**.

The first part is done. Now we have a page layout that, although it looks the same, will have its separate identity since it inherits our custom page content type. Next let's create a page instance that will use our custom page layout:

1. In your Visual Studio solution structure, locate the **Pages** folder and add a new item of type: **Module** called, **HomePage**.

2. Though similar to the module we used in the page layout above, this module will provision pages to the **Pages** folder on the site.

3. Rename the **Sample.txt** file to **Default.aspx** and open the file to replace its content with the following:

LISTING 9-2

```
<%@ Page Inherits="Microsoft.SharePoint.Publishing.
TemplateRedirectionPage

    ,Microsoft.SharePoint.Publishing,Version=14.0.0.0

    ,Culture=neutral,PublicKeyToken=71e9bce111e9429c" %>

<%@ Reference VirtualPath="~TemplatePageUrl" %>

<%@ Reference VirtualPath="~masterurl/custom.master" %>
```

The above code will mark the page as a publishing page. In fact, all of the publishing pages that you create will have exactly the same some content.

4. What appears on the page will be defined in the accompanying module XML file. Let's rename it to **Landing.xml** so we know that this XML definition will provision the landing page. Open the **Landing.xml** and replace its content with the following code:

LISTING 9-3

```
<?xml version="1.0" encoding="utf-8"?>

<Elements xmlns="http://schemas.microsoft.com/sharepoint/">

<Module Name="HomePage" Url="Pages" Path="">

<File Url="Default.aspx"

        Type="GhostableInLibrary"

        Path="HomePage\default.aspx">
```

```
<Property Name="Title" Value="Home Page" />
<Property Name="PublishingPageLayout"
    Value="~SiteCollection/_catalogs/masterpage/
    LandingPage.aspx
    ,MyCustomPage;" />
<Property Name="ContentType" Value="MyCustomPage" />
</File>
</Module>
</Elements>
```

In the above, we defined a module and a file within that module that will be copied over to the **Pages** folder of the site this module will be delivered to. Among other properties, two important ones are:

■ **PublishingPageLayout** – defining the page layout used for this page.

■ **ContentType** – the content type of the page if you use custom one, which we do.

At this point, we did all SharePoint requires to provision a page to the site, but there are few things that happened behind the scenes. If you noticed, all of our modules have relative paths as to where they deploy their contents. There is a very good reason behind this, you can deploy one module a few times in several different places on your site.

Think about the page module we created. It's a generic page that doesn't have any content on it. Yet, we need pages like that, or maybe less generic ones, to create landing pages for our portal. The mechanism by which SharePoint delivers content to the site is using Features. You are already familiar with features from previous discussions. The same approach applies when provisioning pages. If you open the **Features** folder in your Visual Studio site structure, you will see that there have been a few features automatically created with generic names. SharePoint created those features so that they can be activated upon your solution deployed and all of the modules that belong to a feature will get provisioned to their respective places. If you selected the **debug** site to be your local site, all features will be activated on that site and, hence, all the pages with their relative parameters will be deployed to the pages library on your main site. In the next sample, we take a look at how pages tie together with the rest of the site structure to build sites with subsites in them and applicable pages on each site.

Defining Site Templates and Driving Site Content

Usually, provisioning new pages programmatically happens in two situations:

- Your site is deployed using scripted deployment for the first time and it needs all of the relevant pages in the right sites and subsites.

- Your users create new sites as a part of their workflow and those sites provision all the necessary artifacts, including pages, in them.

Apart from the scenarios above, you would either create individual pages in their libraries or your users would create pages using a user interface from the **Site Actions** menu.

The steps to achieve the above two scenarios of automated page deployment start from a single task of defining a site template.

Just as you would define a template for your list in order for users to create instances of it, you will also need to define a site template from which users and automated systems will create new sites and site collection instances. SharePoint comes with variety of available templates, which, in essence, initially all looked the same way; it's the features that get activated on each template that make it unique. Naturally, if one of the out-of-the-box templates resembles 80 percent of your functionality, it makes sense to start with that template and add the missing pieces one by one.

Let's see how we can define a new custom publishing site template with default features first and then attach our custom pages to it later:

1. In your Visual Studio, locate the **Templates** mapped folder and add sub folders to it with the following names and hierarchy:

- 1033
- XML

- SiteTemplates
- MyNewSite
- XML

2. Add a new file to the **1033 -> XML** folder of type **XML** file, and name it **Webtemp.MyNewSite.xml**. This file will make sure SharePoint is aware of the new site template we're going to define next.

3. Open the **Webtemp.MyNewSite.xml** file and replace its content with the following:

LISTING 9-4

```
<?xml version="1.0" encoding="utf-8" ?>

<Templates xmlns:ows="Microsoft SharePoint">

<Template Name="MyNewSite" ID="110111">

<Configuration ID="0"

        Title="MyNewSite"

        Hidden="FALSE"

        ImageUrl="/_layouts/1033/images/template_srch_cntr_
        lite.png"

        Description="A site for delivering the MyNewSite
        experience."

        DisplayCategory="MyCategory" >

</Configuration>

</Template>

</Templates>
```

Above, we defined the name and a few other attributes that will be shown to users if we make the template visible. The important attribute is the **ID**, and it has to be unique within the system and not be the same as other templates located in the template folder located here: *[Drive]:\Program Files\Common Files\Microsoft Shared\Web Server Extensions\14\TEMPLATE\SiteTemplates.*

4. Next, we're going to make a copy of the out-of-the-box publishing site template by including the existing file into our

SiteTemplates->MyNewSite->XML folder. The location of the source file we'll be including is: *[Drive]:\Program Files\Common Files\Microsoft Shared\Web Server Extensions\14\TEMPLATE\ SiteTemplates\PUBLISHING\XML\onet.xml*.

5. Visual Studio will copy the file to your local solution folder. Open the onet.xml to make changes to it.

Take a look at the file structure. Collapse all outlining (**CTRL+M+L**) to make it more readable.

If you expand the Project node, you will see several nodes defining various components of the site. Let's make few changes to match the template with our new site definition:

1. Expand the **<Modules>** node of the structure and remove the **<Module>** definition, but leave the parent node as is.

2. Expand the **<Configurations>** node. You will see two site configurations, expand the one with **ID ="0"**. Change the name attribute of the configuration and make it the same as we defined it in **Webtemp.MyNewSite.xml**. which is **MyNewSite**.

3. Expand the **<Modules>** node of the configuration for which you just changed the name and remove the child module.

   Above, we're taking an out-of-the-box publishing site template and removing any out-of-the-box modules it was using. We also matched some of the attributes we defined in **Webtemp. MyNewSite.xml** to match our site template definition in **onet.xml**.

4. Expand the **<WebFeatures>** node of the site. This section will activate many out-of-the-box features of a publishing site in order to facilitate functionality that comes with publishing sites. Using those features, SharePoint will set navigation and some of the site properties. In fact, we are going to add our own feature references to the list of existing features to drive our content provisioning. Ensure the list of the Web features contains:

LISTING 9-5

```
<WebFeatures>

<!-- Include the common WSSListTemplateFeatures used by CMS -->
```

```
<Feature ID="00BFEA71-DE22-43B2-A848-C05709900100" >
</Feature>

<Feature ID="00BFEA71-E717-4E80-AA17-D0C71B360101" >
</Feature>

<Feature ID="00BFEA71-52D4-45B3-B544-B1C71B620109" >
</Feature>

<Feature ID="00BFEA71-A83E-497E-9BA0-7A5C597D0107" >
</Feature>

<Feature ID="00BFEA71-4EA5-48D4-A4AD-305CF7030140" >
</Feature>

<Feature ID="00BFEA71-F600-43F6-A895-40C0DE7B0117" >
</Feature>

<Feature ID="00BFEA71-4EA5-48D4-A4AD-7EA5C011ABE5">
</Feature>

<Feature ID="22A9EF51-737B-4ff2-9346-694633FE4416">

        <Properties xmlns="http://schemas.microsoft.com/
        sharepoint/">

        <Property Key="ChromeMasterUrl" Value=""/>

        <Property Key="WelcomePageUrl"

            Value="$Resources:osrvcore,List_Pages_UrlName;/
            default.aspx"/>

        <Property Key="PagesListUrl" Value=""/>

        <Property Key="AvailableWebTemplates" Value=""/>

        <Property Key="AvailablePageLayouts" Value=""/>

        <Property Key="SimplePublishing" Value="true" />

        </Properties>

</Feature>

<Feature ID="541F5F57-C847-4e16-B59A-B31E90E6F9EA">

        <Properties xmlns="http://schemas.microsoft.com/
        sharepoint/">

        <Property Key="InheritGlobalNavigation" Value="true"/>

        <Property Key="ShowSiblings" Value="true"/>

        <Property Key="IncludeSubSites" Value="true"/>
```

```
    </Properties>

</Feature>

<Feature ID="94C94CA6-B32F-4da9-A9E3-1F3D343D7ECB">

<!-- Office SharePoint Server Publishing -->

</Feature>

</WebFeatures>
```

You will notice that some features accept no properties and others do accept values. If the feature has feature receivers performing certain actions and getting input from passed properties, those properties would be defined here. If the sole purpose of the feature was to provision modules or definitions, those would not have any properties to drive their behavior.

The only remaining piece left to provision our pages with a site definition is to determine which features are used to provisioned our modules and reference them within our site template definition. If you followed the steps above when creating page layouts and pages, you will probably have a feature called **Feature1** created for you by SharePoint. If you open the feature you will see that its scope is set to a Web and it contains your page layout module and page module. There is nothing wrong in having both of the modules provisioned by one feature. However, when building typical SharePoint solutions, you will end up with many modules with various scope and activated under different levels of hierarchy. In this scenario, it makes sense to create different features to provision different parts of your solution. Here is how we're going to restructure what Visual Studio created for us:

1. Rename your **Feature1** created by Visual Studio to **ProvisionPageLayouts**.

2. Open the feature and change its name.

3. Ensure the only item in the feature is the **MyCustomPage** module that contains page layout definition.

4. Add a new feature and rename its default name to **ProvisionPages**.

5. Ensure the only item in the feature is the **HomePage** module that contains page definition.

6. Finally, add a new feature and rename its default name to **ProvisionContentTypes**.

7. Verify that the only item this feature contains is the **MyCustomPage** module that takes care of our custom content type we created to handle our pages.

You will notice that every time you open a feature, you get an option at the bottom of the page to toggle between **Design** and **Manifest**. If you switch to the manifest mode, one of the attributes for the **<Feature>** node will be an **ID** of the feature. In order for your custom site template to activate the feature, you will need to reference the **ID** of all three features you created for your pages, layouts, and content types in your site template, just like out-of-the-box features referenced; see below:

LISTING 9-6

```
<WebFeatures>

<!-- Include the common WSSListTemplateFeatures used by CMS -->

<Feature ID="00BFEA71-DE22-43B2-A848-C05709900100" > </Feature>

<Feature ID="00BFEA71-E717-4E80-AA17-D0C71B360101" > </Feature>

<Feature ID="00BFEA71-52D4-45B3-B544-B1C71B620109" > </Feature>

<Feature ID="00BFEA71-A83E-497E-9BA0-7A5C597D0107" > </Feature>

<Feature ID="00BFEA71-4EA5-48D4-A4AD-305CF7030140" > </Feature>

<Feature ID="00BFEA71-F600-43F6-A895-40C0DE7B0117" > </Feature>

<Feature ID="00BFEA71-4EA5-48D4-A4AD-7EA5C011ABE5"> </Feature>

<Feature ID="22A9EF51-737B-4ff2-9346-694633FE4416">

        <Properties xmlns="http://schemas.microsoft.com/
        sharepoint/">

        <Property Key="ChromeMasterUrl" Value=""/>

        <Property Key="WelcomePageUrl"

            Value="$Resources:osrvcore,List_Pages_UrlName;/
            default.aspx"/>
```

```xml
<Property Key="PagesListUrl" Value=""/>

<Property Key="AvailableWebTemplates" Value=""/>

<Property Key="AvailablePageLayouts" Value=""/>

<Property Key="SimplePublishing" Value="true" />

</Properties>

</Feature>

<Feature ID="541F5F57-C847-4e16-B59A-B31E90E6F9EA">

<Properties xmlns="http://schemas.microsoft.com/
sharepoint/">

<Property Key="InheritGlobalNavigation" Value="true"/>

<Property Key="ShowSiblings" Value="true"/>

<Property Key="IncludeSubSites" Value="true"/>

</Properties>

</Feature>

<Feature ID="94C94CA6-B32F-4da9-A9E3-1F3D343D7ECB">

<!-- Office SharePoint Server Publishing -->

</Feature>


<!--MyProject.ProvisionPageLayouts-->

<Feature ID="9dd54fa8-5d71-4c9d-bf42-0015d66163ee" > </
Feature>

<!--MyProject.ProvisionContentTypes-->

<Feature ID="86de898b-f875-496a-9cbe-a59b64b6d182" > </
Feature>

<!--MyProject.ProvisionPages-->

<Feature ID="12bacc31-58a2-488e-97a4-b237a2978ee9" > </
Feature>

</WebFeatures>


<SiteFeatures>

<!-- Workflow Expiration -->
```

```xml
<Feature ID="C85E5759-F323-4EFB-B548-443D2216EFB5" />
<!-- DLC Workflows -->
<Feature ID="0AF5989A-3AEA-4519-8AB0-85D91ABE39FF" />
<!-- "A44D2AA3-AFFC-4d58-8DB4-F4A3AF053188" -->
<Feature ID="A44D2AA3-AFFC-4d58-8DB4-F4A3AF053188" />
<Feature ID="A392DA98-270B-4e85-9769-04C0FDE267AA">
<!-- PublishingPrerequisites -->
</Feature>
<Feature ID="7C637B23-06C4-472d-9A9A-7C175762C5C4">
<!-- ViewFormPagesLockDown -->
</Feature>
<Feature ID="AEBC918D-B20F-4a11-A1DB-9ED84D79C87E">
<!-- PublishingResources -->
    <Properties xmlns="http://schemas.microsoft.com/
    sharepoint/">
    <Property Key="AllowRss" Value="false"/>
    <Property Key="SimplePublishing" Value="true" />
    </Properties>
</Feature>
<Feature ID="F6924D36-2FA8-4f0b-B16D-06B7250180FA">
<!-- Office SharePoint Server Publishing -->
</Feature>
<!-- SearchCenter Url feature -->
<Feature ID="7AC8CC56-D28E-41f5-AD04-D95109EB987A" >
    <Properties xmlns="http://schemas.microsoft.com/
    sharepoint/">
    <Property Key="SearchCenterUrl" Value="~SiteCollection/
    Search/" />
    </Properties>
</Feature>
</SiteFeatures>
```

The final step is to provision the site of a custom site template we have created here. Now, all along we have used the Visual Studio mechanism to deploy our solutions; however, with site hierarchy and provisioning this is not the case. We can deploy the solution, and this will make the site template available to create new sites. However, if we want to provision a site automatically using a site template of our choice, we will need to use the script we looked at the very first chapter.

Here is how our deployment will go:

1. Assuming you have set up your Visual Studio to create WSP files on build, execute solution build from Visual Studio.

2. Open the folder you have your Visual Studio solution in and ensure the WSP file that is there is of the latest version (check the time stamp on the file).

3. Assuming your automatic provisioning files: **SetupStructure.bat**, **SetupStructure.ps1**, and **SiteStructure.xml** are in the same folder as WSP open **SiteStructure.xml** in editor and replace its contents with the following:

LISTING 9-7

```xml
<Setup WebAppUrl="http://localhost">
<Solutions>
<Solution WebApplication="False">MyProject.Platform.wsp</Solution>
</Solutions>
<SiteCollection Name="My Project"
        Url="/sites/myproject"
        OwnerAlias="administrator"
        Template="MyNewSite#0">
<Features>
<Feature></Feature>
</Features>
</SiteCollection>
</Setup>
```

In the above, all the attributes are pretty self explanatory; here are some items worth noting:

■ The solution value (in my case **MyProject.Platform.wsp**) will have to match the name of your WSP file and your WSP file will be driven by the **Name** attribute of your **Package** component within your Visual Studio structure.

■ The site collection URL attribute – can be either a root site collection or a subsite collection. If you'd like to deploy to the root, use '/' as your URL value. The **OwnerAlias** is the install account or an account that has privileges to create a new site collection.

■ The template attribute for the site collection is the name that you called your new site template folder within **Template -> SiteTemplates** folder. The '**#**' tag followed by the number determines the configuration you like to use for the site template. In our case, we have just one active configuration, but in some solutions, you may have several if your template has variations and different features activated for different configuration types.

Once you've made all of the changes, save the configuration XML file and run the **SetupStructure.bat** as an administrator. If the deployment is complete, you will see a message in your command window and the site will be opened in your browser window. If you encountered errors, you will get a message describing what might be the cause.

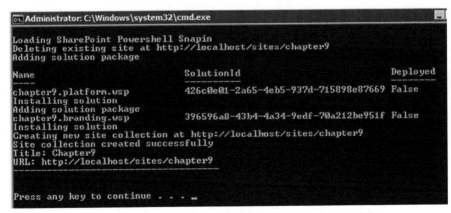

Figure 9-1 Automated PowerShell site deployment complete

The whole point in using an automated script is to be able to create several sites under each site collection, all in one deployment.

Here is how your configuration XML might look like if you choose to create three more subsites under the site collection:

LISTING 9-8

```xml
<Setup WebAppUrl="http://localhost">
<Solutions>
<Solution WebApplication="False">MyProject.Platform.wsp</Solution>
</Solutions>
<SiteCollection Name="My Project"
        Url="/sites/myproject"
        OwnerAlias="administrator"
        Template="MyNewSite#0">
<Features>
<Feature></Feature>
</Features>
        <Site Name="Sub site 1" Url="site1"
        Template="MyNewSite#0">
        <Feature></Feature>
        </Site>
        <Site Name="Sub site 2" Url="site2"
        Template="MyNewSite#0">
        <Feature></Feature>
        </Site>
        <Site Name="Sub site 3" Url="site3" Template="STS#0">
        <Feature></Feature>
        </Site>
</SiteCollection>
</Setup>
```

Each of the sites has a name and a site template assigned to it. Since we inherit access permissions from the site collection, we don't have to specify the owner name. Notice the last site has **STS#0** as the name of the template. This means that rather than using our site template, this site will be using an out-of-the-box team site template. After you run the new script, you will see three more subsites under the main site collection.

Provisioning Page Content to Your Pages Programmatically

From the last example, you've seen how you can provision pages to your sites and create a hierarchy of sites on the site collection. However, all of the sites and pages on them have no content on them, except the site that inherited from the **Team Site** template.

Let's take a look at some of the techniques we can use to add new content to pages. We'll start with adding simple text content by using the content editor Web Part:

1. Navigate to the root of your SharePoint test site and switch to the edit mode of the main page.

2. Locate any of the Web Part zones and click **Add a Web Part**.

3. Click on the **Media and Content** category and select **Content Editor** from the available options.

4. Once the Web Part has been added, type any text into the Web Part editing zone.

5. Click on the **Content Editor** Web Part Maintenance arrow located in the top left hand side of the Web Part chrome and click **Export**.

6. Save the file you're offered to disk. The file is an XML definition of the Web Part along with its state and content you've just typed in.

7. Open the file and copy its entire contents to the clipboard.

8. Switch to Visual Studio and locate the **HomePage** module you created earlier under the **Pages** folder.

9. Open the configuration XML file **Landing.xml**, and locate the section of the file that looks like this:

LISTING 9-9

```
</File>

</Module>

</Elements>
```

The section before the **</File>** is used to define Web Parts and any other components that will go on the pages appropriate sections.

10. Insert the code below right before the **</File>** closing tag from the previous step:

LISTING 9-10

```
<AllUsersWebPart WebPartZoneID="CenterLeftColumn"
WebPartOrder="0">

<![CDATA[

<?xml version="1.0" encoding="utf-8"?>

<WebPart xmlns:xsi="http://www.w3.org/2001/XMLSchema-
instance" xmlns:xsd="http://www.w3.org/2001/XMLSchema"
xmlns="http://schemas.microsoft.com/WebPart/v2">

<Title>Content Editor</Title>

<FrameType>Default</FrameType>

<Description>Allows authors to enter rich text content.</
Description>

<IsIncluded>true</IsIncluded>

<ZoneID>TopZone</ZoneID>

<PartOrder>0</PartOrder>

<FrameState>Normal</FrameState>

<Height />

<Width />

<AllowRemove>true</AllowRemove>

<AllowZoneChange>true</AllowZoneChange>

<AllowMinimize>true</AllowMinimize>

<AllowConnect>true</AllowConnect>

<AllowEdit>true</AllowEdit>
```

```
<AllowHide>true</AllowHide>

<IsVisible>true</IsVisible>

<DetailLink />

<HelpLink />

<HelpMode>Modeless</HelpMode>

<Dir>Default</Dir>

<PartImageSmall />

<MissingAssembly>Cannot import this Web Part.</
MissingAssembly>

<PartImageLarge>/_layouts/images/mscontl.gif</PartImageLarge>

<IsIncludedFilter />

<Assembly>Microsoft.SharePoint, Version=14.0.0.0,
Culture=neutral

        ,PublicKeyToken=71e9bce111e9429c</Assembly>

<TypeName>Microsoft.SharePoint.WebPartPages.
ContentEditorWebPart</TypeName>

<ContentLink xmlns="http://schemas.microsoft.com/WebPart/v2/
ContentEditor" />

<Content xmlns="http://schemas.microsoft.com/WebPart/v2/
ContentEditor">

<![CDATA[Sample Content]]>

</Content>

<PartStorage xmlns="http://schemas.microsoft.com/WebPart/v2/
ContentEditor" />

</WebPart>

]]>

</AllUsersWebPart>
```

It seems like a lot of text, but all we have is an XML copied from the exported Web Part on the site surrounded by the following markup:

LISTING 9-11

```
<AllUsersWebPart WebPartZoneID="CenterLeftColumn"
WebPartOrder="0">
```

```
<![CDATA[

]]>

</AllUsersWebPart>
```

You will notice that Visual Studio has highlighted your XML and claims that it's broken—and it's right. Because the exported XML from the site had **<![CDATA[ ]]>** identifiers for the content of the Web Part, it's conflicting with our Web Part definition **CDATA** section. In this case, it's safe to remove the Web Part property **<![CDATA[]]>** since we already have defined a free form text in our XML earlier.

The markup defines that the containing XML will be a Web Part placed into the **CenterLeftColumn** Web Part Zone. If we had more than one Web Part in that zone, the **WebPartOrder** attribute would set the order of them rendered on the page.

11. Let's build the solution and deploy it with the script we used in the last sample.

After the script has deployed the site, you will see that sites that use our custom template will have a Web Part with our sample content provisioned to each landing page.

One of the things you probably noticed is us knowing the exact name of the Web Part zone where our Web Part will go. To find out the available Web Part zones, you would refer to the **PageLayouts** folder and the module we have defined for the page layout. If you open the **ASPX** file defining the actual page layout, you will see the Web Part zone definitions coming up among the other markup:

LISTING 9-12

```
<WebPartPages:WebPartZone

runat="server"

Title="<%$Resources:cms,WebPartZoneTitle_Center%>"

ID="CenterColumn"  />
```

The above definition tells us the **ID** of the Web Part zone. Since we copied the existing page layout from the out-of-the-box SharePoint layout definition, we know what Web Part zones our definition has. If we add more Web Part zones, those will be named differently and those are the zones we could use to place Web Parts into.

Provisioning Other Web Parts and Views onto the Page

In our last sample, we looked at how you can provision simple Web Parts to the Web Part zone in your page. In fact, you can provision multiple Web Parts in the page the same way.

Let's try to provision a custom Web Part to the page:

1. In Visual Studio, locate the **WebParts** folder and add a new item of type: **Visual Web Part.**

2. Give any name to your Web Part and add it to the solution. Leave all the settings to be default.

3. In a newly create Web Part open **ASCX** control and add a piece of text that will help us identifying the Web Part: **Sample User Control Web Part.**

4. Deploy the solution using a command from Visual Studio. This will only deploy the Web Part to the gallery of available Web Parts and to recreate the site.

5. Navigate to your SharePoint test site and, just as you did with the **Content Editor** Web Part, try to export your custom Web Part.

NOTE:

If you can not locate our custom web part in the list – ensure the Site URL of your Visual Studio project properties is the same URL you're looking to find your web part under.

6. You will notice that the export option is not available.

7. Open the Web Part property pane by clicking **Edit Web Part.**

8. Expand the **Advanced** section from the Web Part editing pane and select **Export All Data** in the **Export Mode** section.

9. Click **OK** to save the setting and try the export option again; you should be able to export your Web Part XML now.

10. Now that you have the XML ready, you can insert it in your Visual Studio module, just as you did with the **Content Editor** Web Part.

11. Before you deploy the solution with our custom script, you need to ensure that feature created by Visual Studio to provision your Web Part is being called from **onet.xml** file. Open the feature Visual Studio created for you and copy the **ID** attribute from the **Manifest** section of feature property page.

12. Switch to the onet.xml file in your custom site template and locate the **SiteFeatures** section.

13. Reference the feature with an **ID** you copied in your **onet.xml** feature list just like all the other site features that exists there are referenced.

14. Since we have site scoped features in our resulting WSP file – SharePoint solution deployment will require you to scope the **Platform** solution to the web application. This means that in your **SiteStructure.xml** file you need to locate the following line and switch the **WebApplication** attribute to **True**:

    <Solution WebApplication="False">Chapter9.Platform.wsp </Solution>

15. Build the solution and deploy it with our custom deploy script. Once the script is finished and the site opens – you will see both web parts added to the page.

One other scenario that you will definitely see is when you need to provision list and library views. When you navigate to your portal and try inserting another Web Part using the ribbon command, one of the first category options you'll see is **Lists and Libraries**. This category will contain the list of all the available instances of lists and libraries you have on your site. Let's for example, add **Documents** as one of the out-of-the-box document libraries that's provisioned with every publishing site. When you add this library to a page and try to export its XML, you will also not see any option to export the component. The reason in this case is not because the export is restricted from the Web Part property pane. The difference here is that we're dealing with list or library view and not the Web Part. List views are provisioned differently to the page and have fewer options available when provisioning them.

Here is how we define the **Documents** library on the page using the XML of the landing page we're working with:

LISTING 9-13

```
<View

        List="Documents"

        BaseViewID="0"

        WebPartZoneID="Header"

        WebPartOrder="1" />
```

In the above, we started with a special node to define a view. One of the attributes we didn't have before is **BaseViewID** defining the view we are going to display for this instance of the page. To determine the view of the list or library, you would reference the **ID** from their respective **schema.xml** file as described in an earlier chapter. For example, the views available for generic document library can be found in this file: *[Drive]:\Program Files\Common Files\ Microsoft Shared\Web Server Extensions\14\TEMPLATE\FEATURES\ DocumentLibrary\DocLib\schema.xml*.

For this library template we have eight views available. The default view **ID** is usually **0** – which unless you need anything else but default, makes the best bet when creating instances of it on the page. All of the other attributes are the same as we've seen in Web Parts.

You can provision as many of the views and Web Parts in one page definition as you need by stacking each definition in any order. The actual rendering of the components will be determined with the **WebPartOrder** attribute.

Below is the example of my custom Web Part provisioned along with the view:

LISTING 9-14

```
<View List="Documents" BaseViewID="0"

        WebPartZoneID="Header" WebPartOrder="1" />

<AllUsersWebPart WebPartZoneID="CenterRightColumn"
WebPartOrder="1">

        <![CDATA[
```

```
    ...
    ]]>
</AllUsersWebPart>
```

Provisioning Several Pages with One Module

A few samples ago, we created a landing page in one of our modules—and you might be thinking about the scenario when we have more than one page on the site. Do we need to create modules for each of them? If all of the pages will end up being deployed to the same page library, it's safe to define their XML in the same module.

Assuming we already have our module that deploys our landing page, here is how we go about adding few other page definitions:

1. In your Visual Studio, locate the module that deploys your landing page on the site.

2. Right click on the **Landing.xml** file and select **Copy**.

3. Right click on the module name and select **Paste**. Your **Landing. xml** page will be copied to the same module.

4. Rename the page with another name; in our case let's call it **Contact.xml**.

5. By default, Visual Studio assumes that the file you just pasted is just a content file and, therefore, when compiling, it will ignore the entire markup and not provision your page, even if you define correct parameters in it. Since Visual Studio assumes you have just added the file and not the XML definition – it's trying to provision a file as content using one of the default modules it created. Select the newly added file and in the file properties window locate the **Deployment Type** property and ensure its value is set to **Element Manifest**.

6. While you have your **HomePage** module structure expanded in the Solution Explorer on the very top of the panel click **Show All Files** button.

7. You will see Visual Studio hidden file show up called **SharePointProjectItem.spdata**. This file keeps track of all the items

and their role in the solution. This is where Visual Studio has taken a note that our newly added **Contact.xml** is now an element manifest file.

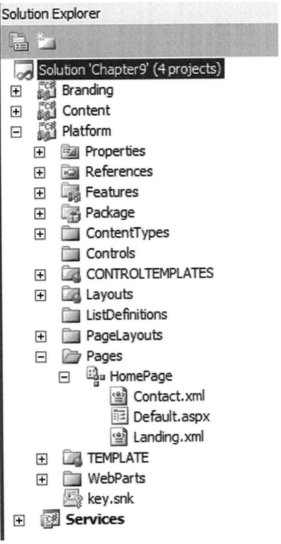

Figure 9-2 Visual Studio solution structure including the module provisioning multiple pages

8. Now open the **Contact.xml** and replace it's content with the following:

LISTING 9-15

```
<?xml version="1.0" encoding="utf-8"?>

<Elements xmlns="http://schemas.microsoft.com/sharepoint/">

<Module Name="HomePage" Url="Pages" Path="">

<File Url="Contact.aspx" Type="GhostableInLibrary"
      Path="HomePage\default.aspx">

<Property Name="Title" Value="Contact Page" />

<Property Name="PublishingPageLayout"
      Value="~SiteCollection/_catalogs/masterpage/
      LandingPage.aspx

      , MyCustomPage;" />

<Property Name="ContentType" Value="MyCustomPage" />

</File>

</Module>

</Elements>
```

Notice how at the beginning of the definition we defined the **URL** attribute of the file to be **Contact.aspx**; this defines the resulting page name. On the other hand, the **Path** attribute is still pointing to **Default.aspx**; this is source location of where the page is copied from:

> *<File Url="Contact.aspx" Type="GhostableInLibrary" Path="HomePage\default.aspx">*

9. Now that we're done with provisioning, we can build the solution and deploy it using our custom deployment script.

After the script is complete, you will notice that two pages are inside the page library and one of them without any Web Parts is **Contact. aspx**. You can provision web parts or other components just like you would to a home page.

Provisioning Web Parts Directly to Page Layouts

So far we looked at how to add your custom Web Parts directly to pages. Although this approach works most of the time, there are scenarios where you would want to have Web Parts provisioned to the page layout that your page instance will end up inheriting. For example, your users want to create pages for a particular type of content and besides just look and feel they want the page to initially have few Web Parts on it. You can provision Web Parts during the automated page provisioning using a feature, but when a user creates a page manually, no Web Parts will be provisioned on a page unless placed into a page layout definition. Let's see how that can be achieved:

1. In your Visual Studio solution structure we have used so far in samples in this chapter, locate the custom page layout module called **MyCustomPage**. Open the **Elements.xml** file.

2. Locate the following node in the XML file:

LISTING 9-16

```
<Property

Name="PublishingAssociatedContentType"
Value=";#MyCustomPage;#0x010100C568DB52D9D0A14D9B2FDCC96666E9
F2007948130EC3DB064584E219954237AF3900bc25837a141242eabc35dc6
a382e3fd6;#" />
```

3. Right after the property definition above, insert the XML of the Web Part you're planning to provision on the page layout. In our case, we provision the **Content Editor** Web Part and our page layout looks like this:

LISTING 9-17

```
<?xml version="1.0" encoding="utf-8"?>

<Elements xmlns="http://schemas.microsoft.com/sharepoint/">

<!-- page layouts -->

<Module Name="PageLayouts" Url="_catalogs/masterpage"

        Path="PageLayouts" RootWebOnly="TRUE">

<File Url="LandingPage.aspx" Type="GhostableInLibrary"

        Path=" LandingPage \ LandingPage.aspx">
```

```
<Property Name="Title" Value="LandingPage Page Layout" />

<Property Name="MasterPageDescription" Value=" LandingPage
Page Layout" />

<Property Name="ContentType" Value="MyCustomPage" />

<Property Name="PublishingAssociatedContentType" Value=";#MyCu
stomPage;#0x010100C568DB52D9D0A14D9B2FDCC96666E9F2007948130EC3
DB064584E219954237AF3900bc25837a141242eabc35dc6a382e3fd6;#" />

<AllUsersWebPart WebPartOrder="0" WebPartZoneID="CenterRightC
olumn" >

<![CDATA[

<?xml version="1.0" encoding="utf-8"?>

<WebPart xmlns:xsi=http://www.w3.org/2001/XMLSchema-instance

        xmlns:xsd=http://www.w3.org/2001/XMLSchema

        xmlns="http://schemas.microsoft.com/WebPart/v2">

<Title>Content Editor</Title>

<FrameType>Default</FrameType>

<Description>Allows authors to enter rich text content.</
Description>

<IsIncluded>true</IsIncluded>

<ZoneID>wpz</ZoneID>

<PartOrder>0</PartOrder>

<FrameState>Normal</FrameState>

<Height />

<Width />

<AllowRemove>true</AllowRemove>

<AllowZoneChange>true</AllowZoneChange>

<AllowMinimize>true</AllowMinimize>

<AllowConnect>true</AllowConnect>

<AllowEdit>true</AllowEdit>

<AllowHide>true</AllowHide>

<IsVisible>true</IsVisible>
```

```
<DetailLink />

<HelpLink />

<HelpMode>Modeless</HelpMode>

<Dir>Default</Dir>

<PartImageSmall />

<MissingAssembly>Cannot import this Web Part.</
MissingAssembly>

<PartImageLarge>/_layouts/images/mscontl.gif</PartImageLarge>

<IsIncludedFilter />

<Assembly>Microsoft.SharePoint, Version=14.0.0.0,
Culture=neutral,
        PublicKeyToken=71e9bce111e9429c</Assembly>

<TypeName>Microsoft.SharePoint.WebPartPages.
ContentEditorWebPart</TypeName>

<ContentLink xmlns="http://schemas.microsoft.com/WebPart/v2/
ContentEditor" />

<Content xmlns="http://schemas.microsoft.com/WebPart/v2/
ContentEditor">
        Sample content</Content>

<PartStorage xmlns="http://schemas.microsoft.com/WebPart/v2/
ContentEditor" />

</WebPart>

]]>

</AllUsersWebPart>

</File>

</Module>

</Elements>
```

4. Build the solution in Visual Studio and deploy it using our custom deployment script, which will open your SharePoint test site.

   As you can see, although we haven't provisioned anything to the right Web Part zone of the page, it still has content because it was provisioned through a page layout.

Rendering Additional Page Specific Metadata during Page Edit

As you remember from last few chapters, we were talking about lists and defining our custom metadata, which later on was rendered on a form so users could fill out all of the additional text boxes and other controls. If you think about your page as a list item, users also may want to define some metadata as they create a page. For example, if we're creating an instance of a News page and want to type out our News text and define the news release date, those additional controls would be very helpful when rendered right there when you're in the middle of typing up your news details.

Let's take a look at how we can define custom fields on the instance of a page when users create it:

1. Assuming we're using the same Visual Studio solution we have used all along, you already have defined a content type and set the page layout to be inherited from the content type.

2. Locate the content type definition within your Visual Studio structure: **MyCustomPage.**

3. Right click the folder of a custom content type to add a new item to it of type: **Empty Element**. This container will take care of provisioning our custom fields to SharePoint. In fact, we could define our custom fields right in the body of the content type definition. However, if you have complex structure, which sometimes you may, you should place your field definitions separately from the content type.

4. Give your empty elements definition a name **Fields**, and once finished, open the **Elements.xml** created.

5. Replace the contents of the file with the following:

LISTING 9-18

```xml
<?xml version="1.0" encoding="utf-8"?>

<Elements xmlns="http://schemas.microsoft.com/sharepoint/">

<Field ID="{B4EC7C97-EB21-4171-9B64-B56CDC7D9EBA}"
```

```
      Name="DepartmentManager" DisplayName="Department Manager"

      Type="User" List="UserInfo"

      SourceID="http://schemas.microsoft.com/sharepoint/v3"

      StaticName="DepartmentManager" Group="MyCustomFields">

</Field>

<Field ID="{B9CC7A6F-3753-4d47-A7CD-B6B88F82B683}"

      Name="NewsDate" DisplayName="News Date"

      Type="DateTime" Format="DateOnly"

      SourceID="http://schemas.microsoft.com/sharepoint/v3"

      Hidden="FALSE" ReadOnly="FALSE"

      Required="TRUE"

      xmlns="http://schemas.microsoft.com/sharepoint/"

      Group="MyCustomFields" >

<Default>[Today]</Default>

</Field>

</Elements>
```

Here we have **Department Manager** and **News Date** defined. Take a look at how both fields were defined and some of the attributes they use for your future reference.

6. Next, we'll reference defined fields in our content type. Open the **Elements.xml** file from your content type and locate the **<FieldRefs>** section in the file; replace the section with the following reference to our custom fields:

LISTING 9-19

```
<FieldRefs>

<FieldRef ID="{B4EC7C97-EB21-4171-9B64-B56CDC7D9EBA}"

      Name="DepartmentManager" />

<FieldRef ID="{B9CC7A6F-3753-4d47-A7CD-B6B88F82B683}"

      Name="NewsDate" />

</FieldRefs>
```

At this point, if we were to deploy our solution with the custom deployment script, the newly provisioned page would show two new fields we have added if you were to switch to the item property view from the **Pages** document library.

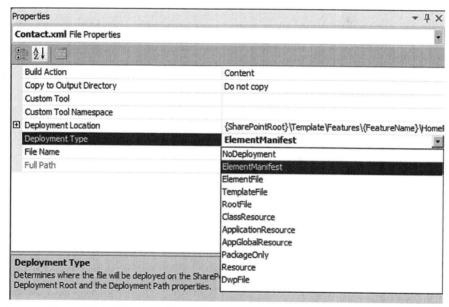

Figure 9-3 Additional fields available to set using an item property page

However, it takes few steps to get to the item in order to modify its properties in the **Pages** document library. Therefore, the next change will take care of offering users to enter the metadata right into the page while users interact with it in the edit mode.

7. Locate the **MyCustomPage** page layout module and open the **MyCustomPage.aspx** file that defines the markup of your page, including Web Part zones. Locate the following section in the file:

LISTING 9-20

```
<PublishingWebControls:EditModePanel runat="server"
CssClass="edit-mode-panel">

<SharePointWebControls:TextField runat="server"
FieldName="Title"/>

</PublishingWebControls:EditModePanel>
```

The above section defines any controls that will be rendered to the user once the page enters edit mode. You can see that we already have one control that is rendered and one reference item title. The item in this case is page, meaning that this control will let you enter the title of the page and save it to the appropriate field in the page library.

8.   Replace the content of the section from above with the following code:

LISTING 9-21

```
<PublishingWebControls:EditModePanel runat="server"

    CssClass="edit-mode-panel">

<legend>Page Metadata</legend>

<SharePointWebControls:UserField id="DepartmentManagerEdit"

    FieldName="DepartmentManager" runat="server" />

<SharePointWebControls:DateTimeField id="NewsDateEdit"

    FieldName="NewsDate" runat="server" />

<SharePointWebControls:TextField runat="server"
FieldName="Title"/>

</PublishingWebControls:EditModePanel>
```

Above, we have added two more controls that bind to the respective field names we have provisioned to the content type. At this point, the page will allow us entering the content to the respective fields, but those fields will not be rendered on the page once it's published because there is no control to render them. If you like the metadata pieces below to be rendered, you will need to place those fields into the markup of the page layout where you want them to appear. Also, because you don't want those fields to appear again when the page is in the edit mode, you can specify that controls will be rendered only in the display mode, as below:

LISTING 9-22

```
<SharePointWebControls:UserField id="DepartmentManagerEdit"

    FieldName="DepartmentManager" runat="server"
    ControlMode="Display" />

<SharePointWebControls:DateTimeField id="NewsDateEdit"

    FieldName="NewsDate" ControlMode="Display"
    runat="server" />
```

9. Last step required for our custom fields to appear on a page is to make sure the content type that defines our custom page with fields will be permitted in a Pages library on a given site. By default having a content type specified in your page XML definition file does not mean this content type will be allowed in the **Pages** library. In order to bind the content type to a library we need to make a binding definition. We can use a new **Empty Elements** module to perform binding or use existing one; the binding needs to be defined only once per Pages library on a site. In our case we will reuse the **HomePage** module Landing.xml file to define a binding.

10. Add the following definition right after Elements node in your XML:

    <ContentTypeBinding ContentTypeId="{ID}" ListUrl="Pages" />

    In here, replace the **{ID}** with the **ID** of our custom content type (**MyCustomPage**); the **ID** is located in **Elements.xml** file of the content type definition.

11. Let's build and deploy the solution using our custom deployment script, which will launch the site when done.

The page will look as before at first. Switch the page to edit mode and you will see two new fields available to edit.

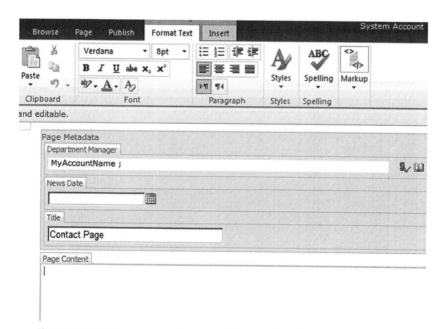

Figure 9-4 Additional properties available to set from the page's edit mode

If you enter valid values into the fields, check in the page, and navigate to the pages library, you will see that entered metadata was preserved in the properties of your pages. Notice how each of our controls has a proper type (**DateTimeField, UserField**, etc). For the list of other controls available, search **Microsoft.SharePoint.WebControls** on MSDN.

Using SharePoint Publishing Site Navigation Properties

When working with SharePoint pages, by default each page will get picked up by navigation controls. This means you will have a link on a top navigation bar for each page you provision to the pages library. Fortunately, there is a tool that allows users to hide any pages from navigation. To access the tool, users will need to do the following:

1. Select the site where they have unwanted pages displayed on the top navigation and click **Site Actions -> Site Settings**.

2. From the settings page, click the **Navigation** link located under the **Look and Feel** category.

3. Users will be able to choose whether pages are shown at all on the site as well as pick individual pages and hide them from the navigation. See the screen capture below:

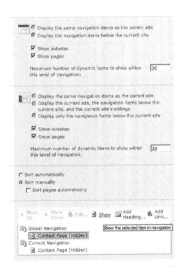

Figure 9-5 Site navigation control settings

Additionally, you can toggle the same settings you have available on this page using the navigation feature available out-of-the-box for publishing sites. When we looked at the structure of publishing site template, there were several features activated; navigation feature was one of them by default and called from **onet.xml** like this:

LISTING 9-23

```
<Feature ID="541F5F57-C847-4e16-B59A-B31E90E6F9EA">

<!-- Per-Web Portal Navigation Properties-->

<Properties xmlns="http://schemas.microsoft.com/sharepoint/">

<Property Key="InheritGlobalNavigation" Value="true"/>

<Property Key="IncludeSubSites" Value="true"/>

</Properties>

</Feature>
```

If you're ever interested where the feature is defined, follow this location: *[Drive]:\Program Files\Common Files\Microsoft Shared\Web Server Extensions\14\TEMPLATE\FEATURES\Navigation*.

But as you can guess, there are far more properties to this feature than in the default version of the publishing site **onet.xml** file. Here is the complete list of accepted properties and their sample values:

LISTING 9-24

```
<Feature ID="541F5F57-C847-4e16-B59A-B31E90E6F9EA">

<!-- Per-Web Portal Navigation Properties-->

    <Properties xmlns="http://schemas.microsoft.com/
    sharepoint/">

    <Property Key="InheritGlobalNavigation" Value="true" />

    <Property Key="InheritCurrentNavigation" Value="true" />

    <Property Key="ShowSiblings" Value="true" />

    <Property Key="IncludeSubSites" Value="true" />

    <Property Key="IncludePages" Value="true" />

    <Property Key="GlobalIncludeSubSites" Value="true" />

    <Property Key="GlobalIncludePages" Value="true" />
```

```
<Property Key="CurrentIncludeSubSites" Value="true" />

<Property Key="CurrentIncludePages" Value="true" />

<Property Key="GlobalDynamicChildLimit" Value="99" />

<Property Key="CurrentDynamicChildLimit" Value="99" />

<Property Key="OrderingMethod" Value="Automatic" />

<Property Key="AutomaticSortingMathod"
Value="LastModifiedDate" />

<Property Key="SortAscending" Value="true" />

<Property Key="IncludeInGlobalNavigation" Value="true" />

<Property Key="IncludeInCurrentNavigation"
Value="true" />

</Properties>
    </Feature>
```

Most of the values are descriptive of their functionality and you can reference the user interface version to get more details about their description. One item that you cannot set right from the navigation feature is whether the individual page is visible or not. The reason behind this is the fact that this is a per-Web feature, and, therefore it doesn't accept any settings for individual pages. In our next sample, we look at exactly how you can manage which pages are visible and which are not, as well as other properties of publishing pages.

Programmatically Hide SharePoint Web from Default Navigation

As you can see from the last sample, there is more to pages than just content. In this sample, we'll take a look at some of the properties of publishing pages and, in particular, how to hide individual page from the navigation.

In this example, we will be using the event receiver to execute our changes:

1. In your Visual Studio solution structure, navigate to the **Features** folder and create a new feature called **HidePagesFromNavigation**.

2. Add a new event receiver to the page and switch to the code behind of the receiver.

3. Add a new project reference assembly called **Microsoft. SharePoint.Publishing**

4. Add a new namespace reference to your feature:

■ using Microsoft.SharePoint.Publishing;

5. Locate the **Feature_Activated** method of the receiver.

6. Replace the code of the method with the following:

LISTING 9-25

```
public override void FeatureActivated(SPFeatureReceiverProper
ties properties)

{

using (SPWeb web = properties.Feature.Parent as SPWeb)

{

PublishingWeb pw =

        Microsoft.SharePoint.Publishing.PublishingWeb.
        GetPublishingWeb(web);

pw.IncludeInCurrentNavigation = false;

pw.Update();


SPQuery query = new SPQuery();

query.ViewFields = "<FieldRef Name='Title' />";

query.Query = "<Where><Contains><FieldRef Name='Title'/>

        <Value Type='Text'>Contact Page</Value></Contains></
        Where>";

SPListItemCollection itemCollection = pw.PagesList.
GetItems(query);

if (itemCollection.Count > 0)

{

        PublishingPage contactPage =

        PublishingPage.GetPublishingPage(itemCollection[0]);
```

```
        contactPage.IncludeInCurrentNavigation = false;

        contactPage.IncludeInGlobalNavigation = false;

    }

    }

    }
```

Above we have two examples. In the first, we get a hold of the current publishing Web and set its navigation properties not to inherit current navigation.

7. The last step to complete is to reference the feature **ID** of the feature you have created in your **onet.xml** of your custom site template. Refer to previous samples to get the feature **ID** and place it under the **<WebFeatures>** category in the **onet.xml** file of your site template.

8. Build and deploy the solution using our custom deployment script.

Assuming you still have the contacts page available in your pages library and the title of the page matches the one we have specified in the query, it will be excluded from the navigation as opposed to the case when our feature is not activated—meaning that the left hand side navigation is relevant only to the current site and doesn't include links from its parent. In the second part of the code, we build a query that looks for pages titled **contact page**, and if it finds any, the first page on the list will be excluded from the global navigation as well as current navigation on the left hand side. Take a look at some of the other properties of publishing Web and publishing page instances and see what other options are there that you might be using in your scenarios.

Hide Unused SharePoint Site Templates

From the last few samples, you have seen us mostly working with pages and some of the properties that we can leverage to enhance the experience of users on the site. One of the items that directly affects users experience when creating new sites is the choice of templates that are available to them. In most cases, having a choice is good but it depends on what circumstances. If you're building a custom intranet portal for you client and have a hierarchy of sites, you probably don't want your users to mistakenly create a team site under the section that is only dedicated to news. In scenarios like this, you would limit templates that users are able to use when creating a new site.

In your **onet.xml** file for your custom template, there is a default feature that looks like this:

LISTING 9-26

```
<Feature ID="22A9EF51-737B-4ff2-9346-694633FE4416">

<!-- Publishing -->

    <Properties xmlns="http://schemas.microsoft.com/
    sharepoint/">

    <Property Key="ChromeMasterUrl"

        Value="~SiteCollection/_catalogs/masterpage/
        v4.master"/>

    <Property Key="WelcomePageUrl"

        Value="$Resources:osrvcore,List_Pages_UrlName;/
        default.aspx"/>

    <Property Key="PagesListUrl" Value=""/>

    <Property Key="AvailableWebTemplates" Value=""/>

    <Property Key="AvailablePageLayouts" Value=""/>

    <Property Key="AlternateCssUrl" Value="" />

    <Property Key="SimplePublishing" Value="true" />

    </Properties>

</Feature>
```

This feature comes with quite a few properties assigned, and some of them have very descriptive names. The one we are interested in is **AvailableWebTemplates**, responsible for managing which templates will be allowed to be chosen by users. The format in which you have to specify your templates might be a bit confusing; here is the format logic:

[LCID]-[TEMPLATE] # [ID]

Above we have the following pieces:

- **LCID** – the language **ID** of the portal. English is **1033**.

- **TEMPLATE** – is the **ID** of the template as defined in your **Site Templates** folder located here: *[Drive]:\Program Files\Common Files\Microsoft Shared\Web Server Extensions\14\TEMPLATE\ SiteTemplates*

- **ID** – is the configuration **ID** of the template you are using; remember each site template has an **onet.xml**, which may have one or more configuration IDs.

For example, if the only template for subsites permitted on my main site is our custom template we've been working on all along, my **AvailableWebTemplates** value will look like this: **1033-MyCustomSite#0**. If you have more than one template you would like to permit, and in most cases you will, you will need to separate the definition shown above with a semicolon with no spaces.

For example: **1033-MyCustomSite#0;1033-AnotherCustomSite#0**.

To finalize your setup and test whether everything works, build the solution with appropriate values in your test **onet.xml** site template definition. Deploy the solution and try creating a new subsite to see whether all the other templates have been removed.

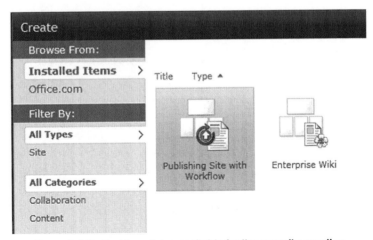

Figure 9-6 Limited templates available for the new site creation

This approach works only on the onet.xml of the configuration where you activate the feature. Therefore, if you have only a few subsites where you would like to limit the list of available templates, you can separate the settings using several configurations in your site template **onet.xml**.

Limiting Allowed SharePoint Page Layouts on a Desired Web

In last sample, we looked at how you can limit site templates available on the site. The same importance has the ability to limit page layouts available on the site for users to change. In the latest version of SharePoint, users are not asked for the layout of the page when they create a new page by default. After the page is created, users can choose its layout by switching to the editing mode of the page and using the **Page Layout** fly out menu fom the **Page** tab on the ribbon. If you have several of your own page layouts plus out-of-the-box page layouts, you might want to choose to limit the available items so that users don't pick up the wrong layout and let it stay like this on their site. In most cases, users will pick the wrong template without noticing anything wrong with it at first. There is an easy way to limit the available page layouts to choose from just by executing code in the feature receiver. Our feature receiver will assume that it's activated through **onet.xml**, and will accept parameters specifying which page layouts will be permitted to show up:

1. Add a new feature in to your Visual Studio features folder and call it **HidePageLayouts**.

2. Add an **event receiver** to the feature and switch to the code behind of your event receiver.

3. Ensure your feature receiver has the following namespace reference statement defined:

■   *using Microsoft.SharePoint.Publishing;*

4. Locate the **FeatureActivated** method of your feature receiver and replace its content with the following code:

LISTING 9-27

```
public override void FeatureActivated(SPFeatureReceiverProper
ties properties)
```

```csharp
{
    using (SPWeb web = properties.Feature.Parent as SPWeb)
    {
        PublishingWeb publishingWeb = PublishingWeb.
        GetPublishingWeb(web);

        string allowedLayouts = string.Empty;

        string[] allowedLayoutArray = null;

        bool subsitesInherit = false;

        bool clearPreviouslySetLayouts = false;

        if (properties.Feature.Properties["AvailablePageLayouts"] !=
        null)
        {
            allowedLayouts = properties.Feature
                .Properties["AvailablePageLayouts"].Value;

            allowedLayoutArray = allowedLayouts.Split(';');
        }
        if (properties.Feature.Properties["ResetAllSubsitesToInher
        it"] != null)
        {
            subsitesInherit =
                properties.Feature.Properties["ResetAllSubsitesToIn
                herit"]
                .Value.ToLower().Equals("true");
        }
        if (properties.Feature.Properties["ClearPreviouslySetLayou
        ts"] != null)
        {
            clearPreviouslySetLayouts =
                properties.Feature.Properties["ClearPreviouslySetLa
                youts"]
                .Value.ToLower().Equals("true");
        }
```

```
PageLayout pageLayout = null;

PageLayout[] pageLayouts;

SPList masterPageList =
    publishingWeb.GetAvailablePageLayouts()[0].ListItem.
    ParentList;

PageLayout[] existingLayouts = publishingWeb.
GetAvailablePageLayouts();

int existingLayoutsCount = existingLayouts.Length;

if (!clearPreviouslySetLayouts)

{

    pageLayouts = new PageLayout[allowedLayoutArray.Length
        + existingLayouts.Length];

    for (int i = 0; i < existingLayouts.Length; i++)

    {

    pageLayouts[i] = existingLayouts[i];

    }

}

else

{

    pageLayouts = new PageLayout[allowedLayoutArray.
    Length];

    existingLayoutsCount = 0;

}

if (masterPageList != null)

{

    for (int i = 0; i < allowedLayoutArray.Length; i++)

    {

    for (int j = 0; j < masterPageList.Items.Count; j++)

    {

    if (masterPageList.Items[j]["Name"].ToString()
```

```
            .Equals(allowedLayoutArray[i]))

    {

        pageLayout = new PageLayout(masterPageList.
        Items[j]);

        pageLayouts[existingLayoutsCount] = pageLayout;

        existingLayoutsCount++;

    }

    }

    }

    publishingWeb.SetAvailablePageLayouts(pageLayouts,
    subsitesInherit);

    publishingWeb.Update();

}

}

}
```

Above, we determine whether the following attributes have been set:

- **AvailablePageLayouts** – semicolon separated names of page layouts as they appear in your solution or out-of-the-box file names located under the following URL relative to your site: _catalogs/masterpage/Forms/AllItems.aspx

- **ResetAllSubsitesToInherit** – true/false depending on whether you want all of the child sites on the current site to inherit the same pattern.

- **ClearPreviouslySetLayouts** – true/false depending on whether you want to clear previously available layout pages, which in most cases you will have set to **true**.

5. Now that our feature receiver is created, we will need to get the feature **ID** of its parent feature and reference the feature ID as a **<WebFeature>** in the **onet.xml** of the site template we are using for testing.

LISTING 9-28

```
<Feature ID="7e90c448-65ce-4a7f-afa7-3e0e9d19d518">

<Properties xmlns="http://schemas.microsoft.com/sharepoint/">

<property key="AvailablePageLayouts"

    value="BlankWebPartPage.aspx;MyCustomPage.aspx" />

<property key="ResetAllSubsitesToInherit" value="false" />

<property key="ClearPreviouslySetLayouts" value="true" />

</Properties>

</Feature>
```

6. Since our feature directly depends on the page layouts being provisioned to the site, we need to establish feature activation dependency to make sure our new feature waits for the page layout feature to provision relevant page layouts. Open the **Design** view of our new feature and scroll down to **Feature Activation Dependencies**. In here, add the feature provisioning layout modules to the list of dependencies.

7. Build the solution and deploy it with our custom deployment script.

When succeeded, navigate to the root of your site and add a new page to the site using **Site Actions -> New Page**. When the page is created, switch to the **Page** tab on the ribbon and click the **Page Layout** fly out button. Under the list of available options, you should see only two page layouts we have specified in our feature.

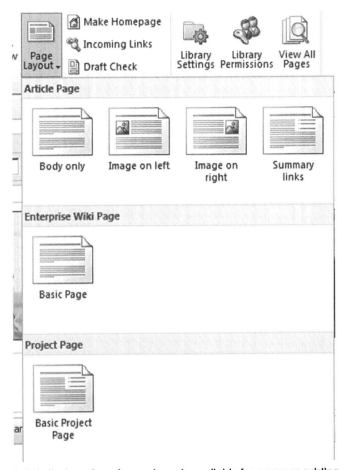

Figure 9-7 Limited number of page layouts available for a new or existing page

Just because we used a feature receiver, it doesn't mean you cannot dynamically assign available page layouts on the site after the site is deployed. By using the same object model as outline in our feature receiver, you can adjust what is going to be allowed for users in terms of site templates and page layouts.

Setting Automatic Page Title for SharePoint Default Pages

When performing automated solution deployment, you will provision many generic pages with the same page layout and possibly some generic content, which users will use to populate their own content. A typical SharePoint site will also have subsites that your client may require to set with generic landing pages where they will add more content. Each of the subsites will have their **Default.aspx** page with a predefined set of Web Parts and other components set up.

In our scenario, we have a feature that provisions the landing page in the site. However, when provisioning a landing page, you won't have the ability to assign properties for each page, such as title. Therefore, the title of your default pages will remain empty; usually that means viewers' browsers will substitute the title of your page with the URL of the site, which throws off the look and feel of the page.

One of the solutions that you may want to implement is to set the title of your automatically provisioned page to be the same as the title of the subsite that is being provisioned.

In our solution, the feature that provisions the landing page is a generic feature that contains just a module, and referenced in **onet.xml**. Since this feature provisions the page, one of the ways to enhance this feature is to add an event receiver to it:

1. In your Visual Studio solution structure, locate the feature we used for page module provisioning.

2. Add an event receiver to the feature and ensure it references the following namespaces:

■ *using Microsoft.SharePoint.Publishing;*

3. Locate the **FeatureActivated** method and replace its content with the following code:

LISTING 9-29

```
public override void FeatureActivated(SPFeatureReceiverProper
ties properties)
{
using (SPWeb web = (SPWeb)properties.Feature.Parent)
{
        // Assuming we activate this feature only on publishing
        pages
        PublishingWeb pubWeb = PublishingWeb.
        GetPublishingWeb(web);
```

```
SPFile defaultPage = pubWeb.DefaultPage;

defaultPage.CheckOut();

defaultPage.Update();

defaultPage.Item["Title"] = web.Title;

defaultPage.Item.Update();

defaultPage.CheckIn("Title automatically set");

defaultPage.Update();

}

}
```

Above, our page is checked out and had the property of it changed to one of the properties of the site.

4. Build your solution and deploy the site using our custom script.

Since we have not added the feature ID to the **onet.xml** for automatic provisioning, you will see no changes to the page title. Let's activate the feature to see how it affected the page:

1. Click **Site Actions -> Site Settings**.

2. Click **Manage site features**.

3. Locate our new feature with the name you have give in it and click **Activate**.

When you navigate back to the home page, you will see that the default page title in the breadcrumb of the site is set to the title of the site rather than original title of **Home Page**. Also, if you navigate to the page library of your site and select to view page version history, you will see that the page has been modify and a comment has been left by the feature receiver to indicate that the page has been modified.

In reality you would want this feature to be activated during provisioning so that when users create new site instances based on your custom template – the title of the page gets set automatically.

This example solves a very specific need, but you can certainly explore some of the other applications of using the same approach in different scenarios.

CHAPTER 10

Adding Custom Logic to Your Site Using Application Pages

Thus far we have looked at various scenarios to customize different parts of SharePoint. In most cases, we utilized out-of-the-box components since SharePoint had enough flexibility to let us extend some of its functionality and saved us from rewriting existing features. There are some other scenarios where you may be migrating custom application to be hosted within SharePoint and, for one reason or another, you just cannot break down the functionality into separate Web Parts. In that case, SharePoint has a nice ability for you to create what is known as application pages. Whether you know it or not, you have been using out-of-the-box application pages quite often to interact with your SharePoint site. All of the application pages are located in the **_Layouts** virtual directory and are relative to the site from which you're calling them.

Application pages are simply **ASPX** pages that allow you to write your custom code behind them and place controls on them. The benefit is that they run within a context of SharePoint and if you need access to SharePoint objects, you can retrieve the content and identify whether the page was called from one subsite as opposed to another. In this chapter, we're not going to take a granular look at custom application pages. We will cover a few interesting features and extensions you can take advantage of.

Limiting the List of Available Page Layouts with an Application Page

An application page is an independent piece of functionality that executes your custom .NET code and has access to some of the context in SharePoint. Application pages should not be confused with SharePoint item forms or rendering templates. The main difference is the fact that item forms have access to the context of an item and, therefore, can host item contextual controls such as rating control. Application pages are not attached to an item; you can, however, pass parameters to a page that will define the item you're working on and access the item in the list that way.

Let's create an application page that will execute one of the samples we looked at in the previous chapter and limit page layouts available for SharePoint pages on the current site:

1. In your Visual Studio solution structure, locate **Layouts** mapped folder and add a new folder to it called **Chapter10**.

2. Add a new item to folder of type **Application Page**. Set the name of the page to **ListPageLayouts.aspx**

3. Open the **ListPageLayouts.aspx** file and take a look at some of the markup there. Beside the definition of the page and reference to code behind file, you will see placeholders for various sections of the page. Locate the placeholder with the following code:

LISTING 10-1

```
<asp:Content ID="Main" ContentPlaceHolderID="PlaceHolderMain"
runat="server">

</asp:Content>
```

4. Replace the above placeholder with the code below, which is a definition of a list of checkboxes and a button.

LISTING 10-2

```
<asp:Content ID="Main" ContentPlaceHolderID="PlaceHolderMain"
runat="server">
```

```
<asp:CheckBoxList runat="server" id="PageLayoutList"></
asp:CheckBoxList>

<asp:LinkButton runat="server" id="LimitPageLayouts"
onclick="LimitPageLayouts_Click">Limit Page Layouts</
asp:LinkButton>

</asp:Content>
```

5. Switch to the code behind of the application page and make the following references in your namespace references section:

- using Microsoft.SharePoint.Publishing;
- using System.Collections.Generic;
- using System.Linq;
- using System.Web.UI.WebControls;

6. Ensure **Microsoft.SharePoint.Publishing** DLL is referenced in your project.

7. Locate the **Page_Load** method in your code and replace it with the following code:

LISTING 10-3

```
protected void Page_Load(object sender, EventArgs e)

{

if (!Page.IsPostBack)

{

SPWeb web = SPContext.Current.Web;

PublishingWeb publishingWeb = PublishingWeb.
GetPublishingWeb(web);

PageLayout[] pageLayouts = publishingWeb.
GetAvailablePageLayouts();

PageLayoutList.DataSource = (from row in pageLayouts.
Cast<PageLayout>()

        select new ListItem

        {

        Text = (string)row.Name,

        Value = (string)row.Name
```

```
  }).ToArray();
PageLayoutList.DataBind();

  }

  }
```

Above, we get a hold of all of the available page layouts on the current Web where the application page is called from, and populate the check box list with their file names.

8. Right below the **Page_Load** method, add the code below, which will handle our link button's click event:

LISTING 10-4

```
protectedvoidLimitPageLayouts_Click(objectsender,EventArgse)

{

SPWebweb=SPContext.Current.Web;

PublishingWebpublishingWeb=PublishingWeb.
GetPublishingWeb(web);

List<string>allowedLayouts=newList<string>();

for(inti=0;i<PageLayoutList.Items.Count;i++)

{

        if(PageLayoutList.Items[i].Selected)

        {

            allowedLayouts.Add(PageLayoutList.Items[i].Text);

        }

}

PageLayoutpageLayout=null;

PageLayout[]pageLayouts;

SPListmasterPageList=

publishingWeb.GetAvailablePageLayouts()[0].ListItem.
ParentList;

PageLayout[]existingLayouts=publishingWeb.
GetAvailablePageLayouts();

intexistingLayoutsCount=0;
```

```
pageLayouts=newPageLayout[allowedLayouts.Count];
if(masterPageList!=null)
{
for(inti=0;i<allowedLayouts.Count;i++)
{
for(intj=0;j<masterPageList.Items.Count;j++)
{
        if(masterPageList.Items[j]["Name"].ToString()
            .Equals(allowedLayouts[i]))
        {
        pageLayout=newPageLayout(masterPageList.Items[j]);
        pageLayouts[existingLayoutsCount]=pageLayout;
        existingLayoutsCount++;
        }
}
}
publishingWeb.SetAvailablePageLayouts(pageLayouts,false);
publishingWeb.Update();
}
}
```

In here, we go through the list of the page layouts that the user has checked from the list of available templates and set them up just like we did in the last chapter through a feature.

9. Next, deploy the solution using Visual Studio deployment feature.

10. Navigate to the application page URL:

    http://localhost /_layouts/Chapter10/ListPageLayouts.aspx

Now you can test the application page functionality by checking only the page layouts that you would like to be available on the site and clicking a button to apply your changes. The next time you refresh the page, you will see only the items you have checked listed as check boxes. Also, if you create a new page and check available page layouts on the new page's **Page** ribbon button, you will see that only the ones you selected are available.

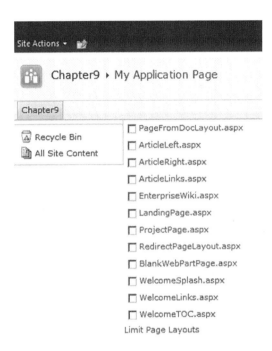

Figure 10-1 Custom application page showing available page layouts

There you have it ... the same action executed from a page. This is also a good example of application pages being used as extensions to administrative interface in SharePoint.

The great feature about application pages is the fact that they are aware of the site context you're running. You notice we established the context of the existing site by calling the following: *SPWeb web = SPContext.Current.Web;*

This means that if our application page was called from the child site collection or a subsite, it would be aware that changes are going to be applied on that site and not on the parent.

Displaying SharePoint "Processing" Page during Your Long Running Operations

SharePoint has a great framework to allow asynchronous operation execution. There are many features that we looked at earlier that allow users to launch a process or a workflow and keep going with their tasks without worrying about the completion of the task. However, in many scenarios, and especially in scenarios when you integrate with other systems, you really want to give that feedback to a user on whether their operation has been completed successfully or not—for example, if it interacts with the Web Part that creates a list item in the list and then the event handler launches to execute some actions of the list item that has just been created by the user. If the event handler has to go out and retrieve data from business connectivity services and at that time the connection with external database is down, user will never know that the execution of their request has failed. In this case, it's best to give our user an indication that something went wrong and they should try it again later, or whatever else the case might be. If the operation is not terribly long, you can use one of the mechanisms that SharePoint uses when it runs important long running operations. Each time you create a new site collection or a site, you are presented with the graphic page letting you know that things are in progress and you should expect your results shortly.

You can incorporate exactly the same mechanism in your solutions too. Let's create a page that will execute a long running operation to demonstrate the case. Our page will provision a new site to the site collection:

1. Locate the **Layouts** mapped folder in your Visual Studio solution.

2. Add a new item to the folder of type **Application Page** called: **DemoLongRunningOperation.aspx** since we already have two pages.

3. Find the content place holder with **ID="Main"** and replace it with the following code:

LISTING 10-5

```
asp:Content ID="Main" ContentPlaceHolderID="PlaceHolderMain"
runat="server">
```

```
<asp:TextBox runat="server" id="SiteName"></asp:TextBox>

<asp:LinkButton runat="server" id="CreateSite"
onclick="CreateSite_Click">Create Site</asp:LinkButton>

</asp:Content>
```

4. Switch to the code behind of your application page and ensure you have referenced the following namespaces :

■ *using System.Web;*

5. Add a new method right below your **Page_Load** method which is going to handle the click event of our button:

LISTING 10-6

```
protectedvoidCreateSite_Click(objectsender,EventArgse)

{

stringcomeBackUrl=SPContext.Current.Site.Url+"/"+

        SiteName.Text.Replace(" ",string.Empty);

using(SPLongOperationoperation=newSPLongOperation(this.Page))

{

        operation.Begin();

        CreateWeb();

        operation.End(comeBackUrl,Microsoft.SharePoint.
        Utilities

            .SPRedirectFlags.DoNotEncodeUrl,HttpContext.
            Current,null);

}

}


privatevoidCreateWeb()

{

SPSitesite=SPContext.Current.Site;

SPWebnewWeb=

        site.AllWebs.Add(SiteName.Text.Replace(" ",string.
        Empty),
```

```
SiteName.Text,SiteName.Text,1033,"STS#0",false,false);

newWeb.Update();

newWeb.Close();

}
```

Above, the **CreateWeb()** functionality is fairly self explanatory; we get a hold of the current site collection and create a new site. The **CreateSite_Click** part warps the functionality of the provisioning function with commands that will display the page when long running operations execute. Since the process of new site creation takes a moment, you will see the **processing** page followed by the redirect to the root of the newly created site.

6. Deploy the solution with Visual Studio deployment option and navigate to the application page URL: *http://localhost /_layouts/ Chapter10/DemoLongRunningOperation.aspx*

7. Fill out the site name and click the button to create a new site to test the behavior of the logic.

As it happened, if you followed the exact steps of the last sample, and other samples for that matter, you didn't get any errors. But we all know that in real life you will get errors and they will not be descriptive. If you worked through the chapter where we discussed how to go about debugging your SharePoint applications, you are one step ahead. However, there is one more detail to application pages that make them unique. Application pages live in the virtual folder that is mapped to a physical folder on your file system: *[Drive]:\Program Files\Common Files\Microsoft Shared\Web Server Extensions\14\ TEMPLATE\LAYOUTS*.

That folder, as does every virtual folder, has its own Web configuration settings file, which overwrites some of the setting you outlined in the web.config of your root SharePoint site folder.

If you locate the **web.config** (*[Drive]:\Program Files\Common Files\ Microsoft Shared\Web Server Extensions\14\TEMPLATE\LAYOUTS\ web.config*) and open it, you will see that its debugging setting is set to show custom SharePoint errors. To save you a lot of trouble when writing custom application pages, set the value like this:

<customErrors mode="Off" />

CHAPTER 11

Extending Visual Studio 2010 to Speed Up and Standardize Your SharePoint 2010 Projects

You've come a long way reading about all of the samples and applications you can build with SharePoint. Throughout the process, we have used Visual Studio quite a bit. Mostly to take advantage of its features and templates that it provides. It's time to talk about the Visual Studio alone and see what else it is good for beyond creating SharePoint solutions. One of the great new features in Visual Studio is an ability to add new features to it. By extending your development environment, you can make the process of creating new solutions easier and have shortcuts and templates available for reuse. If you spent several hours trying to figure out how to create a new time job for SharePoint and you finally got it, six months down the road you will need to create a new time job you can just fire off the template you created before, and then you're all ready to go. That's when you work alone. If you work in a team, no matter smaller or larger, you probably already have standards and code guidelines and, in general, certain rules about how people write their solutions. Just by creating a solution or item template, you already saved quite a few hours just by making things easier for your team to implement. Plus you get it done your way and all of your standards are preserved. Think your solution is worth more than saved time, now you can upload your extensions to the Visual Studio gallery online and there you go—you have your first product for developers. Now if you think that creating all of those standardized templates and extensions is hard work, you will see through the two samples below that things are quite easy.

Extending Visual Studio Server Explorer Window with New Nodes

If you don't remember what the Visual Studio Server Explorer window is, you're probably someone like me. There was not much use in a server explorer window before, and especially there was no use for it for a SharePoint developer. Now, the server explorer window has a new node specifically targeted for SharePoint; the window now looks like this:

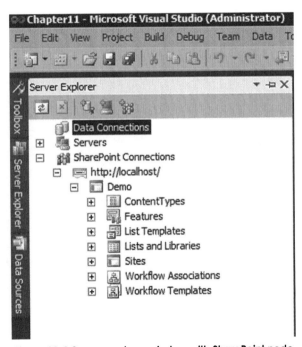

Figure 11-1 Server explorer window with SharePoint node

Knowing what's in your SharePoint site and knowing the properties of items is something you need all the time. There were few tools in past versions of SharePoint and Visual Studio that helped with site exploration; but now that you have server explorer SharePoint connections that you can extend, things will be much easier when doing your development.

Let's start with setting up your first Visual Studio Server Explorer extension.

1. Search the internet for **Visual Studio 2010 SDK** and download a copy of it. Make sure you download and install a release version of SDK and not Beta or RC version.

2. Launch a new instance of a Visual Studio and create a new project of type: **Other Project Types -> Extensibility -> Visual Studio Package**.

3. Follow the wizard and select the programming language of your package and other product information; pick all the rest of the options as defaults.

As a result, Visual Studio will generate a project, and some of the projects for unit testing and integration testing if you accepted all of the default choices from the wizard.

Let's now add some functionality to our extensibility package:

1. In the Visual Studio solution you created in previous steps, add a new project of type: **Class Library**; ensure you select .NET Framework 4.0 for your platform target.

2. Rename the default class that was created to **SiteNodeExtension.cs**; this will represent a new node that will show up in our server explorer SharePoint connection.

3. Add the following namespace references to the class:

- *using System.Collections.Generic;*
- *using System.ComponentModel.Composition;*
- *using Microsoft.SharePoint.Client;*
- *using Microsoft.VisualStudio.SharePoint;*
- *using Microsoft.VisualStudio.SharePoint.Explorer;*

4. Add the following project references to your project:

- *Microsoft.SharePoint.Client*
- *System.ComponentModel.Composition*
- *Microsoft.VisualStudio.SharePoint*
- *Microsoft.SharePoint.Client.Runtime*

5. Enter the following code in to the body of your new class right under the namespace reference declarations:

LISTING 11-1

```
namespaceMy.DevTools.SharePointExplorerTools.WebPartNode

{

[Export(typeof(IExplorerNodeTypeExtension))]

[ExplorerNodeType(ExplorerNodeTypes.SiteNode)]

internalclassSiteNodeExtension:IExplorerNodeTypeExtension

{

privateSystem.UrisiteUrl=null;

publicvoidInitialize(IExplorerNodeTypenodeType)

{

        nodeType.NodeChildrenRequested+=NodeChildrenRequested;

}

privatevoidNodeChildrenRequested(objectsender,ExplorerNodeEv
entArgse)

{

        siteUrl=e.Node.Context.SiteUrl;

        e.Node.ChildNodes.AddFolder("WebPartGallery",My.
        DevTools

            .SharePointExplorerTools.WebPartNode.Properties.
            Resources

            .WebPart.ToBitmap(),

        CreateWebPartNodes);

}

privatevoidCreateWebPartNodes(IExplorerNodeparentNode)
```

```
{
try
{
        ClientContextcontext=newClientContext(siteUrl.
        AbsoluteUri);
        ListwebPartsGallery=
           context.Web.GetCatalog((int)ListTemplateType.
           WebPartCatalog);
        ListItemCollectionwebParts=
           webPartsGallery.GetItems(newCamlQuery());
        context.Load(webParts,listItems=>
           listItems.Include(i=>i.FieldValuesAsText));
        context.ExecuteQuery();
        if(webParts!=null)
        {
        foreach(ListItemwebPartinwebParts)
        {
        varannotations=newDictionary<object,object>()
        {
        {typeof(ListItem),webPart}
        };
        parentNode.ChildNodes.Add(WebPartNodeTypeProvider
           .WebPartNodeTypeId,
           webPart.FieldValuesAsText.FieldValues["Title"],anno
           tations);
        }
        }
}
catch{}
}}}
```

6. Create a new class with the following file name: **WebPartNodeTypeProvider.cs**

7. Add the following reference to the project:

- *System.Windows.Forms;*

8. Declare the following namespace references:

- *using System.Windows.Forms;*
- *using System.ComponentModel.Composition;*
- *using Microsoft.SharePoint.Client;*
- *using Microsoft.VisualStudio.SharePoint;*
- *using Microsoft.VisualStudio.SharePoint.Explorer;*
- *using System.Net;*
- *using System.IO;*

9. Replace the contents of the existing name space declaration with the following code:

LISTING 11-2

```
namespaceMy.DevTools.SharePointExplorerTools.WebPartNode

{

[Export(typeof(IExplorerNodeTypeProvider))]

[ExplorerNodeType(WebPartNodeTypeProvider.WebPartNodeTypeId)]

internalclassWebPartNodeTypeProvider:IExplorerNodeTypeProvider

{

internalconststringWebPartNodeTypeId="My.WebPart";

publicvoidInitializeType(IExplorerNodeTypeDefinitiontype
Definition)

{

typeDefinition.DefaultIcon=My.DevTools.SharePointExplorerTools

.WebPartNode.Properties.Resources.WebPart.ToBitmap();

typeDefinition.IsAlwaysLeaf=true;

typeDefinition.NodePropertiesRequested+=NodePropertiesRequest
ed;
```

```
typeDefinition.NodeMenuItemsRequested+=NodeMenuItemsRequested;
}
privatevoidNodePropertiesRequested(objectsender,
ExplorerNodePropertiesRequestedEventArgse)
{
        varwebPart=e.Node.Annotations.GetValue<ListItem>();
        objectpropertySource=
            e.Node.Context.CreatePropertySourceObject(
                webPart.FieldValuesAsText.FieldValues);
        e.PropertySources.Add(propertySource);
}
privatevoidNodeMenuItemsRequested(
objectsender,ExplorerNodeMenuItemsRequestedEventArgse)
{
        e.MenuItems.Add("CopyXML").Click+=MenuItemClick;
}


privatevoidMenuItemClick(objectsender,MenuItemEventArgse)
{
IExplorerNodeparentNode=e.OwnerasIExplorerNode;
if(parentNode!=null)
{
        varwebPart=parentNode.Annotations.GetValue<ListItem>();
        WebClientclient=newWebClient();
        StreamoutputStream=newMemoryStream();
        client.Credentials=CredentialCache.DefaultCredentials;
        StreamwebpartDef=null;
        stringdocumentUrl=string.Format(parentNode.Context
            .SiteUrl.AbsoluteUri
```

```
    +webPart.FieldValuesAsText.FieldValues["FileRef"]);

    webpartDef=newMemoryStream(client.
    DownloadData(documentUrl));

    using(StreamReadersr=newStreamReader(webpartDef))

    {

        Clipboard.SetText(sr.ReadToEnd());

    }

    MessageBox.Show("WebpartXMLcopiedtoclipboard.","Webpart
    XMLCopy");

    }

}

}}
```

10. Next, we'll add an image your code is referencing to represent a Web Part node and an individual Web Part. Right click on the project name and choose **Properties**.

11. Click Resources tab and select a link to add new resources.

12. Switch resource type from **Strings** to **Images**.

13. From the top panel, click **Add Resource -> Add New Icon**. Give it a name: **WebPart**.

14. In your Solution Explorer, find a newly created **WebPart.ico**, and from its properties, select **Embedded Resource** as a value for **Build Action**.

15. Navigate to the project properties page of the initial Visual Studio Extensibility project and ensure that under **Application**, the **Default Namespace** is set to: *My.DevTools.SharePointExplorerTools.WebPartNode*.

16. Ensure the same value of namespace as above is set on the supporting **Class Library** project.

17. In the Solution Explorer of your Visual Studio Extensibility project locate: **source.extension.vsixmanifest** and open the file.

18. Scroll down to **Content** section and click **Add Content**.

19. For the **Content Type**, set **MEF Component**; and for the **Source**, select **Project**. Pick the name of your supporting **Class Library** project. Click **OK**.

At this point we can take two routes to see results of our new solution:

■ Debug the solution just by pressing F5 in your Visual Studio.

■ Build your solution and navigate to an output folder (*bin/ Debug*) of the **Extensibility Project** root to install package file with **VSIX** extension. Usually the name of the file will equal the assembly name you have specified in your Visual Studio Extensibility project.

If you chose to install the package using the **VSIX** file – restart the instance of the Visual Studio.

Once ready and Visual Studio has restarted or new instance started in debug mode – navigate to server explorer SharePoint connections tab to verify that you see a new node called Web Parts under your local SharePoint test site.

When you right click on the Web Part from the Web Parts node, you will be able to copy the XML of the Web Part definition to the clipboard and then use it in your code.

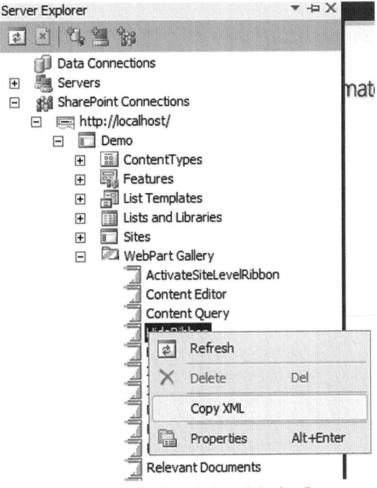

Figure 11-2 Extended Server Explorer window in action

This sample illustrates how you can create your own nodes in server explorer and create options for users to interact with the interface. In fact, I recommend you check our Visual Studio online extension gallery. **Click Tools -> Extension Manager** to access the existing extension list. If you ran through this sample, you will see your custom extension installed, and this is where you can uninstall it. If you click **Online Gallery** option, and in the right hand side of the window search for **SharePoint**, you will see many solutions available for download. Most of those were created by developers like you trying to improve the development experience.

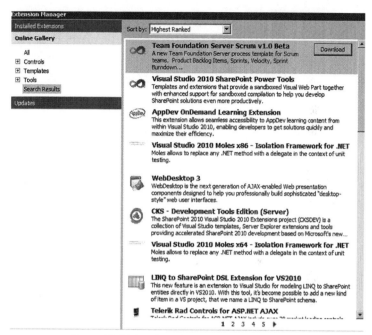

Figure 11-3 Visual Studio online gallery browser

LEARN MORE:

Video screencast: Extending Visual Studio 2010 with custom tools for SharePoint 2010.

http://vimeo.com/9749665

Creating Visual Studio Project and Item Templates

Code standards are great to improve your code quality and have a library of solutions you researched best practices around and know how to implement. Now make a comparison of what's easier:

- Read this book, other books, read blog articles – then put them all together to create a standard solution or template in the form of another step-by-step instruction.

- Read this book, other books, and blog articles, then put all the knowledge together to create a sample solution and save it as a Visual Studio template that you can share with others or just yourself.

If your answer is later, take a look at how easy it is to create a Visual Studio template:

1. Let's assume you already have your solution created in Visual Studio. In our example, we'll use a solution from the last sample where we created a server explorer extension.

2. Click **File -> Export Template.**

3. Pick Project Template since our new template will be a new project. We'll use the extension class library project from the previous sample. As you remember, we went through quite a bit of steps to get it set up, so it's nice to have it saved as a template.

4. Leave all the default settings on the next step of the wizard and click Finish.

5. Visual Studio will open a folder where your template has been saved.

Next, we will create a new Visual Studio extensibility package and add our custom template to it so that it can be distributed to others as a single package:

1. Launch a new instance of a Visual Studio and create a new project of type: **Other Project Types -> Extensibility -> Visual Studio Package.**

2. Follow the wizard and select the programming language of your package and other product information; pick all the rest of the options as defaults.

3. After you click Finish, Visual Studio will open the package definition window. Scroll down to the **Content** area and click **Add Content.**

4. From **Select Content Type** pick **Project Template.**

5. For Source, pick a file from the location that was given to you from the Visual Studio when you exported your template.

6. Click **OK** and build your solution.

7. When built, Visual Studio will generate a **VSIX** package in the output folder of the project (*bin\Debug*). This file is your distributable project template.

Just as in the previous sample, you can now distribute the package, and upon users installing it, they will be able to add new projects with the same template you have created in your solution.

At this time of this book being edited, there has been yet another extensibility module release by Microsoft called **Export Template Wizard**. The module is available from Extension Manager Online Gallery and it allows you to export any project or an item to an external **VSIX** package right away without having to export it in native format and then create manual **VSIX** package.

Once you have the module installed – while having a project loaded (any project you want to export) click **File -> Export Template as VSIX**. This is great one stop solution allowing you to easily create and distribute allof your packages. The module will even create a preview image for you so that your **VSIX** module looks more exciting.

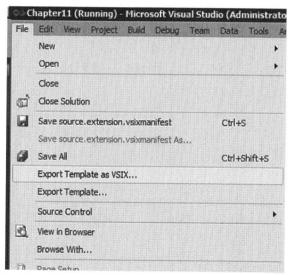

Figure 11-4 Extensibility module launched and available in Visual Studio

... etc

There we are ... now you are familiar with the functionality and features of the latest version of SharePoint. Hopefully you have got a complete coverage on what's available for you in the new release. If you haven't already, be sure to check out the source code for each chapter at www.sharemuch.com. That's where you can also reach me and tell me what you liked and didn't like about the book. I do hope you found this book resourceful and complete with examples that closely resemble your scenarios and everything actually worked from the first time.

Good Luck!

INDEX

#

_Layouts, 274

A

Add a Web Part, 86
add functionality to search
    results, 213
add new page content
    programatically, 213
AlternateCssUrl, 263
Application pages, 274
assign new rendering template, 74
asynchronous operation
    execution, 279
AutomaticSortingMathod, 259
AvailablePageLayouts, 262
AvailableWebTemplates, 262
average rating, 150

B

BaseViewID, 245
BCS Operations, 99

BDC Explorer, 99
BDC Method Details, 105
BDC Model, 98
**BDC Provisioning Event
    Receiver**, 113
BDC Provisioning feature, 111
Branding Project Root, 3
BSC, 90
build tasks, 96
Business Connectivity Services, 90
**Business Data Connectivity
    Service**, 98

C

Calculated Field Formulas, 37
Composite Field, 65
Configure Diagnostic Logging, 26
Content Project Root, 3
Content Sources, 207
content type, 35
ContentType, 227
CoreProperty, 136
Correlation ID, 24
Crawled property, 207

Crawling, 207
create a list instance, 31
CreatePackage command, 8
creating a solution template, 286
CurrentDynamicChildLimit, 259
CurrentIncludePages, 258
CurrentIncludeSubSites, 258
custom action buttons, 71
custom application pages, 274
Custom Permissions Levels, 44
custom rendering template, 64
Custom Save Item, 69
CustomAction, 175

D

DateTimeField, 257
debug Service Job execution, 126
Debugging SharePoint Applications, 24
Deploy command, 10
Display Properties, 213

E

Edit form, 61
Element Manifest, 247
Embedded Resource, 293
EnableAttachments, 43
EnableFolderCreation, 43
Enable-SPFeature, 18
Event receiver, 40
exclude lists from search crawl, 43
existing SharePoint fields, 32

Export All Data, 296
Export Template, 296
Export Template Wizard, 297
Export Web Part definition, 87
Export WebPart, 240
Extending existing properties, 132
extending your development environment, 286
Extensibility Project, 295
Extension Manager, 295
External Content Type, 94
external item query threshold, 118
External list, 98
External System, 94

F

Farm Configuration Wizard, 131
Feature Activation Dependencies, 141
Feature Activation Dependenices, 142
Feature Manifest, 233
Fetched Properties, 211
Filter Category Definition, 203
Fly out anchors, 176

G

Global Assembly Cache, 19
GlobalDynamicChildLimit, 258
GlobalIncludePages, 259
GlobalIncludeSubSites, 258
Grant list Permissions, 44

H

HitHighlightedSummary, 211

I

Import BDC Model, 117
IncludeInCurrentNavigation, 260
IncludePages, 258
IncludeSubSites, 258
InheritCurrentNavigation, 259
InheritGlobalNavigation, 259
item property page, 254
Item-level Permissions, 41

J

JobDefinitions, 124

L

layout page, 222
Limited page layouts, 268
List Event Receivers, 49
List Item Validation, 37
List Queries, 52
List Relationship, 47
list schema file, 36
List Unique Permissions Threshold, 119
List View Lookup Threshold, 119
List View Threshold, 119
List View Threshold for Auditors and Administrators, 120
log file, 24
long running operation, 280

M

Manage Service Applications, 99
Manage User Profiles, 136
Managed Metadata service, 163
managed property, 205
mapped folder, 6
MappedProperty, 205
MEF Component, 295
metadata properties, 222
Modal window, 196

N

New form, 61
New Managed Property, 207
New-SPWeb, 18

O

OrderingMethod, 260
out-of-the-box ribbon control definitions, 190

P

page layout, 225
page libraries, 222
page's edit mode, 257
Platform Project Root, 2
PowerShell commands, 27
processing page, 282
Project Template, 296
properties driven by metadata, 139
provision rating feature, 153

provisioning custom Web Part, 83
provisioning new pages, 228
Publishing Navigation Feature, 258
PublishingAssociatedContentType, 225
PublishingPageLayout, 227

Q

query an external list, 115

R

Rating controls, 150
Rating settings, 151
rating synchronization, 152
ReadSecurity, 43
Referenced Assemblies, 19
Refinements Web Part, 203
Registration ID, 175
Registration type, 175
RelationshipDeleteBehavior, 49
Remove-SPSite, 14
ribbon button, 175
ribbon groups and tabs, 182

S

Sandoxed Solution, 4
Search Core Results, 211
Security Aware Composite Field, 65
Service Jobs, 122

Services Project Root, 3
setting list security
    programmatically, 41
SharePoint Designer, 74
SharePoint ribbon, 172
SharePointProjectItem, 247
SharePointWebControls, 256
ShowSiblings, 258
SimplePublishing, 263
Site Collection Search Center, 204
Site Collection Search Results Page, 204
site definition, 229
site level ribbon, 187
Site navigation control, 257
Site Templates, 263
Social Data Maintenance Job, 164
Social Rating service, 150
solution structure, 1
SortAscending, 260
status message Web Part, 149
Stop Inheriting list permissions, 44

T

Taxonomy Term Store, 163
TemplateAlias, 185
Term Store Management Tool, 163
Throttling options, 119
Time Jobs, 122
TypeDescriptor, 103
types of templates, 61

U

Uninstall-SPSolution, 16
User Profile Service application, 131
**User Profile to SharePoint Full
  Synchronization**, 152
User Properties, 131
UserField, 257
UserProfileConfigManager, 136

V

verbose logging, 25
View form, 61
Visual Studio 2010 SDK, 290
Visual Studio gallery, 285
Visual Studio Module, 83

Visual Studio Package, 286
Visual Studio Server Explorer, 286
Visual Web Part, 53

W

Web Application scope, 20
Web Part zone, 243
WebPartOrder, 245
WriteSecurity, 43
WSP, 8

X

XSL link, 80
XSL template, 76

10720494R0

Made in the USA
Lexington, KY
16 August 2011